JOHN SINGLETON

INTERVIEWS

CONVERSATIONS WITH FILMMAKERS SERIES
PETER BRUNETTE, GENERAL EDITOR

JOHN SINGLETON
INTERVIEWS

EDITED BY CRAIGH BARBOZA

UNIVERSITY PRESS OF MISSISSIPPI / JACKSON

www.upress.state.ms.us

The University Press of Mississippi is a member of the Association of American University Presses.

Copyright © 2009 by University Press of Mississippi

First printing 2009

Library of Congress Cataloging-in-Publication Data

John Singleton : interviews / edited by Craigh Barboza.
    p. cm. — (Conversations with filmmakers series)
    Includes index.
    ISBN 978-1-60473-115-6 (cloth) — ISBN 978-1-60473-116-3 (pbk)
        1. Singleton, John, 1968– —Interviews. 2. Motion picture producers and directors—United States—Interviews.   I. Barboza, Craigh.
    PN1998.3.S539A3   2009
    791.4302'33092—dc22

                                                                    2008032362

British Library Cataloging-in-Publication Data available

CONTENTS

INTRODUCTION

J O H N S I N G L E T O N, the Oscar-nominated director of *Boyz N the Hood* and *Four Brothers*, conquered the Hollywood studio system by making movies from an African American perspective that are packed with explosive storylines, sociological insight, and hip-hop attitude. A product of South Central Los Angeles, he literally talked his way into the movie business in the early 1990s only to emerge a headline-grabbing iconoclast. His early inspirations were George Lucas and Steven Spielberg, but at a time when black youth culture was becoming a force in the mainstream, Singleton demanded that movies reflect contemporary street life. In his works, he turned the camera on subjects rarely dealt with on celluloid (drive-by shootings, inner-city romance, the violent legacy of slavery) and captured the drama of the human condition, the pain and hopelessness, as well as the vibrancy. Singleton makes films that really matter; they sum up the times, rattle audiences and introduce future stars. In an era of oversize studio productions, he has helped prove that movies with substance can be just as entertaining as slick, would-be blockbusters. As Roger Ebert, Pulitzer Prize-winning critic for the *Chicago Sun-Times*, says, "Singleton is a born filmmaker."

Over a relatively short period, Singleton already has been responsible for a dozen motion pictures (about one every eighteen months) that have generated nearly three quarters of a billion dollars at box offices worldwide. He has thrived by alternating between genres. His films include one featuring the poetry of Maya Angelou, *Poetic Justice*, and the blockbuster *2 Fast 2 Furious*, which set a record for the highest-grossing movie with a black director. "Everyone in Hollywood seems to think you have to make films for Hollywood," Singleton says. "I never thought, 'What do the studios want me to make?' If I did that, I wouldn't have a career. Instead, I think, 'What do I want to do;

what do I want to see?' I grew up in the hood, so I came at it from a whole other perspective."

As one of the few black directors to find steady work inside the studio system, Singleton has had a far-reaching impact. He created opportunities for blacks and other minorities behind the scenes, hiring them in key positions such as producer, set designer, costumer, and development executive. Equally important, he gave several unknown actors, who for years were relegated to minor or supporting parts, leading roles in which they could shine and which catapulted them to stardom. Singleton is the director who cast Cuba Gooding Jr., Ice Cube, Nia Long, and Taraji P. Henson in their first major movie roles. In the mid-'90s, when Jennifer Connelly was on nobody's A-list and years away from winning an Oscar, he cast her in *Higher Learning*. He is the director who showed the romantic sides of Tyrese Gibson, Ving Rhames, and Tupac Shakur, as well as the producer who tapped Terrence Howard for his Oscar-nominated role in *Hustle & Flow*. Other performers, including Angela Bassett, Laurence Fishburne, Jeffrey Wright, and Chiwetel Ejiofor, have delivered some of their most memorable work in his movies.

This book will detail John Singleton's personal arc from film school sensation to seasoned filmmaker with his own star on the Hollywood Walk of Fame. From the start of his career, Singleton sat for hours of interviews with both the American and foreign press. In discussions that date back to 1991 and continue through 2007, the man and his achievements come into sharp focus. We learn which movies fascinated Singleton as a child and hear him describe in vivid detail the early experiences that formed his point of view. He talks about shuttling between his parents before an incident at school forced him to move in with his father for good. He explains his love for hip hop and his disdain for the LAPD. Perhaps most important, we find out that the first time Singleton picked up a film camera was the summer before his senior year in high school. He later directed an 8mm short about a black teenager who kills himself over a blond-haired white girl. Singleton tells *Why We Make Movies* author George Alexander that he submitted the short to a film competition for the National Association for the Advancement of Colored People and, not surprisingly, didn't win. "I don't think that [story] went over too well with the NAACP," he says, laughing. Among other things, Singleton discusses the basis for his feature films, working in Hollywood, and why he considers himself an "old school director." The nearly three-dozen interviews that appear here are arranged chronologically and have not been edited in any significant way. Repetitions should be viewed as evidence of Singleton's focus at that point in his life.

Singleton will forever be known for *Boyz N the Hood*, his modern classic set on the streets of South Central Los Angeles, where he grew up amid gang violence. Made for a modest $5.7 million, it took in nearly $60 million in the U.S. alone, making it one of the most profitable films of 1991. Only twenty-three at the time of the film's release, Singleton was hailed as a wunderkind in the press and compared to the likes of Orson Welles. Critics praised his skill at winning natural performances from his actors and his confident camera-work. The film earned him a pair of Academy Award nominations for original screenplay and directing. His nod in the directing category made Singleton both the first African American and the youngest person ever to compete for the award. (Welles, the esteemed auteur, had previously held that distinction for directing his 1941 masterpiece *Citizen Kane* at the age of twenty-five).

Timing is everything, and Singleton's rise in the movie business benefited in some ways from what a *New York Times Magazine* cover story described as Hollywood's sudden open-door policy toward black filmmakers. In the mid-to-late 1980s, Spike Lee (*Do the Right Thing*), Robert Townsend (*Hollywood Shuffle*), the Hudlin brothers (*House Party*), Charles Lane (*Sidewalk Stories*), and Wendell B. Harris (*Chameleon Street*) set the stage for a kind of black film renaissance reminiscent of the 1970s, the last time major studios produced black-themed stories en masse. In 1991, an unprecedented nineteen films with black directors were released in theaters. *Boyz N the Hood*, which caused a sensation at the Cannes International Film Festival that May, was unlike anything that had been seen before. It was a major studio film that was exclusively about black characters, written and directed by a black man, and filmed on location with a crew that was 90 percent black. More significantly, it acted as a bridge between commercial movies and hip hop, which was fast becoming a dominant art form in America.

The rise of rap music created a hunger not only for fresh faces, but also for a new black identity on the screen, one that struck its fans as authentic and uncompromising. This was precisely the attitude that Singleton envisioned for *Boyz N the Hood*. While he was by no means the earliest director to capitalize on hip hop, or to cast its stars in movies, he became the first to translate the politics and passion of the music into an artfully woven story that didn't speak down to its audience. Talking to Peter Brunette in *Sight and Sound* magazine, the director says what matters most to him is that his film is authentic to "the brothers and the sisters I made the film for. The people on the street." The success of *Boyz N the Hood* did more than win Singleton an armful of trophies from the New York Film Critics Circle, the Los Angeles Film Critics Association, and the MTV Movie Awards; it pointed to the box-office bankability of hip-hop stars and created a new genre—hood movies—that helped define the era.

Music is clearly a deep source of inspiration for Singleton, who's been called the first director of the hip-hop generation. In a *Rolling Stone* article by Alan Light, Singleton credits a Public Enemy CD with "changing his life." Later, in a *Washington Post* feature, the director tells Kristal Brent Zook, "My goal [with *Baby Boy*] was to try to make a film that was kind of like a rap album: audacious, young, brash . . . funky." During long delays in filming on location, Singleton has been known to pull out a boom box and turn on some music (Rick James's "Super Freak," for instance) at "block-party decibel level." For a short period, he had a record division within his company, New Deal Productions, and he toyed with directing music videos. His first was the lavish video clip for Michael Jackson's hit song *Remember the Time*, which was set in ancient Egypt and featured an all-star cast including Eddie Murphy, Magic Johnson, and supermodel Iman.

Singleton, a short (5 feet 7), wiry, and energetic man with a shaved head, swaggering gait, and laidback persona, resists categorization. As a journalist once pointed out, he challenges you to define him and then defies all who try. In conversation, he has an infectious enthusiasm and comes across as a supreme strategist who is always planning two moves ahead on the game board. He's been described as defiant, brash, thoughtful, guarded, and, above all, determined. After months of unsuccessfully shopping around a musical-drama about a Memphis pimp (Terrence Howard) who dreams of rap stardom, Singleton decided to bankroll the movie with $3 million of his own money. Studio executives "couldn't see past the stereotypes and see the humanity in these characters," he explains to Lola Ogunnaike of the *New York Times*. "Everybody thought I was crazy." All that changed when director Craig Brewer's *Hustle & Flow* turned out to be a major hit at the Sundance Film Festival in 2005, just as Singleton had envisioned; its rights sold for a cool $9 million and Singleton signed a $7 million two-movie deal with Paramount and MTV Films. *Hustle & Flow* was also nominated for two Oscars, winning for best original song (the catchy street anthem *It's Hard Out Here for a Pimp*).

Considering his place at the forefront of black film as well as his reputation as a tastemaker, to say nothing of his historic achievement as the first African American nominated for a best director Oscar, it's remarkable that not one film historian has engaged in a comprehensive study of John Singleton's work. Scholars aren't alone. Many serious film journals (think: *Cineaste*, *Film Comment*, *Fade In*, *American Cinematographer*) also have neglected to cover Singleton's films in any significant way. Instead, the majority of the critical analysis of African Americans in film tends to focus on color-line-breaking performers such as Dorothy Dandridge and Sidney Poitier. Black directors, with the exception of Spike Lee, have been ignored in large part by academia.

This lack of attention is all the more troubling because historically black directors have had a notoriously difficult time breaking into the studio system. Gifted filmmakers such as Charles Burnett (*Killer of Sheep*) and Julie Dash (*Daughters of the Dust*) have won critical acclaim but continue to struggle. Even movies with a high-profile producer like Oprah Winfrey (*The Great Debaters*) behind them rarely get the backing that they deserve. Part of the problem, Singleton explains to Patrick Goldstein of the *Los Angeles Times*, is that Hollywood retains a white-dominated studio structure. Things haven't changed all that much from the days of Louis B. Mayer and Jack Warner. "The film industry," Goldstein writes, "is full of all sorts of progressive causes, but when it comes to hiring people of color, it betrays a huge gap between its ideals and its actions."

Singleton, who is trying to do for South Central L.A. what Spike Lee did for Brooklyn, has lived and worked for nearly his entire life just a short car ride away from Hollywood. He was born on January 6, 1968, the only child of teenage parents. His father, a real estate broker, and his mother, a pharmaceutical sales executive, never married but remained close and took turns raising him. A latchkey kid, he spent a lot of time reading comic books and watching movies shown at a nearby drive-in theater out of his apartment's back window. When *Star Wars* was released in 1977, Singleton's father took him to see the sci-fi fantasy and the film made a huge impression. After seeing the movie about a dozen times, he began to break down how a film was made. Before long, he and a friend began making illustrated stories in class using notepads or the margins of books. They would draw their favorite comic book characters (Spider-Man and Power Man) and invent new adventures for them, or they would make up another episode of *Star Wars*. They called them flip books.

"In my neighborhood when we sat around talking about what we wanted to be when we grew up, everyone would say that they wanted to be a basketball player or a football player," Singleton remembers. "When I'd say that I wanted to be a film director, they'd say, 'Film director? What's that?' I'd tell them and they'd say, 'Ain't no white people gonna let no black people make no damn movies.'"

Singleton, however, grew up convinced that he could accomplish whatever he set his mind to. He started hanging out at a revival movie house. While his friends were selling drugs and getting into trouble, Singleton was getting into art films. He began studying Francis Ford Coppola, Akira Kurosawa, Martin Scorsese, and Woody Allen, directors who told stories that were culturally specific. "Like François Truffaut, who said that films saved him from being a delinquent, films saved me from being a delinquent," Singleton says.

After reading *Skywalking*, Dale Pollock's biography of George Lucas, Singleton decided to apply to Lucas's alma mater, the University of Southern California. As one of the few black students in its prestigious film program, and one who was not about to kiss up to anyone, Singleton felt alienated. (That sense of being an outsider is something Singleton, despite his achievements, has continued to struggle with ever since.) At school, he was seen as the "militant black dude that everybody thinks is a weirdo" and he says that he specialized in "busting people's chops." Some schoolmates who were rich and well connected took pleasure in telling him that he would never make it. In a Playboy article by David Resin (September 1993), Singleton remembers being eager to prove them wrong, and that he began studying film the way an athlete would devour game tapes of an opponent. Singleton would go on to win several writing awards, attracting the attention of the Creative Artists Agency, which signed him while he was still an undergraduate. "I want[ed] to come out of school just like a first-round draft pick, but in a filmic sense," he said. "I'm not going to let nobody get in my way."

Inspired by *Do the Right Thing*, Singleton decided to pen a hard-hitting drama that captured the essence of South Central L.A. He pitched a semiautobiographical coming-of-age drama to his screenwriting class as his magnum opus, and he sat down to write it listening to the gangsta rap of N.W.A. Every character, every sound in his script is rooted in the working-class neighborhood he called home, a place where young black males were an endangered species. Growing up, Singleton had to live with the sputter of automatic gunfire in the distance and the rumble of crime copters overhead. During the Reagan years, gangs turned the area into an urban war zone. Crack-addicts wandered the streets and the alleys were littered with garbage and, sometimes, dead bodies. There was always the sound of hip-hop booming from passing cars. Singleton took all of those day-to-day gritty life experiences and compressed them into *Boyz N the Hood*. Growing up like that, he tells Goldstein during a tour of his childhood haunts, "makes you not think in terms of the future, because who knows if you'll be around. So you say, 'Not next year. Not next week. I'm going to get mine now.'"

Between classes at U.S.C., Singleton began taking meetings with studio executives interested in optioning his script, which was creating a buzz around town. Despite his inexperience behind the camera (he had made two silent 8mm shorts), Singleton insisted that only he would direct the movie. He didn't trust Hollywood directors. The movie *Colors*, released a few years earlier, angered him, and when the film's producer visited U.S.C. for a preview screening Singleton stood up and attacked him for billing it as a movie about L.A. gangs when it was actually about two white cops. "Well, Ice-T wrote the music," the producer said. And Singleton responded, "Well, Ice-T didn't write the fucking script." Hollywood is notorious for making movies such as *Mississippi Burning*, in which African Americans seem like extras in their own stories, and Singleton wasn't about to let yet another well-meaning, out-of-touch white director reshape his script. "Look," he says in an early interview. "In this business you get hired for your vision, and your vision begins with your script. I'm a writer first, and I direct in order to protect my vision."

Cheap comedies and exploitative action movies have never interested him. Instead, Singleton has always admired directors who make personal movies about subjects close to them. He understands the power of the imagery and the responsibility of making movies. Through his work he has striven to present a more balanced depiction of African American life. In interviews, he has talked about the wealth of black literature that could be mined by directors. "Everybody wanted to get rich, but nobody wanted to work to get there," he says about his film school days. "I wasn't into film to get money. I just wanted to make classic films about my people in a way no one had ever done."

After a string of contemporary dramas based on his own screenplays, Singleton was approached in 1995 by producer Jon Peters to direct *Rosewood*. The harrowing story of black genocide proved to be a major departure for the director: there was a large cast and logistically complicated shots involving a speeding train and gunmen on horseback. Filming took place in the swamps of Florida, where two small towns from the 1920s were replicated. The production employed a number of whites from the Deep South. "We had a lot of crackers on the crew. Dozens," Singleton says. Some questioned the need to retell the story of an all-black community that was destroyed by a lynch mob more than a half-century before.

While directing *Rosewood*, Singleton thought a lot about *Schindler's List*, Steven Spielberg's 1993 Holocaust masterpiece, which he respected for its attention to detail and multidimensional villains like Ralph Fiennes's SS commandant. Singleton wanted to avoid turning what actually happened in Rosewood into a tale of "fire-breathing racists and holier-than-thou blacks." In his vision of the horror, he decided to stick closely to the actual events but Singleton admits to Jay Carr of the *Boston Globe* that he struggled to find something positive in the black response. This had to be a movie that black audiences would want to go to see, and as such Singleton felt it was important to show some of the black residents fight back. A fictional character named Mann was added to exemplify black heroism. Singleton explains that Ving

Rhames's character was "a spectrum of black men in American history . . . who never really get anything to do in American cinema."

Early in his career, Singleton says, he was dubbed a "serious filmmaker," and it is not difficult to see why someone might come to that conclusion. In spite of his flair for storytelling, it becomes obvious watching some of Singleton's work that he is determined to say something of critical importance. That ambition, critics say, sometimes works against his best instincts. *Higher Learning*, Singleton's racially and sexually charged look at college life, was accused of overreaching and dealing more with symbols than characters. Others have accused him of being preachy. Singleton countered that he is a director of movies, not messages but that he believes that movies could affect people's lives. "Films serve different purposes," he tells *Sight and Sound*'s Peter Brunette. "Some are meant just to entertain but there's also room for other films that inform as well."

Things have not always gone Singleton's way. After the initial success of *Boyz N the Hood*, Singleton's next three films failed to generate any substantial box office. *Rosewood* even lost money. The problem, he admits, is that he "kept feeling like each film had to be more serious than the last one." Eventually, he came to a point where he wanted to just relax and make the kind of fun movie that people watch while munching on popcorn. It was not an easy transition. During the making of *Shaft*, his tribute to the '70s icon with Samuel L. Jackson, Singleton openly feuded with producer Scott Rudin over the title character's sexuality and the film's action sequences. The original became a phenomenon by introducing a new kind of take-charge African American hero; Shaft (played Richard Roundtree) was a black private dick who's a sex machine to all the chicks. Rudin, who is white, and the successful producer behind *Clueless* and *The Addams Family*, wanted a family-friendly movie. "It was very evident. Nobody tried to conceal that [there was tension] on this movie," says Christian Bale, who portrays the movie's wealthy, murderous thug, in an *Entertainment Weekly* cover story written by Steve Daly. The tension started when white screenwriter Richard Price was brought on board to rework some of Singleton's earlier drafts, which were deemed too risqué. "Price didn't have a clue about the attitude of Shaft," Singleton says in a *Los Angeles Daily News* article by Glenn Whipp. "He took out all the flavorful dialogue. He just didn't get it. His pop culture references were stuff like 'Bulldog Drummond.' Now what does that have to do with John Shaft?"

Unlike most filmmakers of his generation, Singleton does not normally draw his inspiration from other films. An acute observer, Singleton often gleans his stories from the streets and conversations he's had. He places great value in the African oral storytelling tradition and tries to explore the black community through his characters, several of whom are modeled after friends and others around him. "I always want people to point to the screen and say my cousin is like that, or my brother's like that," he says. "The film should get responses, good or uncomfortable." He's attracted to ambiguous characters; they're usually working-class types or people drifting in the margins of society: neighborhood dope boys, poetry-writing beauticians, reformed ex-cons, ambitious postal workers, college feminists, and thrill-seeking gear heads. He has an insatiable curiosity. The drama *Baby Boy*, about the infantilization of black men, was inspired by a visit to the Crenshaw Mall, in South Central L.A. "I'd be sitting up at the mall, watching these cats walk around the mall rubbing their chests, talking to these fifteen-, sixteen-year-old girls," he says. "Those guys in their twenties are the ones that foster all these teenage pregnancies. So I just figured, damn, I want to tell a story about a guy like that."

Black manhood is one of Singleton's dominant themes. He's interested in showing how black men define themselves, how they relate to one another, and the effects of the larger social forces on their lives. He's interested in the evolution of the character. Whereas in the past, black men in movies were generally depicted as one-dimensional, without character arcs of their own, in Singleton's work they are allowed to grow and change. In *Baby Boy*, Jody starts out as a womanizer who is unemployed and living off of his mother, but he later becomes a self-sufficient, responsible father who is monogamous.

In his films audiences meet a variety of black men, some strong-willed and loving. The men in his movies refuse to allow others to dictate who they are, and they demand respect. If they make a change, it's because they've come to that point. There is an inner strength to black men that movies often ignore. In *Shaft*, the title character confronts a colleague for making a racially insensitive remark while locking up a thug and later goes outside of the corrupt system to bring a bad guy to justice. He's a man of action. Just as important, in that strength he also shows that black men can be vulnerable. In one particularly unsettling scene in *Boyz N the Hood*, a self-loathing black officer pulls over Tre's car and harasses him to the point where the boy is moved to tears. He later breaks down in front of his girlfriend.

Oftentimes violent incidents are a rite of passage for his characters. They are victims of violence, not just perpetrators of it. Singleton shows that black men can be on both sides of the gun. And it's not just the men in his movies who are affected. *Poetic Justice* opens with Janet Jackson's character losing a loved one who is murdered at a drive-in theater, and the film shows how she copes with her loss.

Although violence permeates the world of his characters, Singleton is not the type of director who includes gunplay for casual, bang-bang effect. There are very few acts of gratuitous violence in his movies. When bloodshed is depicted, it carries a range of meanings. There is the cathartic violence of Doughboy in *Boyz N the Hood* gunning down his brother's killers, or the murder of an angelic foster mother in *Four Brothers*. Even in a movie like *2 Fast 2 Furious*, where Singleton is at his giddiest and tricked-out cars are as much characters in the film as the actors, the violence is never trivialized even when the movie's villain uses a metal wastebasket, a torch, and a rat to torture an uncooperative detective on his payroll. Perhaps because of the way in which he grew up, Singleton is extremely sensitive to the effects of violence.

For the past few years, Singleton has been focused on expanding his oeuvre and nurturing young filmmakers like *Hustle & Flow*'s writer-director Craig Brewer and Franc. Reyes, another double-threat whose film *Illegal Tender* was produced by Singleton in 2007. Future projects for Singleton include the Halle Berry drama *Tulia*, which is based on Nate Blakeslee's book about a small Texas town in which 10 percent of the black population was incarcerated on trumped-up charges. He is still trying to adapt a film about Marvel Comics' black superhero *Luke Cage*. His next feature, scheduled for release in 2009, is *The A-Team*, a big-budget action movie based on the 1980s hit TV show.

I want to thank the following people for all their support and guidance with the book: My family (Salaama, Langston, and Sadie), my father, Anthony, and my brothers (David, Tommy, Robert, Steven, Ken, Ron, and Timmy). Shout outs to Tom Lent, Reyhaneh Fathieh, and Jeffrey Ressner for your contributions, and a special thanks to everyone kind enough to waive the permission rights to their stories, without which there would be no book.

CB

CHRONOLOGY

1968   Born John Daniel Singleton on January 6, 1968 in Los Angeles,
California, to Danny Singleton and Sheila Ward-Johnson.

1986   Graduates from Blair High School in Pasadena, California.

1990   Graduates from the University of Southern California School
of Cinema-Television as a filmic writing major.

1991   Writes and directs *Boyz N the Hood*, starring Larry Fishburne,
Cuba Gooding Jr., Ice Cube, and Angela Bassett, his impressive
debut feature film. Singleton won the New York Film Critics
Circle Award for Best First-Time Director and was nominated
for two Academy Awards for Best Original Screenplay and Best
Directing.

1992   Writes and directs "Remember the Time," Michael Jackson's
big-budget music video set in ancient Egypt. Jackson plays a
court sorcerer opposite Eddie Murphy (the pharaoh), Earvin
"Magic" Johnson (a guard), and Iman (the queen).

1993   Writes, directs, and produces *Poetic Justice*, with Janet Jackson
and Tupac Shakur. Jackson's song "Again" was nominated for
Best Song at the Academy Awards.

1995   Writes, directs, and produces *Higher Learning*, with an ensemble cast that includes Omar Epps, Ice Cube, Jennifer Connelly,
Michael Rapaport, and black supermodel Tyra Banks in her
movie debut. (Singleton began dating Banks before filming,
but the couple broke up shortly after the film's release.)

1996   Rapper/actor Tupac Shakur is killed in a Las Vegas drive-by
shooting. Singleton had planned to make several movies with
Shakur, including *Baby Boy*, which he had written with Shakur
in mind. The director saw Shakur as "my Robert De Niro," his
alter ego on screen.

1997   Directs *Rosewood* with Jon Voight, Ving Rhames, Don Cheadle, Esther Rolle. It is Singleton's first time directing a script written by someone else and also the first time he had ever shot a film outside of California. The film is one of his best reviewed since *Boyz* but does poorly at the box-office.

1998   Produces *Woo* for Daisy von Scherler Mayer, with Jada Pinkett and Tommy Davidson. Singleton's first turn as producer is not commercially successful.

2000   Directs, co-writes and produces *Shaft*, starring Samuel L. Jackson, Vanessa Williams, Jeffrey Wright, and Christian Bale. Despite lukewarm reviews, Singleton's update of the 1971 blaxploitation classic was a summer crowd-pleaser.

2001   Writes, directs, and produces *Baby Boy*, with Tyrese Gibson, Taraji P. Henson, Omar Gooding, Ving Rhames, and Snoop Dogg. The film is shot on a tiny budget and considered a companion piece to *Boyz*.

2003   Directs *2 Fast 2 Furious* with Tyrese Gibson, Paul Walker, Eva Mendes, and Ludacris. The sequel to the 2001 blockbuster movie generates $242 million at box-offices worldwide, the biggest showing for a black-directed movie at the time.

2005   Directs *Four Brothers* with Mark Wahlberg, Tyrese Gibson, Andre Benjamin, Chiwetel Ejiofor, and Terrence Howard. The film is a modest hit at the box-office. Uses more than $3 million of his own money to produce *Hustle & Flow* for director Craig Brewer. The film, with Terrence Howard, Anthony Anderson, Taryn Manning, and Taraji P. Henson, won the Audience Award at the Sundance Film Festival and the Academy Award for Best Original Song for the rap act Three 6 Mafia. Howard also earned an Academy Award nomination for Best Actor. Singleton was awarded the "Behind the Lens" Award by DaimlerChrysler, which celebrates the achievements of individuals who work behind-the-scenes in the entertainment world.

2007   Produces *Black Snake Moan*, his second film with director Craig Brewer. Despite some controversial material and a cast that includes Samuel L. Jackson, Christian Ricci, and Justin Timberlake, the film never finds an audience.

2007   Produces *Illegal Tender* for director Franc. Reyes. The film stars Rick Gonzalez, Millie DeLeon, Dania Ramirez, and Tego Calderon.

FILMOGRAPHY

As Director

1991
BOYZ N THE HOOD
Columbia Pictures Corporation
Producer: Steve Nicolaides
Director: **John Singleton**
Screenplay: **John Singleton**
Cinematography: Charles Mills
Art Director: Bruce Bellamy
Editing: Bruce Canon
Music: Stanley Clarke
Cast: Doughboy (Ice Cube), Tre Styles (Cuba Gooding Jr.), Ricky Baker
(Morris Chestnut), Furious Styles (Larry Fishburne), Brandi (Nia Long),
Reva Devereaux (Angela Bassett), Brenda Baker (Tyra Ferrell), Shalika
(Regina King)
Color
112 minutes

1993
POETIC JUSTICE
Columbia Pictures Corporation
Producers: Steve Nicolaides, **John Singleton**, Dwight Alonzo Williams
(associate)
Director: **John Singleton**
Screenplay: **John Singleton**
Poetry: Maya Angelou
Cinematography: Peter Lyons Collister

Production Design: Keith Brian Burns
Editing: Bruce Canon
Music: Stanley Clarke
Cast: Justice (Janet Jackson), Lucky (Tupac Shakur), Jessie (Tyra Ferrell), Iesha (Regina King), Chicago (Joe Torry), Heywood (Roger Guenveur Smith), Markell (Q-Tip), Aunt June (Maya Angelou)
Color
109 minutes

1995
HIGHER LEARNING
Columbia Pictures Corporation
Producers: **John Singleton**, Paul Hall, Dwight Alonzo Williams (co-producer)
Director: **John Singleton**
Screenplay: **John Singleton**
Cinematography: Peter Lyons Collister
Production Design: Keith Brian Burns
Editing: Bruce Canon
Music: Stanley Clarke
Cast: Malik Williams (Omar Epps), Kristen Connor (Kristy Swanson), Remy (Michael Rapaport), Taryn (Jennifer Connelly), Fudge (Ice Cube), Wayne (Jason Wiles), Deja (Tyra Banks), Scott Moss (Cole Hauser), Professor Maurice Phipps (Laurence Fishburne), Monet (Regina King), Dreads (Busta Rhymes)
Color
127 minutes

1997
ROSEWOOD
Warner Brothers
Producers: Jon Peters, Tracy Barone (executive), Penelope L. Foster (co-producer), Russ Kavanaugh (associate), Peter A. Ramsey (associate)
Director: **John Singleton**
Screenplay: Greg Poirier
Cinematography: Johnny E. Jensen
Costume Design: Ruth Carter
Production Design: Paul Sylbert
Editing: Bruce Canon

Music: John Williams
Cast: John Wright (Jon Voight), Mann (Ving Rhames), Sylvester (Don Cheadle), Duke Purdy (Bruce McGill), James Taylor (Loren Dean), Aunt Sarah (Esther Rolle), Scrappie (Elise Neal), Lover (Robert Patrick), Sheriff Walker (Michael Rooker), Fanny Taylor (Catherine Kellner), Jewel (Akosua Busia)
Color
142 minutes

2000
SHAFT
Paramount Pictures
Producers: Scott Rudin, **John Singleton**, Adam Schroeder (executive), Paul Hall (executive), Steve Nicolaides (executive), Eric Steel (co-producer), Mark Roybal (associate)
Director: **John Singleton**
Screenplay: Richard Price, **John Singleton**, Shane Salerno
Cinematography: Donald E. Thorin
Production Design: Patrizia von Brandenstein
Editing: John Bloom
Music: David Arnold and Isaac Hayes
Cast: John Shaft (Samuel L. Jackson), Carmen Vasquez (Vanessa Williams), Peoples Hernandez (Jeffrey Wright), Walter Wade, Jr. (Christian Bale), Rasaan (Busta Rhymes), Jack Roselli (Dan Hedaya), Diane Palmieri (Toni Collette), Uncle John Shaft (Richard Roundtree), Jimmy Groves (Ruben Santiago-Hudson)
Color
99 minutes

2001
BABY BOY
Columbia Pictures Corporation
Producers: **John Singleton**, Dwight Willaims (executive)
Director: **John Singleton**
Screenplay: **John Singleton**
Cinematography: Charles E. Mills
Production Design: Keith Brian Burns
Editing: Bruce Cannon
Costume Design: Ruth Carter

Music: David Arnold
Cast: Jody (Tyrese Gibson), Yvette (Taraji P. Henson), Sweatpea (Omar
Gooding), Peanut (Tamara LaSeon Bass), Miss Herron (Candy Ann Brown),
Juanita (A. J. Johnson), Melvin (Ving Rhames), Rodney (Calvin "Snoop
Dogg" Broadus, Jr.)
Color
134 minutes

2003
2 FAST 2 FURIOUS
Universal Pictures
Producers: Neal H. Moitz, Lee R. Mayes (executive), Michael Fottrell
(executive), Heather Lieberman (co-producer)
Director: **John Singleton**
Screenplay: Michael Brandt, Derek Hass
Cinematography: Matthew F. Leonetti
Production Design: Keith Brian Burns
Editing: Bruce Cannon, Dallas Puett
Music: David Arnold
Cast: Brian O'Conner (Paul Walker), Roman Pearce (Tyrese Gibson), Monica
Fuentes (Eva Mendes), Carter Verone
(Cole Hauser), Tej (Chris "Ludacris" Bridges), Agent Markham (James
Remar), Agent Bilkins (Thom Barry), Slap Jack (Michael Ealy)
Color
108 minutes

2005
FOUR BROTHERS
Paramount Pictures
Producers: Lorenzo Di Bonaventura, Ric Kennedy (executive), Erik Howsam
(executive)
Director: **John Singleton**
Screenplay: David Elliot, Paul Lovett
Cinematography: Matthew F. Leonetti
Production Design: Keith Brian Burns
Costume Design: Ruth Carter
Editing: Bruce Cannon, Billy Fox
Music: David Arnold
Cast: Bobby Mercer (Mark Wahlberg), Angel Mercer (Tyrese Gibson),
Jeremiah Mercer (Andre Benjamin), Jack Mercer (Garrett Hedlund),

Lt. Green (Terrence Howard), Detective Fowler (Josh Charles), Sofi (Sofia Vergara), Evelyn Mercer (Fionnula Flanagan), Victor Sweet (Chiwetel Ejiofor), Camille Mercer (Taraji P. Henson)
Color
108 minutes

As Producer

1998
WOO
New Line Cinema
Producers: Beth Hubbard, Michael Hubbard, **John Singleton** (executive), Howard Hobson (executive), Bradford W. Smith (executive), David C. Johnson (co-producer), Bill Carraro (co-producer)
Director: Daisy V. S. Mayer
Screenplay: David C. Johnson
Cinematography: Jean Lepine
Production Design: Ina Mayhew
Editing: Nicholas Eliopoulos, Janice Hampton
Music: Michel Colombier
Cast: Woo (Jada Pinkett), Tim (Tommy Davidson), Frankie (Duane Martin), Romaine (Michael Ralph), Hop (Darrel Heath), Lenny (Dave Chappelle), Claudette (Paula Jai Parker), Darryl (LL Cool J), Tookie (Aida Turturro)
Color
90 minutes

2005
HUSTLE & FLOW
Paramount Vantage
Producers: **John Singleton**, Stephanie Allain, Dwight Williams (executive), Preston L. Holmes (associate)
Director: Craig Brewer
Screenplay: Craig Brewer
Cinematography: Amelia Vincent
Production Design: Keith Brian Burns
Editing: Billy Fox
Original Score: Scott Bomar
Cast: Djay (Terrence Howard), Key (Anthony Anderson), Nola (Taryn Manning), Shug (Taraji P. Henson), Shelby (DJ Qualls), Skinny Black (Chris

"Ludacris" Bridges), Lexus (Paula Jai Parker), Yevette (Elise Neal), Amel
(Isaac Hayes), Tigga (Jordan Houston)
Color
115 minutes

2007
BLACK SNAKE MOAN
Paramount Vantage
Producers: **John Singleton**, Stephanie Allain, Ron Schmidt (executive)
Director: Craig Brewer
Screenplay: Craig Brewer
Cinematography: Amelia Vincent
Costume Design: Paul A. Simmons
Production Design: Keith Brian Burns
Editing: Billy Fox
Music: Scott Bomar
Cast: Lazarus (Samuel L. Jackson), Rae (Christina Ricci), Ronnie (Justin
Timberlake), Angela (S. Epatha Merkerson), Reverend R. L. (John Cothran),
Tehronne (David Banner), Gill (Michael Raymond-James)
Color
115 minutes

2007
ILLEGAL TENDER
Universal Pictures
Producers: **John Singleton**, Preston L. Holmes (executive), Dwight Williams
(executive)
Director: Franc. Reyes
Screenplay: Franc. Reyes
Cinematography: Frank Byers
Costume Design: Rahimah Yoba
Production Design: Keith Brian Burns
Editing: Tony Ciccone
Music: Heitor Pereira
Cast: Wilson DeLeon, Jr. (Rick Gonzalez), Wanda De Jesus (Millie DeLeon),
Ana (Dania Ramirez), young Millie DeLeon (Jessica Pimentel), Wilson
DeLeon, Sr. (Manny Perez), Randy (Antonio Ortiz), Choco (Tego Calderon)
Color
108 minutes

JOHN SINGLETON

INTERVIEWS

His New Hood Is Hollywood

PATRICK GOLDSTEIN/1991

CRUISING AROUND his old neighborhood is dredging up memories for John Singleton. As he swings onto Century Boulevard, he points out Red's Liquor Store, where he bought comic books and swiped copies of *Players* magazine. Driving by an aging apartment complex, he gestures toward a row of one-way street signs. "They used to be regular two-way streets, but when crack came in, they made them one-way so it'd be easier for the cops to chase the drug dealers."

At twenty-three, Singleton is relishing his first taste of Hollywood heat with the release of his debut film, *Boyz N the Hood*. But the movie business is far from the brash young writer-director's mind right now as he takes a visitor on a tour of his childhood haunts in South-Central Los Angeles.

Singleton says he was often one of the smallest kids in the playground. But when he was threatened, he felt obligated to respond. "The thing that made me different from my friends was that I had a strong commitment to not back away from a fight," he says, driving past his first home on West 60th Street, the gang turf he says is the Rolling 60s. "I wasn't big but"—he taps his skull—"I could (mess) with people's heads."

In elementary school, if a kid gave Singleton trouble, he would simply inform his adversary that the Earth was spinning so close to the sun that they were about to collide and destroy the entire universe.

"That usually did it," he says coolly. "They'd start screaming and go running off to the teacher. I didn't do anything stupid. I used my brain. I guess I was a lucky kid. If I did something bad, I never got caught. And if I did something good, everybody noticed."

Singleton has taken his brainpower—and his unflinching ambition—and focused it on his dream of making a film portrait of his boyhood adventures. Though a graduate of USC Film School, a Hollywood factory that has produced such young directors as Phil Joanou and James Foley, Singleton's only student-film experience was directing a pair of silent 8-millimeter movies. But his film-school scripts were impressive—Singleton won the Jack Nicholson Writing Award two years in a row. His accomplishments created the kind of industry buzz that got him signed to CAA, Hollywood's hottest agency—and wooed by Columbia Pictures.

All along, Singleton had insisted that, despite his inexperience, his script for *Boyz N the Hood* could be directed by only one person—himself. And after a lengthy meeting on the Columbia lot, he earned a powerful ally—Columbia studio chief Frank Price.

"I thought John's script had a distinctive voice and great insight," says Price. "But when we met, I was really impressed. He's not just a good writer, but he has enormous self-confidence and assurance. In fact, the last time I'd met someone that young with so much self-assurance was Steven Spielberg. We had John do some test scenes with several actors and they turned out so well that I became completely convinced—I thought he'd do a terrific job as director."

With Columbia Pictures behind it, *Boyz N the Hood* emerges as the first all-black movie about L.A.'s urban strife to be bankrolled by a major studio. More important, it's one of the first times a young African-American filmmaker has dealt with the searing issues of his generation—family disintegration, gang turf wars, and crack addiction.

It's the cinematic flip side to Steve Martin's *L.A. Story*, a razor-sharp portrait of violence and retribution set against a family's struggle to provide their son with the tools of survival. Presented at the Cannes Film Festival in May, the film earned a tumultuous ovation—with critical praise to match. Calling it a film of "extraordinary maturity and emotional depth," *Chicago Sun-Times* critic Roger Ebert hailed the movie as "not simply a brilliant directorial debut, but an American film of enormous relevance."

Shot in various neighborhoods last winter, *Boyz N the Hood* is a South-Central coming-of-age story that traces the growth of three childhood pals—Tre Styles, played by Cuba Gooding Jr.; Doughboy, his gang member pal, played by rap star Ice Cube; and Ricky, a budding football star, played by Morris Chestnut.

Of the three, only Tre has an active father figure, Furious Styles (played by Larry Fishburne), who steers his son away from gangland temptations, preaches black-pride sermons ("Never respect someone who doesn't respect you back") and offers a steely sense of parental discipline and dignity. The film's dramatic question: Can the bonds of family and friendship survive on the mean streets of South-Central Los Angeles?

As a stark reminder of the stranglehold of violence in this society, Singleton floods the soundtrack to *Boyz N the Hood* with the crackle of gunfire and the whir of police helicopters. The film opens with a volley of shots from a drive-by shooting. Wherever Tre Styles goes, someone is putting a gun to his head, whether it's a local Crips gang-banger or a bullying black cop. Doing her homework, Tre's girlfriend is startled by staccato gunfire. When she and Tre make love, we see the copters circling overhead, flashing their searchlights.

Singleton knows this environment firsthand, having grown up in several South-Central neighborhoods. "I've heard the copters all my life," he says, driving down Crenshaw Boulevard. "It's an incredible kind of psychological violence. It makes you not think in terms of the future, because who knows if you'll be around. So you say, 'Not next year. Not next week. I'm going to get mine now.' The only reason I ever thought about the future was because my Moms and my Pops made me think about it. I didn't get involved with gangs, like some of my friends. If I'd joined a gang, my Pops would've kicked my ass."

Singleton turns off Crenshaw and heads toward a neighborhood where he spent his pre-teen years, living with his mother. Down the street is Darbey Park, a major playground hangout for Singleton and his friends. He points to a fence around the park with a padlocked gate.

"Around 1984, after Reagan had been in office for a few years and after crack started coming in, everything changed here," he says. "They ran out of recreational funds, so the park ceased to be a recreational facility. It became a turf for the gangs. And if you went there and weren't with the right crowd, you could get hurt."

Singleton slows the car to a crawl, staring off into the park. "That's what I mean about how things have changed down here. When I was little, you could fight with somebody, kick their butt, and then you could still become friends. But after crack and the gangs took over, it all changed. If you beat somebody up and kicked their ass, they'd go get one of their friends with a gun and come back and shoot you.

"All I know is that ever since black people were brought here—dragged, kicking and screaming, out of the motherland—we've been under some police state, whether it's slavery or the LAPD."

The cutting edge of today's black culture, whether in the ferocious rap broadsides of Ice Cube and Public Enemy, the white-hot films of Matty Rich and Mario Van Peebles or the icy private-eye thrillers of Walter Mosley, explores the chilling specter of rage and violence. For Singleton, sipping an Orange Julius at the Crenshaw Mall, the rage is born of little indignities.

"I could leave this mall, roll up Crenshaw (Boulevard) and if I was talking on the phone to my girlfriend, some cop could take me for a suspected drug dealer," he says with a shrug. "Can you imagine that—it's bad for me to have a cellular phone, even in my line of work? It's psychological lynching."

It's a measure of Singleton's disdain—and alienation—that the most hated authority figure in *Boyz N the Hood* is a black cop. He complains that when the LAPD "virtually lynched" Rodney King, one of the first groups to support Police Chief Daryl Gates was the Black Policemen's Assn.

"I can't change white cops," he says. "But I think I can change the minds of some black cops. They shouldn't care more about doughnuts and coffee than they care about the people in their community."

The central character in *Boyz N the Hood*, Tre Styles, is patterned after Singleton. But the character he often identifies with the most is Doughboy, the neighborhood's gun-toting enforcer. First seen as a chubby neighborhood delinquent, Doughboy returns from prison with a fatalistic film noir-style sense of doom, cruising the 'hood with a posse of bloods, ogling women and sizing up rivals.

"Sometimes I really feel like Doughboy," he says quietly. "I think it has a lot to do with the need to strike out and not think about your actions. I've been in situations where I was so mad that I wanted to stab somebody—I wanted to kill them."

He sighs. "But I couldn't do it because I thought too much about the consequences. I knew I'd go to jail. I knew someone could die. At times, ignorance is freedom. Doughboy didn't have a father like Furious Styles, who would make him think about his actions before he did them."

Singleton takes great pride that his parents, though living apart, provided him with a strong family bond—and nurtured his dreams as a budding filmmaker.

When he was a kid, he was in awe of the black bourgeoisie who lived in View Park. Now he has home there. When he was fourteen he went back to see *E.T.* over and over, saving the ticket stub from each theater he'd seen it in. Now he visits Steven Spielberg on the secrecy-shrouded set of *Hook*, sitting with him between takes, talking about his favorite pictures.

To an outsider, this volatile mixture of sweetness and wrath can be unsettling—one minute Singleton is waxing nostalgic about *E.T.*, the next minute he's dismissing his hometown as a police state. But coming of age in South Central has given him a radically different cultural compass from

his white filmmaker contemporaries. They share the same pop culture influences: Singleton was transfixed the first time he saw *Star Wars*, he openly
idolizes Spielberg and Francis Ford Coppola, and when he was shooting *Boyz
N the Hood*, you could often find him on the set, between shots, buried in a
Spiderman comic book.

It's Singleton's life experience that sets him apart. He's survived, but not
without scars. His favorite childhood movies may have been fantasies, but
he doesn't embrace movie escapism. As a filmmaker, Singleton searches for
inspiration—and affirmation—on the grim street corners of his home turf.

Singleton has always been an outsider, whether when being bused to white
high schools or when mingling with ambitious young white film students
at USC. So it comes as no surprise that when you first meet the baby-faced
director, he seems guarded and detached, almost aloof. Once he gets warmed
up, he proves to be an outspoken guy—with a sense of mission. When a
salesman at a local clothing store asks if he enjoyed directing a movie, Singleton responds, without hesitation: "It was the first job I ever had where I got
to work early everyday."

Consider him a filmmaker still wrestling with the complicated furies of
youth. Wandering through the mall, he jumps from a dissection of black
economic problems ("We need an organized infrastructure in our community so we can be self-sufficient") to a ranking of the area's female populace
("The Crenshaw Mall has the finest women anywhere").

Singleton's office is on the Columbia Pictures lot, but his heart remains in
South Central. Unimpressed by the trappings of Hollywood—he still drives
his mother's car—he's a loner with few close friends. He calls his new home
his "fortress of solitude." When searching for inspiration, he'll often visit the
Crenshaw Mall with a notebook and 3x5 cards, where he can "brainstorm"
for fresh ideas while munching on a Hot Dog on a Stick.

Still, Singleton is enjoying this first burst of acclaim. At Cannes, he was
impressed by the respect the French paid visiting filmmakers. "They treat you
like a king, like a dignitary," he says. "It doesn't even matter how good your
film is!"

He wryly noted that the Cannes paparazzi had trouble distinguishing him
from a considerably better-known black film director. "It was funny to see
these photographers come racing across the street to take my picture," he
recalls. "And then when I'd sign autographs, they'd all say, 'Oh, no, you're
not Spike Lee.'"

Once Singleton gets comfortable, his youthful bravado begins to show.
Asked if he worried about studio interference with his film, he breezily pro-
nounces, "If your dailies are good, they leave you alone." He said the studio

brass stopped dropping by the set after the first few weeks. "I'm sure they saw I was doing OK, but I did tell them horror stories about what happens down here—shootings, drive-bys. They didn't want to come around much after that.

"It's funny," he continues. "When I was working on my movie, Columbia fired directors off of two other pictures." He flashes a mischievous grin. "But I wasn't worried. I figured, if they fire me, who are they going to get to finish the movie—Alan Parker?

"Gangs are just a symptom of the problems in the black community. They're a rite of passage to manhood. Every society has that. For black youths in South Central, it's joining a gang. In another society, it's joining a football team. The problem with the rite of passage in South Central is that it can get you killed.

"Wow, they've really fixed up that house over there," says Singleton, walking around his father's old neighborhood at Vermont near 101st Street. "It's painted and everything—that was the first crack house around here. I remember when it was a mess."

Armed with an invitation to *Boyz N the Hood*'s Hollywood premiere, Singleton is visiting his childhood pal, Michael Winters, who is Singleton's model for Doughboy, the neighborhood enforcer. The two haven't seen each other since Singleton started shooting his movie. But they've been friends since sixth grade, when they were learning to skateboard, riding the bus downtown to see triple-feature movies and starting to take an interest in girls.

Watching Winters roam around his house, looking for a pack of cigarettes, you can imagine how this cheery guy with the soft, round face could inspire a nickname like Doughboy (actually his childhood moniker was Fat Back). An avid storyteller, Winters eagerly recalls their boyhood adventures, many of which are recounted, with some dramatic license, in the movie.

"John and I were going through puberty at the same time so we were always interested in the same girls," Winters recalls with glee. "Remember Gigi?"

Singleton notes that a Gigi-style character is in the film. "You'll recognize a lot of things. Remember that time my Pops shot at that guy trying to rob our house one night—and put a big hole in the wall? That's in the movie too."

Winters is open about having been in gangs when he was younger. "Yeh, I was doing all that stuff, smoking weed and hanging out. I was in the 107th Street Hoover Crips. It's part of growing up around here—hanging around with the in-crowd.

"I remember going to see John when he was living in Inglewood and you'd get hassled by the guys over there. If you went into a Bloods neighborhood, you'd get real sweated. You know, they'd say, 'What's up, cuz?' And you had to get a pass to stay over there."

On gang turf, violence comes with the territory. "Remember Robbie Springer?" Singleton says. "He was the big bully of the neighborhood—our protector. He got his reputation by breaking into everybody's houses. But once people got to know him, he was OK. He was seventeen, but he seemed a lot older."

Springer didn't make it past seventeen. "He was in the Hoovers," Winters explains. "And one night, some other gang came out here and shot him." He points out the window. "Right over there in that alley. It left a big impression on people. Everyone was saying, 'Damn, he's gone. He ain't here no more.'"

Winters has considered moving out of the neighborhood, but he feels anchored there. "I've been here eighteen years," he says. "It's my block, my street. My name's written out there in the cement. The gangs are still here, but when you get older, you get out of that stuff. You start thinking about making money and doing something else with your life."

As Winters is talking, Singleton walks over to the window and gazes out at a large shade tree in the front yard. "When the crime copters would fly over here, looking for somebody, I used to love to stand under that tree and watch their lights," he says. "I'd go run out in the street, trying to attract the helicopter, so we could play in the spotlights. It was really beautiful. When they'd point the searchlights at the ground, the light would come through that tree in hundreds of tiny little shafts, dappling through the leaves."

Once Singleton lingered too long in the lights and got caught. "Suddenly five or six police cars converged on us—it was like out of a movie. They pulled their guns on us, searched us and everything. They'd say, 'Don't we know you from somewhere? Didn't we pick you up last week? Don't you have a big brother in a gang?' Finally, when they realized we were just a couple of kids, they'd tell us not to mess with them and let us go."

Winters shakes his head. "I remember once, sitting on the curb, when a cop car drove by and I went, 'Oink. Oink!'" He laughs. "Man, that car squealed back so fast, right up to us. And they said, 'You got something to say? 'Cause if you do, we'll pull your ass in here and beat the (expletive) out of you!'"

"When I was a kid I got teased a lot for wearing glasses, so I always carried a little razor in my pocket to protect myself. Not a big thing, just a box-cutter I'd got from my dad when he worked at Thrifty's. When you're in the eighth grade, if you threaten a kid with a razor, he'll know what's up. You had to do something. It's either that or sit home a lot."

Back at the Crenshaw Mall, Singleton is in high spirits. He's just picked up a batch of snapshots from Cannes, including some of him posing with Spike Lee and Bill Duke, director of *A Rage in Harlem*. (Ever the perfectionist,

Singleton made the photo store develop the shots twice—they were too washed out the first time.)

As a director, Singleton says his biggest role model has been Lee, who has graciously offered film tips—and how's this for clout—took Singleton to the fifth game of the NBA championships, where he had front-row seats. "If it wasn't for him, I wouldn't be making movies. He's the one filmmaker who's made it and stayed black. We're obviously different in some ways—he's East Coast, I'm West Coast. But if people want to compare me to him, that's an honor."

Singleton isn't particularly impressed by all the attention given to the recent wave of movies by black filmmakers. "If people think they can make money with black movies, they'll keep making them," he says. "And if they stop making money, you watch—they'll stop making them."

If any one man had a major influence on Singleton's career ambitions, it would be his father, Danny Singleton, whom John has admiringly dubbed the Samurai of South Central. His father is now a real estate broker ("and he still thinks I oughta get into real estate," Singleton says with a grin).

As a child, John lived with his mother—his parents never married—but when he was twelve, he moved in with his dad. "My father said that he couldn't afford to pay child support, but he could pay moral support," Singleton remembers. "He taught me just what you hear Furious Styles say in the movie—never respect someone who doesn't respect you back, and when you talk to someone, always look them in the eye."

When Singleton was nine, his father took him to a movie he'd never forget. He wanted to see the latest Disney *Herbie* movie, but his father said, "No, you've got to see this movie. We stood in line for over an hour and when the movie came on, it was *Star Wars*. Man, the visuals were so strong—the whole movie was just amazing."

At USC, Singleton went to film school and started an African-American film association. He doesn't pretend to have many warm film-school memories. "All the little white boys thought I was arrogant because I was so self-determined."

Singleton bridled at anything holding him back. While at USC, he got a six-month TV directing internship at *The Arsenio Hall Show*. Unhappy that he was being treated like a lowly gofer, he rebelled immediately.

"The show's director, Sandy Fullerton, was really friendly," he says. "But outside of her, I was just tolerated. I remember the first day I was in the booth, they were taping the show and they tried to get me to Xerox all these scripts and I said, 'Hell, no! I'm a directing intern!' I stood my ground, but it caused a real stink."

Singleton also did an internship at Columbia Pictures, where a young studio executive named Stephanie Allain read two scripts Singleton had written—and when she asked to see more, he showed her *Boyz N the Hood*. Allain took the *Hood* script to studio chief, Frank Price, who greenlighted the film.

At a cost of less than $6 million, the film is not a huge financial risk. Still, the studio is hoping it can reach beyond young black moviegoers and attract a sizable percentage of young white rap fans, aided by the presence of rap star Ice Cube.

"No other actor that exists on this planet could have played Doughboy," Singleton says of Ice Cube, who declined to be interviewed. "What Toshiro Mifune was to Akira Kurosawa, Ice Cube is to me. He brings the perfect attitude to the part. Cube knows how to get across all the things that I'm writing."

It's a compelling image—Ice Cube as rap's samurai warrior, guarding the 'hood from evil invaders. In fact, Singleton owes much of his samurai fascination to his father, who schooled him in the ways of great warriors.

"We used to have long talks about all sorts of metaphysical things—life, death, the origins of the universe," Singleton recalls. "That was my father's hero—Toshiro Mifune. My dad's a big man, 6-3 and 230 pounds. He was so big he could scare me into doing things."

Singleton falls silent for a moment as he drives north, heading back to the studio lot, leaving his old neighborhood far behind. "And when I got to the point where I wasn't scared anymore, that was when I became a man."

They Gotta Have Us

KAREN GRIGSBY BATES/1991

JOHN SINGLETON pulls his slightly battered silver Peugeot into the empty two-car garage of his new house in Baldwin Hills, a prosperous black neighborhood of contemporary homes sitting high above Los Angeles. The house itself, with impressive views from each oversize window, is mostly un-furnished, testament to a recent windfall and a lack of time to spend it. Single-ton, whose first feature film, *Boyz N the Hood*, opened nationally on Friday, lives alone, except for an albino cat who floats down the stairs to greet him.

"That's White Boy," Singleton says, stooping to rub the cat behind his translucent ears.

The metaphor is irresistible: at the moment, John Singleton, a twenty-three-year-old black man, has the notoriously insular and mostly white Hol-lywood establishment purring.

It was just over a year ago that Singleton, then a student in the Filmic Writing Program at the University of Southern California, sent his script for *Boyz*, a coming-of-age story set in the tough Los Angeles neighborhood where he grew up, to Columbia Pictures. What followed has already become a Hol-lywood legend. When the Columbia chairman, Frank Price, offered to have the studio develop his script, Singleton agreed—with the understanding that he would direct it himself. "It's my story, I lived it," says Singleton. "What sense would it have made to have some white boy impose his interpretation on my experience?"

Not only did Singleton get a $6 million budget to direct *Boyz N the Hood*, he signed a three-year contract with Columbia that enables him to make as many movies as he can during that period.

From the *New York Times Magazine* (July 14, 1991). Reprinted by permission of Karen Grigsby Bates.

"The Singleton thing," as it's referred to in current Hollywood parlance, is the latest bold-relief example of Hollywood's sudden open-door policy toward black filmmakers, particularly those telling black stories. Several studios—among them Warner Brothers, Columbia, Goldwyn, New Line, and Island World (which is releasing *Juice*, the first feature by Ernest Dickerson, Spike Lee's longtime friend and cinematographer)—have black films in the pipeline. By year's end nineteen will have been released, more than in all of the previous decade. The frenzy for black product that allowed Singleton, who has no previous professional credits, to direct his own film has become so great that black film properties may be to the nineties what the car phone was to the eigthies: every studio executive has to have one.

But along with the new opportunities come some troubling questions for black filmmakers: Will Hollywood learn how to market and promote these films effectively? If the black films prove to be a gold mine, will black filmmakers be the beneficiaries? And given Hollywood's fickle nature and short attention span, will the filmmakers have the opportunity to become part of the Hollywood power structure?

"This is a critical time for black cinema, which, really, is in its infancy," says Spike Lee, who echoes the caution of many black filmmakers. "This opportunity brings with it a special responsibility—because a lot of people who are more talented than we were didn't get a shot at doing this. So it's important for new black filmmakers to be correct with their craft. If one black filmmaker messes up, the rest of us will be made to feel it."

Black filmmaking goes back to the all-black Lincoln Motion Picture Company, established in Los Angeles around 1916. Then, during the Harlem Renaissance in the 1920s and into the 1940s, the independent producer and director Oscar Micheaux created many films for black audiences. These films—romances, comedies, dramas, and adventures—depicted black people in their rich variety, from the pious bourgeoisie to less savory characters. For the next thirty years there were sporadic Hollywood films about blacks— almost always directed by whites—and of course the ascension of Sidney Poitier. In the 1970s, the "blaxploitation" films—like *Superfly*—became the first black movies to receive significant attention from the general public, though these films, too, were frequently made by whites. Star vehicles for Bill Cosby, Richard Pryor, and Eddie Murphy followed.

The current crop of films is breaking new ground in their subject matter and their politics. For the studios, these are tales from a new world, presented with an often harrowing, if occasionally hyperbolic, realism. Such films as Spike Lee's *Jungle Fever*, Mario Van Peebles's *New Jack City*, *Hangin' with the Homeboys*, a tale of the Bronx from twenty-eight-year-old Joseph B. Vasquez,

and *Straight Out of Brooklyn*, the angry first feature from the startlingly precocious nineteen-year-old director Matty Rich, are stridently confrontational in
their depiction of a problem-riddled urban culture in conflict with a white
mainstream.

Boyz N the Hood, the story of a group of teenagers growing to manhood on
a block in south central Los Angeles beleaguered by drugs, crime, and gang
violence, stands squarely at the center of the trend. The film focuses on Tre
Styles (played by Cuba Gooding Jr.), who has the advantage of a father's guidance, and two half brothers who don't. The brothers—Ricky, a football star
(played by Morris Chestnut) favored by his mother, and Doughboy (a complex creation, stirringly portrayed by the rapper Ice Cube), whose intelligence
and street eloquence do battle with a penchant for self-destruction—are ill
fated, which may be a commentary on the plight of fatherless black families
but one that is no less powerful for its didacticism.

Boyz N the Hood is an ambitious film that fulfills much of its ambition, one
that most critics have concurred deserves its good fortune for having arrived
simultaneously with the Hollywood hunger for it.

Singleton himself seems to understand that. Slender and often laconic to
the point of being Cooper-esque, he masks a passion to bring the stories of
life in black communities to the screen. He concedes that five years ago, before Spike Lee's seminal low-budget first film, *She's Gotta Have It*, proved that
black-made films on black subjects could be financially successful, he'd have
encountered resistance to his directing demand. And yet he bristles at any suggestion that his big break is the result of anything but creative talent. "Look,"
he says. "In this business you get hired for your vision, and your vision begins
with your script. I'm a writer first, and I direct in order to protect my vision.
Boyz is a good story, a real story, and they wanted it. Simple as that."

Like Tre Styles, the protagonist in his film, Singleton grew up in south
central Los Angeles. His mother, Shelia Ward, a sales executive for a pharmaceutical company, and father, Danny Singleton, a mortgage broker, never
married. Nevertheless, they lived near each other and for several years he
split his time between them.

Singleton began going to movies early on—"I'm a child of *Star Wars*,
Raiders of the Lost Ark, and *E.T.*, he says—and decided to make them himself
by the time he was nine. He gorged on films by Orson Welles, François Truffaut, Steven Spielberg, Akira Kurosawa, John Cassavetes, Martin Scorsese, and
Francis Ford Coppola.

"The christening scene at the end of *The Godfather* is my favorite," he says
with uncharacteristic animation. Singleton imitates the priest's solemn reci-
tation of the Roman Catholic christening vows: " 'Michael Corleone, do you

renounce Satan?' 'I do.' And at the same time, everybody's getting shot! I love scenes like that. I strive toward saying things visually—that verbal stuff is for TV. In a way, that scene in *The Godfather* influenced how I ended *Boyz*."

In high school, he started to learn the inner workings of Hollywood. "Somebody told me that the film business was controlled by literary properties," he says. "After that, I worked to strengthen my writing skills." And that is when things took off. He won a spot in the prestigious Filmic Writing Program at U.S.C. By the time he graduated in 1990, he had made a few 8-millimeter short films, but, more important, he had won several writing awards. The powerful Creative Artists Agency signed him while he was still an undergraduate. It was his agent, Bradford W. Smith at CAA, who sent the script of *Boyz* to Columbia in May 1990.

Given the material, it seems remarkable that *Boyz N the Hood* and the other so-called homeboy movies have found their way through the cultural cocoon of Hollywood's executive offices to the screen. Sean Daniel, a white independent producer and former production executive at Universal Pictures, says studios continue not to know what the next big "It" is, which is to the advantage of as-yet-untested people who want to make movies.

Warrington and Reginald Hudlin, who produced and directed the surprise teen-age comedy hit of 1990, *House Party*, say Hollywood is attracted to the freshness of black filmmakers' visions. Hollywood has "told all their own stories," says Warrington. "They're tapped out. How many sequels can you do?" Adds Reginald: "White America knows very little about us, and very few of our stories have been told. People want to see them."

Another reason for Hollywood's intense interest in black culture comes from simple arithmetic. "If, within the next thirty years, America is going to be predominantly a nation of people of color, then white studio executives had better begin to understand who their consumer is going to be," Warrington says.

Already, blacks make up 12 percent of the nation's population but 25 percent of America's movie-house audiences, says Ken Smikle, the publisher of *Target Market News*, a Chicago-based publication that tracks black consumer patterns. "The black population is younger, and is growing faster than other segments of the U.S. population, other than Latinos," he adds, "so our future numbers look even better to studios, because young people buy the bulk of movie tickets."

In addition, there is the "crossover" factor, the influence of black culture on whites, particularly young whites, demonstrated by their tastes in music, clothing, even language. The success of rap music in such largely white environments as MTV has paved the way for acceptance of black film, says

Elvis Mitchell, a film critic for National Public Radio and one of the few black critics in the mainstream. "When Hollywood realized that white kids were really into rap—and don't kid yourself, that's the audience the studios are really lusting for—a little light went on: 'Hey, we can make money from black culture!' " Mitchell says.

Studio executives don't necessarily dispute those reasons. New Line Cinema made *House Party* for a stingy $2.5 million. (A Hollywood film costs between $15 million and $20 million on average.) To make a profit on its investment, a film must earn twice what it cost to produce. *House Party* earned more than $26 million. Now New Line may be the studio most heavily invested in black films, with three projects—*House Party 2, Hangin' with the Homeboys,* and *Talkin' Dirty after Dark*—to be released this year and nearly a dozen more in development.

But it took an earlier New Line venture, the wildly successful horror film *Nightmare on Elm Street,* and its four sequels, to stir up the studio's interest in projects like the Hudlins'.

"*Elm Street* helped us identify our market niche," says Janet Grillo, New Line's East Coast vice president of creative affairs. "Our research said there was a significant segment of young blacks attending these films. So we began to think of other movies that they—as well as others—might find appealing." Grillo, who served as executive producer on the recently released *Hangin' with the Homeboys,* adds that the studio is now "constantly eliciting and soliciting ideas from minorities and minority talent."

Despite, or perhaps because of, this rush for black stories, some black film makers worry that the nineties may just become the seventies redux, with an episodic deluge of black product followed by another drought. But Charles Lane, maker of the 1989 black-and-white silent film *Sidewalk Stories* and of the comedy *True Identity,* which will be released in August by Touchstone, observes that "the Berlin Wall, having been pulled down, will not be re-erected."

Neal Gabler, a cultural historian and the author of *An Empire of Their Own: How the Jews Invented Hollywood,* believes that blacks are in a difficult position vis-a-vis the industry. "Outsiders have succeeded in Hollywood before, because their ultimate goal was successful assimilation into what was considered back then a cultural norm," he says. The vision many Americans hold of their country, Gabler claims, is largely due to the influence of early American cinema—made by men who were, in many cases, immigrants and who presented a highly idealized portrait of their new homeland. "Today, there is no longer a desire for a national cultural consensus; we're now much more pluralistic. So the black filmmaker has been placed in what has been the route for success in a cultural climate that's currently going against that."

Some blacks are hedging their bets about assimilation anyway. Warrington Hudlin, for instance, is co-founder of the Black Filmmaker Foundation, which he started more than a dozen years ago because "as young filmmakers who made documentaries, we ran into a wall of institutional disenfranchisement." From its start as a self-help networking organization, BFF has evolved into an association with more than 2,000 members, most of whom are involved in some aspect of black cinema.

While these networks are developing, however, blacks remain supplicants at the studio altar. Even Spike Lee, whose 1989 film, *Do the Right Thing*, earned $27.5 million and whose current hit, *Jungle Fever*, has already brought in more than $23 million in domestic ticket sales, feels the pinch. For his next project, *Malcolm X*, Lee is seeking foreign financing to supplement an investment by Warner Brothers that he feels is inadequate. The question of who will ultimately control and profit from the black film explosion is a resonant issue. The argument goes that from jazz to early rock and roll to rap, whites have taken black art forms and styles and appropriated them. What's to prevent the same thing from happening with black films?

Mark Canton, an executive vice president of Warner Brothers and the studio's chief of production, says he doesn't see "that Elvis thing" happening in film. Black directors will not be shut out of projects that, logically, they should have been asked to handle because of their familiarity with the subject matter, he says. Yet a current Warner Brothers production, *A Class Act*, a black teen comedy, is being shot by Randall Miller, a white director with only a few television episodes under his belt. Canton says he was "hoping for a black director," but that he "had no luck."

In its roster, the Directors Guild of America has a full-page list of about a hundred minority directors, at least half of whom are black. Most have extensive television directing experience; several have done small or independent features. "And," says one, "it is not unusual for film studios to reach back to theatrical directors if they can't find what they want on the D.G.A. roster." Curiously, one of the companies co-producing *A Class Act* is Gordy de Passe, the reconstitution of Motown Productions. If Berry Gordy doesn't insist on getting black directors, it's a small wonder major studios don't feel the need to. Paramount, for instance, holds the rights to August Wilson's Tony-and-Pulitzer-Prize-winning play, *Fences*. Wilson insists that only a black director can do justice to the film adaption. The studio has not found a suitable director, and thus the project has been delayed for about four years.

Bill Duke, whose credits include the award-winning PBS American Playhouse production of *A Raisin in the Sun*, says: "Appropriation is a fact of life; no point in complaining about it. But if that's the way the game's being played, let's do it on both sides. I don't want some white guy making *A Rage in Harlem III* if I can't do *The Godfather V* or *E.T. III.*" Duke's point is largely one of economic fairness. Still, *E.T. III* is one thing; a film like *The Color Purple* is something else. Many in the black film community remain irritated by what they viewed as a fantasy adaptation (by Steven Spielberg) of Alice Walker's searing novel about an abused black woman in the rural South.

"Anybody can direct anything—but the point of view will be different," Duke says. He argues that he has enough humanity and anger in him to handle a film about Jews in Nazi Germany, though his point is finally that lines ought to be crossed with some sensitivity. "I could direct a very decent Holocaust film," Duke says, "but I don't have the same experience as a young boy who was rocked to sleep in the lap of a grandmother who had a tattooed number on her arm, who told him stories of the people who disappeared, the relatives she never saw again, as he drifted off with his cheek nestled next to that number. It's those cultural nuances—and the ability to recognize and comprehend them—that make the difference."

Another conflict has arisen at the back end of the film business—marketing and promotion. The studios, the black directors say, are ill informed about black moviegoers' relationship with the black news media. Poor marketing works against black films in particular because of the industry practice of tallying the first two weeks of box-office receipts to gauge a film's progress in the open market. "Usually, you have some idea of how a picture is going to do by the end of the second week of its release," says Philip Garfinkle, senior vice president of Entertainment Data, a Beverly Hills-based firm that compiles box-office returns. If it's not doing well by then, it won't be around much longer.

But this time frame may be punitive for black films. Without aggressive and effective promotion, viewership will naturally crest later in the release cycle. Beyond that, there is research to show that black movie-going habits are different from those of whites. Black attendance, not only for black films, tends to build more slowly.

"Attracting black audiences means allowing for sufficient time for word of mouth to build interest," notes Ken Smikle, whose information comes from advertising surveys, many commissioned by studios. Blacks, he adds, are not predisposed to see a film the weekend it opens.

Charles V. Richardson, president of Tri-Ad Communications Group, a Manhattan-based agency that specializes in marketing to the black community, says the studio market people "are not accustomed to dealing with black product, so they're not familiar with what makes things work. There are more than 187 black newspapers in the U.S., in thirty-six states, representing more than 100 major markets," Richardson says. "But because nearly all of these papers are weekly, they cannot be expected to generate film interest on the same basis as white dailies." The black weeklies, Richardson notes, often plan feature articles long in advance.

"And frankly," adds one independent black publicist who has worked with the studios, "why should the papers jump when the studios want them to?" The studios, she adds, don't place ads in those papers for general-release movies that would appeal to blacks.

Another frustration is the failure of the studios to take advantage, in any systematic way, of the influence of black radio. Matty Rich, for instance, raised $70,000 from private black investors when, on the advice of Allen Black, a friend and businessman, he made a sample loop of *Straight Out of Brooklyn* and approached WLIB, a New York AM station. After viewing the loop, the talk-format station agreed to interview Rich; it also broadcast several spots urging potential contributors to come to a free screening. The station's support and the subsequent contributions it engendered, says Rich, enabled him to shoot more film.

The marketing of Charles Burnett's *To Sleep with Anger*, an independently made film distributed in 1990 by the Samuel Goldwyn Company, is cited by many directors as an example of studio incompetence. Burnett's drama centers on the tensions raised in a working-class family in Los Angeles when an old friend from the Deep South makes a surprise visit. It received nearly universal critical acclaim but did poorly at the box office, particularly with adult black audiences, its major targeted market. Burnett contends Goldwyn's "lack of knowledge" of how to market the movie helped kill it. The studio spent little money on publicity, Burnett says, neglected to contact the black print media until the eleventh hour, and showed virtually no comprehension of how the black press works.

Leonie de Picciotto, Goldwyn's vice president for publicity, says that "traditionally, the black press sometimes takes forever" to get down to the studio to watch a filming, to come to a screening, to write the review. Goldwyn held several screenings of the film, including one at the National Association of Black Journalists convention last August. The reception was "at best lukewarm," de Picciotto says. "No one," she adds, "has been able to create a black art-film audience." Burnett counters that *To Sleep with Anger* was not an art film. "No one had to interpret anything," she says. And it had a recognizable star, Danny Glover.

Although Richardson had been retained by Goldwyn to target the black market, he was hired only seven weeks before the film's release, which was not enough time to generate the interest the studio hoped for. Several people indicated that Goldwyn could have tapped into the black market for *To Sleep with Anger* by running ad spots on gospel stations, or transit ads at bus and subway stops, both designed to appeal to people who don't read local papers regularly.

When Mario Van Peebles's *New Jack City* opened in March, there were violent skirmishes outside theaters in a few cities. These were variously attributed to some theater owners who sold more tickets than they had seats and to the audiences who arrived hyped-up in anticipation of the film's violence, which is considerable. In the controversy that followed, at least two theaters pulled the film, and the discussion redoubled a fear that many blacks in film have about the viability of certain kinds of stories that are beginning to proliferate—namely, those from the violence-ridden urban world in which many of the nation's blacks live. Van Peebles himself notes that in New York, someone was killed while seeing *The Godfather Part III* but nobody wanted to pull it from theaters. "They are changing the rules of the game," says Van Peebles. "We made a film, it's commercially successful, and now they want us to police the audience too?"

Interestingly, some of the younger directors object to the film on other grounds, claiming that *New Jack City* is TV-gangster stuff, and not an accurate reflection of the real street life in crack-infested poor black neighborhoods. All of which makes the release of *Boyz N the Hood* a crucial test case. On the one hand, its cinematic power ought to strip away any fears that audiences will dismiss it as another example of current Hollywood chic. "The impression the media is giving is that anybody black can pick up a camera and make a movie," says Van Peebles. "As it is, we're looked upon as the cinematic equivalent of a track-and-field team."

It's also a challenging film, a disconcertingly gritty peek into a facet of life to which virtually no white audiences have been privy—and that a fair number of black middle-class viewers will find alien as well. Which is exactly what Singleton intended. "Homeboys and hip whites will see it and like it," he says, "but it will probably make a lot of bourgeois blacks real uncomfortable."

Nonetheless, Columbia Pictures has put the full weight of its marketing and promotion power behind it. According to Paula D. Silver, president of marketing, $8 million has been spent on advertising and publicity for *Boyz*, which was released in 850 theaters nationwide. Most of the promotion budget is being spent in the black community, the target market for the film, and directed at black males under twenty-five years old.

The *Boyz* crew was 90 percent black, extraordinary even for a black film. "I didn't ask anybody if I could," Singleton says. "I just did it." (He is in sharp contrast to Eddie Murphy, who insists that he simply doesn't have the clout to demand more minority staffing on his movies.) And as Singleton attests, there was no pressure put on him to make *Boyz N the Hood* more palatable to a white audience.

"Their chief interest was in making a good film, and they let me do that," he says. "I feel fortunate that my studio supported me and believed in me." Singleton's next project for Columbia will center on "a nineteen-year-old black woman in South Central."

"Nobody's really told a story from a black woman's point of view," he says. "In film, they've been fairly invisible."

This, of course, is true. Not only have there been few substantial roles for black women in mainstream films, but many black filmmakers have been criticized for an inability to portray black women convincingly. One obvious redress would be more black women directors, but there are precious few of those. After her 1984 independent film, *Sugar Cane Alley*, was released to some acclaim, Euzhan Palcy, a black woman from Martinique, was hired by MGM/ UA to direct *A Dry White Season* in 1989; Julie Dash's *Daughters of the Dust* a portrait of turn-of-the-century Gullah life on the Georgia Sea Islands, will premiere on PBS's *American Playhouse* later this year. Romell Foster-Owens is negotiating the distribution of her first film, a black parody of *The Three Musketeers*. And the television directors Helaine Head, Neema Barnette, and Debbie Allen are reported to be under studio consideration for upcoming projects. But as Anita Addison, a black television producer-director, says, "There are very, very few white women directing features, so you can imagine how much tougher it is for women who are black."

Singleton believes that his own acceptance by Hollywood may help "a lot of brothers and sisters get their films done, which wouldn't have happened before." In the meantime, he says, "I just think about telling a good story about my people, because in the last seventy-five years of American cinema, we've been dogged out." Perched in a sunny window of his new house, less than twenty minutes away from the' hood of his adolescence, and poised on the brink of influence, the director smiles. If "the Singleton thing" is a burden, Singleton himself doesn't show it. He has gotten offers to do films that are not specific to the black community, he says tolerantly, but "that's not where my interests are right now."

Singleton's Street Noises

PETER BRUNETTE/1991

PRESENT AT THIS YEAR'S Cannes festival for the world premiere of his first film, *Boyz N the Hood*, a sophisticated if somewhat preachy account of three young boys' violent coming of age in the black ghetto of South Central Los Angeles, twenty-three-year-old John Singleton is clearly enjoying the attention.

When I arrive for our scheduled interview, he is on his way back to his room. He suggests that we talk as we walk along the Croisette, Cannes' jam-packed main thoroughfare. We try this for about ninety seconds, and it's clearly not going to work. I propose instead that we reschedule with the publicist and he is instantly, genuinely grateful. Despite what the folks back home think, Cannes is hard on everyone.

Boyz N the Hood is a tough, raw film. The sense of frustration and urgency expressed is so great that at times Singleton's characters seem to mount invisible soapboxes to address the audience directly and shake some sense into them. Judged from a strictly aesthetic viewpoint, these moments are flaws: in this film, paradoxically, they add to the overwhelming feeling of real life and direct witness. Singleton quietly observes that "films serve different purposes, some are meant just to entertain, but there's also room for other films that inform as well."

Unsurprisingly, the film is being heavily promoted as "authentic," which for Singleton means "that people are seeing some stuff they've never seen before." But what matters to him, in the end, is that *Boyz N the Hood* is authentic "to the brothers and sisters I made the film for. The people on the street. I got the supreme compliments from brothers in Inglewood and Compton and South Central" (black ghettos in Los Angeles). Singleton says that *Boyz*

From *Sight & Sound* (August 1991). Reprinted by permission of *Sight & Sound*.

allows them to "see themselves on film and they can reflect upon it. Think about their situation and the situation of their friends and their family."

Does he think that because of the unflattering way black characters within the film are portrayed, he will be criticized for producing negative images or for blaming the victim? "Maybe I'll be criticised by older black people, but the younger black people will know what I'm talking about. The older generation won't like the language in my film, anyway, but actually I'm just saying the same thing that the hard-core rappers are saying. They say it on wax, and I'm saying it on film."

After the press screening, some North American male critics objected to the treatment of women—perhaps with more than a little of a 'more-feminist-than-thou' tone. Singleton's response is that "the men in the film treat women differently according to what their backgrounds are. Tre [the chief protagonist, played by Cuba Gooding Jr.] doesn't treat women the same way that Dough Boy [a violence-prone teenager played by rap musician Ice Cube] does, you see. I was trying to show real life, in the streets. The women don't just stand there and take it. They talk shit back.

"I was trying to show that there's a certain schism between black men and black women right now," he continues. "Things have been made easier for black women but not for black men, so what I'm trying to say is that we need to stick together instead of fighting each other."

The young men in the film regularly call each other "bitch" and "cunt," as though women were the lowest form of life. Singleton, however, says that "that's too much of an analytical observation. It's just an attack on one's manhood, like if you would call someone a faggot, they'd say bitch. They have their manhood attacked so often they attack each other's manhood in various ways, verbally and physically."

The film's greatest weakness is, in fact, Singleton's uncritical worship of manhood and maleness, which at times approaches an obsessive level. But first films, like first novels, perhaps need to be autobiographically obsessive on some level in order to get made. Singleton says he closely modelled Tre's father, Furious Styles (played by Larry Fishburne of *The Color Purple* and *School Daze*), the film's strongest character, on his own father, whom he describes as "awesome."

I mention the recent controversial news story about a black educator in Los Angeles who, because he felt that the necessary discipline could not be instilled in a co-educational setting, decided to set up an "academy" that would only admit boys. "I think he's right. I had a couple of black male teachers, in addition to my father and my mother, who set me straight on the right path. It's like a woman can't teach a young boy how to be a man, only a man can teach a young boy that. That's what was most on my mind in the film. That's the whole thing."

One of the points the film effectively makes is that violence of all varieties is the everyday reality for these young men simply trying to survive long enough to grow up. Besides the gang violence and the verbal violence, there is a constant psychological violence expressed most effectively in the subconsciously annoying whumpa-whumpa of unseen police helicopters that runs throughout the film. "Yeah, you get it, you're smart, man, you're smart," Singleton responds. "But there are a lot of stupid people in the world, and they're not going to get that. They'll say, why is it so noisy. They won't know that that's there to add to the atmosphere, and that's just how the atmosphere is."

Singleton himself is both smart and a survivor. On the basis of having received several prestigious writing awards while in film school, he signed with Creative Artists Agency while still a student. A young executive at Columbia got hold of his screenplay, passed it along to studio head Frank Price, and a meeting was set up for the next weekend. "I just pitched myself to direct my own film. I figured that if you could tell your story to anybody on the street, orally, you could tell any studio executive."

When I ask if he has any recommendations for other young black filmmakers trying to break into the industry, Singleton emphasises that it was his writing ability that got the studio interested. "I never did a film at USC. All they teach you in school is theory. This film was my chance to put it into practice. And know your history, know where you're from. It gives you a firm foundation and you don't feel you're on shaky ground with anybody or anything."

Not Just One of the Boyz

ALAN LIGHT/1991

WITH HIS BREAKAWAY HIT MOVIE *Boyz N the Hood*, twenty-three-year-old first-time director John Singleton makes it clear that he's not about to let Hollywood Shaft him.

The audience at Harlem's Apollo Theater is notoriously hard to please, but on this night Ice Cube is wearing the place like a suit. The crowd yells every word of every song back to "AmeriKKKa's Most Wanted" gangsta rapper. The theater is getting sweatier by the minute. Then Ice Cube stops the show.

"How many of y'all seen *Boyz N the Hood*?" Cube asks, and the Apollo roars its approval for the controversial film in which he co-stars. "And how many thought it had a positive message?" Again, loud screams. "I want to bring out the man who wrote and directed the movie," Cube continues. "They're blaming this man for some brothers starting static at some of the theaters!" A compact, beaming young man ambles onstage, tossing BOYZ N THE HOOD T-shirts to the cheering crowd.

"They clapped for me!" a still-astonished John Singleton says the next week, back in his native Los Angeles. "A filmmaker, not a rapper, from L.A., not New York, walked onstage at the Apollo, put my fist in the air, and they all pumped their fists!"

Such unexpectedly warm responses are becoming common for the twenty-three-year-old Singleton. On the way to this interview, he ran into Living Colour guitarist Vernon Reid, who began raving about *Boyz*, compared Singleton to Orson Welles and offered—practically begged—to contribute music to the writer-director's next project. In a ritual that was oddly appropriate for this meeting of young black cultural warriors, Reid removed a gris-gris (a protective voodoo locket) from around his neck and hung it on the visibly moved Singleton.

Not everyone, however, has taken so kindly to John Singleton or his movie. Though his debut feature about three friends' coming of age in the killing fields of South Central L.A. took in over $22 million during its first two weeks of release (maintaining a higher per-screen average than even *Terminator 2*) and won stunning critical notices, what most of America knows about *Boyz N the Hood* is that thirty-three people were wounded and one killed at theaters across the country on its opening night.

This movie about the tragic condition of the black American family, which opens with the warning "One out of every twenty-two black American males will be murdered each year" and ends with the blessing "Increase the Peace," is being condemned as a "gang movie." *Boyz* has come to represent black American cinema at a crossroads: An unprecedented number of movies by black filmmakers are being released this year—some tremendously successful—but violence outside theaters has led many observers to fear for the future of black film.

Singleton says the attention that's focused on violence is a smoke screen. "People in the media don't want to deal with the issues at hand," he explains. "They don't want to deal with the fact that the high crime and murder rates are directly related to the illiteracy problem, the homeless problem, problems in the American educational system." Theater security, he says, is simply a matter of finding the appropriate measures for potentially explosive films. He cites the Baldwin Hills Theater, a black-owned movie house near South Central, where the management installed metal detectors, addressed the crowd before each show and asked gang members to check their colors at the door. There were no incidents there, but, says Singleton, "you don't see them reporting that."

After the opening-night violence, some blamed the movie's preview for pandering to a hyped-up gang audience by promising an action-oriented film. Indeed, the trailer shows virtually all of the film's gunplay and spends little time on the powerful father-son relationship that stands as the movie's center. Singleton, who helped cut the trailer himself, stands by the strategy. "It got mother-fuckers in the theater," he says. "That's the bottom line. If the trailer for *Terminator 2* showed the part where he agreed not to kill anyone, nobody would have gone to see it." In fact, Singleton feels the tactic makes the movie's message even stronger. "People went with lower expectations; they thought it was the same old bullshit action-adventure in the streets of South Central L.A. But when they saw it was more, they really watched it."

The violence associated with the movie seems to have scared away (at least initially) the white audience that Columbia Pictures hoped to attract. But Singleton thinks the studio's obsession with crossing over is misguided, given that black Americans, who represent only 12 percent of the population, constitute a disproportionate 25 percent of the moviegoing audience. "Everybody else copies young black men," he says. "If I reach them, everything else will fall into place." Normally soft-spoken and restrained, Singleton lights up when describing a recent trip to L.A's marina. "These little white kids came over, screaming my name," he laughs. "You know something's happening when you're a young black man making movies and a little white kid comes up and tells you, 'When I grow up, I want to be just like you!'"

When Singleton was growing up, his dreams were probably just as remote. In a story similar to *Boyz*'s, he moved at the age of twelve from his mother's house to the home of his father, a mortgage broker, in South Central. Inspired by *Star Wars* and *E.T.*, Singleton began devouring movies, fantasizing about someday making them himself. Then in 1986, the eighteen-year-old Singleton saw a movie called *She's Gotta Have It*, by a young director named Spike Lee, and everything changed. "That was the turning point in my life," he says. "I met Spike at the opening night in L.A., and it solidified everything I'd dreamed about already."

That fall, Singleton enrolled in the University of Southern California's filmic writing program. "USC was a cultural wasteland," he says. "Everybody wanted to get rich, but nobody wanted to work to get there." Singleton's purpose, however, was clear: "I wasn't into film to get money. I just wanted to make classic films about my people in a way no one had ever done." He began studying movies voraciously, transforming himself into a self-professed "filmic soldier" and twice winning the school's Jack Nicholson Writing Award.

During his senior year, Singleton was interning at Columbia Pictures, reading scripts ("wack-ass screenplays," he says, "straight-up booty"). He complained about the quality of the writing until the director of the program asked to read his work. She read two of Singleton's scripts and brought them to a friend at Creative Artists Agency one Friday.

On Monday, the agent called Singleton in for a meeting and announced that CAA wanted to sign him. Singleton coolly accepted, then drove to a gas station and shouted for joy. He was most excited, he says, "because I knew I could talk more shit at the film school."

As graduation neared, he met with Russell Simmons, the chairman of Def Jam Records, who was negotiating a production deal with Columbia Pictures. Simmons read Singleton's latest script—entitled *Boyz N the Hood*, after an N.W.A lyric—on the plane back to New York and immediately called

Columbia's Jon Peters to express his enthusiasm for the project. Meanwhile, somebody at the studio began circulating a copy of the script. *Boyz* generated such a buzz that Columbia decided to offer Singleton, rather than Simmons, a multipicture deal.

Though Singleton had only directed a couple of Super-8 films before, he insisted that he be allowed to direct *Boyz N the Hood* in order to "protect his vision." Columbia Pictures chairman Frank Price was quickly persuaded. "A lot of people in this business don't respect vision—or even recognize it—because they don't have any," Singleton says. "But Price used to be a writer himself, so he still has it."

Singleton's perspective is one that remains unique in Hollywood. "I'm like a child born of two things—hip-hop music and film," he says. Along with his beloved movies, he credits Public Enemy's landmark album *It Takes a Nation of Millions to Hold Us Back* with changing his life. The day after Ice Cube's Apollo concert, Singleton was part of a panel discussion entitled "Hip-Hop as an Art, a Style and a Culture," at New York's annual New Music Seminar, where he said: "The music reflects the condition of the culture. Film is an extension of the music." Growing up with hip-hop, he says, has given him a different relationship to the music than older directors can have: "A lot of these people doing so-called hip-hop films just do it about the culture. They think if they put the word homeboy in there twenty-five times, it's a cool film. In *Boyz N the Hood*, nobody's rapping, but it's a hip-hop film because it has the political as well as the cultural aesthetic that rings true."

Like his rapping contemporaries, Singleton has come under some fire for his depiction of women in *Boyz*. Though he denies any unfair portrayal ("There aren't really good or bad characters in my film"), he will turn his attention to "the politics of black love" in his next film. He is already halfway through a script about "the war between black men and women on the economic and sexual levels" set in South Central and Oakland. Singleton promises that his second film will be much more experimental visually—he's watching Buñuel, Fellini, and Coppola movies for inspiration. "It's gonna be so good," he says. "Imagine *Apocalypse Now* with women!"

Singleton also notes the absence of women from the current black-filmmaking boom. "The power structure seems to want to keep black women from expressing themselves on a canvas as large as film," he says. He talks of using his production company to help women get their work to the screen, as well as possibly branching out to television someday. "The more of a hand I can deal in the media," he says, "the more power I have against a system that's trying to dehumanize my family."

It seems Hollywood may actually be open to Singleton's New Deal. This year, nineteen movies by black filmmakers will be released, more than in the entire previous decade. Singleton sees this growth as representative of a more widespread change in American cinema. "In the late sixties and early seventies, everybody was asking questions of themselves and the society around them," he says. "So we had films that were serious and tackled issues, and it was profitable to do that because that was in vogue. Then in the eighties we were told, 'Don't worry, be happy' by our government, and cinema reflected that. Now, they're still trying to tell us that, but we know we've got a lot of problems. Thought went out of vogue in the eighties, but I think it's coming back."

John Singleton—driven, blazingly intense, focusing on the future even as the spectacular box-office numbers for *Boyz N the Hood*'s second week roll in—knows that real credibility in Hollywood is hard to come by. His biggest fear is that the studios will sense a quick buck in the "Afro-centric new wave" and exploit it with inferior product. But he asks for no concessions. "Real acceptance comes when you make a good film, and it gets widely accepted as a good film," he says. "It's not about the novelty. Of course, there's a lot of new black filmmakers now, but I ain't no fucking novelty. I'm in it for the long haul. And if you ain't in it for the long haul, you ain't in it."

Not Just One of the Boyz

JANICE C. SIMPSON / 1992

THE *TODAY SHOW* calls to schedule an interview. The White House phones about its invitation to dinner. Director Francis Ford Coppola's office rings to discuss a date for a visit to his Napa Valley ranch.

In the movie business, they say the calls you receive are a barometer of your importance. If so, it would probably be wise to declare a storm watch around John Singleton. What's keeping his phone line sizzling is the phenomenal success of his debut feature film, *Boyz N the Hood*. When it opened last July, *Boyz*'s commercial survival seemed threatened by sporadic violence at theaters across the country. But ultimately the film's own passionate condemnation of violence won out. Made for a modest $6 million, it has grossed more than $57 million domestically, making it the most profitable movie of 1991.

Boyz is a poignant, semiautobiographical story of young men coming of age in the mean streets of South Central Los Angeles. It is also one of nineteen movies released by black filmmakers last year, many of them dealing with similar themes. But Singleton's film rose above the competition by presenting vividly individual characters instead of stereotypes, dialogue that hummed with the rhythms of the way people really talk, a powerful story and the reassuring message that parental love and guidance can still rescue black youths from drugs, gangs, and the despair of the inner city. Last month the filmmaker received Academy Award nominations for Best Original Screenplay and Best Director. He is the first African American and the youngest person ever nominated for an Oscar in the directors' category.

The exhilarating whoosh of success has left Singleton racing to catch up with himself. At times he keeps pace, knowingly talking shop with Coppola, Spike Lee, and Steven Spielberg, once childhood idols, now professional confidants; or he adopts a man-of-the-world tone as he kindly reassures audi- tioning actresses that none of the women in his new script are "prostitutes, maids, or welfare mothers," the demeaning roles that black women are usu- ally required to play in films.

At other times he falls behind and is just a kid who pulls out a comic book to read or a portable video game to play when he grows bored during meet- ings with studio executives or interviews with journalists. One is reminded that, though he may be successful and street-smart, he is hardly sophisti- cated: his appearance at last year's Cannes Film Festival was the first time in his life he had been outside the U.S.

A short (5-ft. 6-in.), wiry figure, Singleton dresses and talks like any casual, bright twenty-four-year-old. He peppers his conversation with an abrupt, ex- clamatory laugh and punctuates almost every sentence with the rhetorical question "You know what I'm saying?" In meetings he is usually the young- est person present, but he is often the most decisive.

Even before the Oscar nominations were announced, Singleton had be- gun sampling the heady rewards of having a big-time hit. He moved into a spacious six-bedroom house in the southern part of Los Angeles, which he shares with two cats, White Boy and Mulatto, and three people: his fiancée and, at least temporarily, the production manager for his new film and a childhood friend who was recently discharged from the Army. He treated himself to a Pathfinder, three personal computers and thousands of dollars' worth of videodiscs ("the best way to see movies at home," he insists).

But, keeping his head, Singleton reminds himself that the movie industry is notorious for plumping up its young with praise and then turning around and eating them. He is convinced that the only way he will survive in the business is on his terms. "My attitude is that this can all go in a day," he says of his success. "But I'm still going to be me."

Singleton comes by this determined sense of self—which sometimes bor- ders on cockiness—naturally. "The confidence is in the genes," declares his father Danny Singleton, the model for the compassionate father in *Boyz*. Says his mother Sheila Ward: "John takes pride in who he is."

Like Tre, the lead character in the film, Singleton is the child of teenage parents who never married and who took turns raising their son in separate households. He moved in with his father just before his twelfth birthday. Both parents eventually put themselves through college. Ward, now forty-two, is a sales representative for a pharmaceutical company; Singleton, forty-one, is a real estate broker.

Both parents worried about the temptations of the street when young John was growing up. But Singleton, bolstered by the companionship of the two friends who would serve as models for the characters Doughboy and Ricky in the film, steered clear of gangs. Acquaintances of his were hurt in gang fights, and one was killed in an alley near his house, but the closest Singleton ever came to committing a violent act was in seventh grade, when a bully tried to take his money. He took a box cutter to school and threatened to cut the boy's throat if the harassment didn't stop. "He never tried to ask for money again," Singleton says proudly.

A shy, precocious child, young John learned to read during the long weekends he spent at the library with his mother as she studied for a medical-technology degree. Quickly graduating from picture books to adult books, he whipped through *The Autobiography of Malcolm X* and Anne Moody's *Coming of Age in Mississippi* while still in elementary school.

When he was nine, his father took him to see *Star Wars*. Like many thousands of youngsters, he went back as often as he could scrape up the money for another ticket. But while other kids fantasized about becoming Luke Skywalker or Princess Leia, Singleton's hero was director George Lucas. He soon began drawing scenes on sheets of paper and flipping the pages to create crudely animated "movies." During his senior year in high school, inspired by an English teacher with a passion for good writing, he decided on an alternate route to filmmaking: screenwriting. He enrolled in the Filmic Writing Program at the University of Southern California. "Any fool can figure where to point the camera," he says. "But you have to have a story to tell."

His condescending attitude didn't make Singleton popular with his fellow film students, many of whom found him "arrogant" and "too intense." His professors, however, were won over by his determination to master the elements of structure, dialogue, and character development that go into the craft of a good screenplay. "In his freshman year I wouldn't have predicted his success, but John used this program," says Margaret Mehring, who recently retired as head of the writing program. "He was driven to communicate certain ideas, and he was not about to take no for an answer." By the time he graduated in 1990, Singleton had twice won the school's prestigious Jack Nicholson award for best feature-length screenplay and had been signed up by the powerful Creative Arts Agency.

He had been out of school just a month when Columbia Pictures made a bid to buy *Boyz N the Hood*. Instead of gratefully accepting the offer, Singleton insisted that he be allowed to direct the film. His entire directorial experience at that point consisted of a few homework assignments with an 8-mm camera. "So many bad films had been made about black people, and most of them had been done by people who weren't African American," he says. "I wasn't going to let some fool from Idaho or Encino direct a movie about living in my neighborhood. If they didn't want to do the movie with me directing, they didn't want to do the movie." Impressed by the young man's moxie, Frank Price, then head of the studio, gave him the go-ahead. Says Price: "The last time I saw someone with that kind of confidence, it was Steve Spielberg when he was about that age."

Price's huge risk paid off handsomely, but it still exacted a price: expectations for Singleton's future projects will be even higher. So far, Singleton seems to be handling the pressure nicely. Earlier this year, he directed Michael Jackson, Eddie Murphy and Iman in the lavish music video "Remember the Time." The director gave himself a cameo role as a camel driver. Next month Singleton will get down to more serious business when he begins shooting his original screenplay *Poetic Justice*, a lyrical look at relationships between black men and women.

Friends and relatives say he seems more relaxed than he did when filming began on his first feature. "He knows what he's doing now," says his mother. "People got his ideas the first time, and now he's refining his presentation."

Singleton has found encouragement in the experiences of other onetime wunderkinds who have weathered the vicissitudes of a Hollywood career. He recalls that when he first met Coppola, the older director was screening Jean Cocteau's *Orpheus* in an attempt to learn how filmmakers achieved special effects in the days before high-tech computer graphics. "What real filmmakers do is they study films, they study their craft," Singleton observes. "No matter how much success they encounter, they are always in the process of studying." Singleton himself watches at least one film a day, a practice he equates with taking vitamins. "Nobody is an expert at filmmaking," he says. "Anyone who tells you he is, is lying. I'm still a student." Yes, but for the moment at the head of his class.

Poetry in Motion

VERONICA CHAMBERS / 1992

Simi Valley, Calif. — April 29, 1992

Today an all-white jury in this predominantly white community found a group of police officers charged in the beating of Rodney King innocent. As the old folks would say, It is the Day of Reckoning. Generation after generation of African Americans in Los Angeles had grown up saying don't trust the police, and, finally, the videotape of King's beating showed millions outside the hoods just what they'd been talking about. President Bush would later declare on prime-time television that he found the verdict "hard to understand." Whether or not the system failed, things certainly look that way.

Hard thoughts run through John Singleton's mind as he hears the verdict on the radio in his Pathfinder all-terrain vehicle. He's driving to the set of his new Columbia Pictures film, *Poetic Justice*. Singleton, the twenty-four-year-old director of last summer's explosive, money-making *Boyz N the Hood* is livid. Impulsively, he decides to drive directly to the courthouse. With him is his assistant, a 6'7" man named Shorty, who used to work for Tone-Lōc and was hired to keep Singleton insulated from the masses that besiege him during a shoot.

On the courthouse steps, Singleton and Shorty are immediately pressed by newspaper and television reporters barking questions. In the quiet, steady voice he adopts to make a point, Singleton tells them: "The judicial system feels no responsibility to black people—never has, never will, We have too many lawyers who don't practice true law. They had a chance to prove the system works and they messed it up." His piece said, he heads for the Pathfinder.

From *Vibe*, Fall 1992. Reprinted with permission of Vibe Media Group.

Back on the set, everyone tries to carry on business as usual. But the King verdict has turned Los Angeles into a tinderbox, and film crews are not immune. Some crew members say they feel there's a schism between whites and blacks on the set, though there are no overt incidents. The blacks are visibly angry, the whites either silent or apologetic. The racial split on this crew is about fifty-fifty, unusually integrated for a big-studio production. But holdovers from *Boyz*, whose crew was almost entirely black, feel the added white presence.

It doesn't help that, on a street only yards away from the set boundary, a dozen police patrol in full riot gear. It's almost as if they think Singleton might lead a riot, then and there.

The first shot goes up. The scene is set in an old-fashioned open-air drive-in theater. Because the initial shot is panoramic and doesn't involve any of the actors, most of the crew, including Singleton, aren't directly involved. They spend the time crowded around Singleton, who's sitting in his director's chair holding a small television on his lap. The two dramas unfold concurrently— one starring Janet Jackson, the other starring the angry throngs of Los Angeles. On the small television, the riot looks surreal, a Hollywood concoction of burning buildings, cars on fire, helicopters circling and people in the streets.

All three days shooting continues in Simi Valley as the riots rage on. Although the physical violence never reaches this suburban area, other kinds of violence do. The whole time, crew members alternate between watching the news and the scene being filmed. By the weekend, the worst of the riots have passed, but upon returning home, many of the cast and crew find that their neighborhoods have been hit hard. Singleton's own neighborhood of Baldwin Hills, a pleasant middle- and upper-middle-class black area, was only brushed by the violence. It takes days for the blunt anger to dull and the miasma to lift. To many on the set, the whole idea of making a movie amidst all the destruction of property and spirit seems an aberration.

But, like everyone else in Los Angeles, the cast and crew must get back to work.

Flashback

John Singleton sold *Boyz N the Hood* shortly after graduating from the University of Southern California's film school. Because of its relatively minuscule $5.7-million budget, it generated the most pure profit any film last year. *Boyz* was straight-up family drama—with the twist that it was set in the hellish epicenter of South Central Los Angeles. Its sleeper success started a tsunami brewing, one that Roger Ebert promptly dubbed the black new wave. To Hollywood, it proved there was a new way to sell pictures. And it earned Singleton all of the town's most valued perks, including creative freedom, numerous ducats and representation by Hollywood's most powerful agency, CAA. It also created for his second picture the kind of expectations that can only be called unrealistic.

Poetic Justice is the story of a young black woman named Justice who has known more than her fair share of tragedy. She writes poetry, hence the movie's title. Through a blind date and a crazy roadtrip, the winsome poet is thrown together with Lucky, an around-the-way boy who teaches her a thing or two about men. But make no mistakes, *Justice* couldn't have been directed by John Hughes. It is populated by black women you know and love: mamas, aunts, and grandmas; best friends and sisters; rappers and chit chats, divas and hootchies. After the male-heavy *Boyz*, Singleton decided to focus on women's stories this time around.

Even before casting began, Singleton and casting director Robi Reed were besieged by black actresses asking to read for parts—from the famous (Robin Givens, Lisa Bonet) to the vaguely familiar (Jada Pinkett from *A Different World*) to the unknown. It has been said that sexism is a bigger monster than racism in Hollywood. For black actresses, who must deal with both, meaty roles that move beyond simple stereotypes (hooker, welfare mother) are few and far between. In the end, the lead went to pop singer Janet Jackson. She did not supply her own poems, however—they were penned by Dr. Maya Angelou.

Jackson isn't new to acting, of course. As a child and teenager, she appeared on such television shows as *Good Times, Diff'rent Strokers,* and *Fame.* Understandably, there were doubts that the Encino-bred Jackson could play a girl from South Central. But Jackson, sporting the de rigeur Fendi bag and Nefertiti-like braids, went to town in the screen test. The head honchos at Columbia were duly convinced.

In the movie, Jackson is teamed with another musician, rapper Tupac Shakur. On a recent solo spin from Digital Underground, Shakur landed a smooth one-two earlier this year with a hit movie, *Juice,* and a boomblasting debut album, *2pacalypse Now.* Ice Cube, for whom Singleton wrote the role of Lucky, turned it down because he was "too busy." Ultimately, Shakur and Singleton made a fine match. The scene in his video "Brenda's Got a Baby," In which Shakur's seen holding an infant, reminded many of Singleton's point in *Boyz* that the black man must be a real father to his children.

Poetic Justice also features *Boyz* co-stars Tyra Ferrell, Baha Jackson, and Regina King, Roger Smith (*Do the Right Thing, Deep Cover*) gets a lot of laughs—at singer and co-star Keith Washington's expense. It's a very musical cast that also includes rappers Q-Tip from A Tribe Called Quest, Tone-Lôc, Dina D., Miki Howard, and a cameo by rapper Nefertiti. Singleton insists that the musicians were the best actors that auditioned, (Likewise, music videos have become a stage for many would-be actors.) He's also confident that this movie will be better than his first because "it has rhythms—ups and downs, drama and humor, like a good song."

Los Angeles—Spring 1992

The song begins. It's the first day of principal photography, and, because the crew hasn't become comfortable with one another yet, tension hangs in the air. Everything is brand-new, including the director's chair. The logo on the back of the cast's and crew's chairs reads: POETIC JUSTICE: BACK TO THE HOOD. Singleton is dressed in his usual B-boy uniform of T-shirt, baggy jeans and baseball cap, a Malcolm X pendant dangling from his neck.

We're in a predominantly black Los Angeles community, near where many of the scenes in *Boyz* were shot. It's a street scene: Lucky is driving up the street to visit somebody he knows in the neighborhood, and on the way he runs into a few old friends. While that encounter unfolds in the street, non-actor neighbors peer out of their windows and around the corners of buildings, out of range of the cameras.

The street is full of cars and people. But it' s hard to tell which are the studio cars, which people are actors, and which live in the area. In some circles in Hollywood, fantasy is out and reality is in. Particularly African-American reality. Singleton knows his strengths: every hour or so, he says to whoever wants to listen, "This is *it*, this is the *real shit*."

As a practical matter, the experience of shooting *Boyz N the Hood* made Singleton a stronger filmmaker. He admits, "With *Boyz*, I didn't know how to direct a movie. I just went with my feelings. Somehow, it came out right. I was really intense in film school, a lot more intense than I am now. Whenever someone foils a person's ability to be creative, they make that person dangerous. A lot of people should be glad I'm making movies. I could be out somewhere robbing cars."

Culver City—Later

Singleton drives onto the Sony Pictures lot, blasting Leaders of the New School on his sound system. He is happy because *Boyz* is up for two big Academy Awards— Best Original Screenplay and Best Director. He is the youngest person ever to be so honored.

As Singleton approaches the lot's gate, two young brothers guarding it shout, "Whaddup?" They give him dap for the nominations, obviously proud, even a little in awe of him. Singleton thanks them, shaking their hands.

"'These are the people I make movies for," he says, driving on, "the regular brother and sister on the street."

Many expected the writing nomination, but best-director is a surprise, With it come two firsts. Not only is Singleton the youngest director ever nominated (Orson Welles was twenty-five when he was nominated for *Citizen Kane*), but he is also the first African-American director to be recognized by the Academy.

The latter is a fact that makes him both proud and uneasy. He says, "it's all political. Spike should have got it first. If not for *School Daze*, then for *Do the Right Thing*." Spike Lee and Singleton have a close friendship, with Lee functioning as a mentor to the younger filmmaker.

Lee is many things, but he is not a darling of the movie industry. He lives in Brooklyn and doesn't play on Hollywood's social lots; he's a no-show at industry parties and refuses to join the Directors Guild. On the other hand, Singleton is Los Angeles born and bred. Although he won't win an Oscar this year, the industry *likes* the USC grad. If nothing else, they like the fact that he made a movie for $5.7 million that took in ten times that much at the box office. Politics, racism, and class struggle go over a lot of these people's heads. Money does not.

Los Angeles—One Week Later

The cast and crew have moved to a different location, a residential block in a more upscale neighborhood. This neighborhood is also predominantly black, but it has bigger houses, with pretty gardens and lavish, rolling lawns around back. About fifty people, cast and crew, stand disconsolately inside and around a comfortable-looking house, doing nothing, burning up studio dollars and valuable production moments. It's a couple of hours after lunch, and Singleton is sitting outside, quietly fuming.

The trouble is, an important video segment hasn't arrived as scheduled. Today's scene can't be shot without it. It's a scene in which Justice sits in the living room of her home watching television; the missing segment contained the images that were supposed to be played back on the television. Production assistants point at one another, saying, "I thought you were supposed to bring it," and, "Like hell I was." Because of the timing and location, there's nothing else that can be done until the tape shows.

Singleton is characteristically even-tempered. Sanguinely, he says, "it should've set us back an hour, but it's taking most of the afternoon."

While many directors habitually rant and rave, Singleton has never been known to blow up. He admits to getting frustrated and says he often wants to vent. But he doesn't believe overt anger has ever made something happen more quickly on a set.

For some reason, the delay has raised the tension level to its highest pitch yet. It's still relatively early in shooting, and the crew has yet to settle in. Everybody looks uncomfortable. Trying to cope, Singleton locates a box. He puts on Rick James's "Super Freak" at block-party decibel level. A few of the crew members start dancing. Singleton says, "I should have thought of this sooner. Play some music when things are getting tense. We used to do this all the time on *Boyz*." The earlier film was shot in six furious weeks; the box was out a lot.

The *Poetic Justice* shoot must be going smoothly, because he hasn't had to pull out Rick James until today.

Los Angeles—The Next Day

A twelve-year-old girl visits the set with her mom and two brothers in tow. She wears a key on one of her hoop earrings and a "Rhythm Nation World Tour" T-shirt. Looking around anxiously, she explains that she is "Janet Jackson's biggest fan." Her little brother pipes in, "You should see her room. Janet Jackson everything."

The girl explains that she met Singleton last year when he visited her elementary school. When she heard Jackson was co-starring in Singleton's new film, she wrote him a letter asking to meet her. "John liked the letter and invited me to the set," she say. The girl keeps one eye cocked, looking for Jackson at all times. She spots Jackson's chair and squeals, "Oooooo. She's here. This is her chair." Like Goldilocks in the Three Bears' house, the girl and her two brothers take turns sitting in Jackson's chair.

Singleton comes out and greets the family as respectfully as he would any studio vice president. Then Jackson comes out to meet her fan, trailing two bodyguards who try to stay unobtrusive. She looks like any of the very pretty black woman on set, the sort of girl who's always told she should be a model or an actress. Face to face, and not projected larger-than-life on a video screen or dancing around a stadium stage, you realize that she's a real person. It's oddly comforting and reassuring.

Although not very tall, Jackson has an almost regal grace and posture. Perhaps the most-avoided subject on the set is the fact that she's the youngest member of America's First Family of Soul. Clearly, to this little girl, meeting Jackson is like meeting the Queen. After burbling a few compliments, the girl and her family is shuttled offset so that the actress and director can continue. The meeting is a rarity; the schedule is so tight that every interruption, be it from fans or press or studio heads, takes away precious minutes.

Los Angeles—Two Weeks Later

A month into shooting, the barrage of visitors continues: press, industry, and financial-types, hangers-on and hopefuls, most of them gunning for Singleton. The array of suits constantly dogging him includes his legitimate Sony colleagues, as well as the enemy—writers and producers who bluff their way onto the set and try to woo Singleton with big talk and outrageous promises.

So, the two white men in suits standing near the camera truck could be any body. They're talking to another white guy, a member of the camera crew. The suits, who obviously haven't read the *Poetic Justice* script, ask him what the movie is about. "It's a love story," the camera guy says. The suits pause.

"So it's a nice story?" one of them asks.

"Did you see *Boyz N the Hood?*" the camera guy says, looking at them dubiosly.

"No." The suit shakes his head, "But I saw *New Jack City*."

It's a minor moment, but it makes you think. There will always be those who throw Singleton's work into that big grab bag called Films About Black Folks. Those who will never be able to tell the difference between *Superfly* and *Lillies of the Field*.

Baldwin Hill—Two Weeks Later

On location in a Baldwin Hills hair salon, Singleton is reading *Rising Sun* by Michael Crichton between takes. A fictional diatribe against a perceived Japanese threat to our way of life, the book is being made into a film—a major production—starring Wesley Snipes and Sean Connery. So Singleton is especially curious about this novel, though he is always working his way through one book or another. That is, when he isn't playing Lynx, a hard-held video game system. Either way, he has the ability to concentrate on the book or game despite the bustle of activity surrounding him.

The mood on the set is light. It usually is while shooting scenes in the hair salon, where Justice works. They are typical on-the-job comic riffs, like sitcom set pieces—*Cheers* meets the ghetto. *Shampoo* for afros. Today's scenes strike the giddy crew, at least, as the film's funniest so far.

Singleton looks up from his book and shouts, "Action!" Jackson and Tyra Ferrell cut up, almost losing their self-control in a maelstrom of giggles. Their timing is right-on, but after film stops rolling, Peter Collister, the director of photography, says that the shot was no good because one of the screens used for lighting purposes shows in the shot.

"Maybe it will just show a little bit," Singleton says, hopefully.

Don Wilkerson, unit production manager and first assistant director, shakes his head. "John, at a drive-in, that screen will look a block long."

Singleton looks annoyed. "But the performance was so good. It gets no better. *Damn,* I hate when this happens."

Seizing an opportunity to nag, Collister says, "Now if we were on a soundstage. . . ."

Singleton just smiles at him, acknowledging the point. He fought for location shooting, even though Hollywood lots make work much easier. Defiantly, Singleton says, "I didn't want to be on a soundstage. It's too artificial. I wanted to be on location. *With my people.*" To emphasize his point he turns and hugs the person standing next to him. He does this a lot.

The screen is cleared and the picture's up again. Singleton whispers directions to the actors between shots.

After one good take, he yells from his chair, "Now that was *perfect.* Let's do it again."

The cast and crew groan. They've heard the line before. And they've also heard what comes next: "I love you and I love myself. *Action!*"

Great Expectations:
John Singleton Returns with *Justice*

MARY ANN FRENCH / 1993

> *Alone. Lying, thinking. Last night. How to find my soul a home. Where water is not thirsty. And bread loaf is not stone. I came up with one thing. And I don't believe I'm wrong. That nobody. But nobody can make it out here alone.*
>
> —*Maya Angelou*

He looks more inhospitable than he is, with a face closed to scrutiny, eyes locked behind small round shades. That's primarily because John Singleton, like many other young African Americans, sees the world at large as "tha police." The government, the media, law enforcement, anyone with a piece of the Establishment's power—they're all "tha police," all interconnected and poised to pounce on anyone who looks like him. So why give them an opening?

"[Expletive] tha police," Singleton says matter-of-factly. "I'm just a twenty-five-year-old black man, you know, living in America, no criminal record, two feature films to my credit, two Academy Award nominations under my belt . . ."

Boyz N the Hood, Singleton's first feature, was a low-budget, high-grossing film about boys becoming men in the disaster that is south-central Los Angeles. It's about "growing up in the Reagan era," says Singleton, who used many scenes from his own young life to make the story grippingly real. *Boyz* bagged him Oscar nominations in 1992 for best original screenplay and best director. He thus became the first African American ever nominated in

From *The Washington Post* (July 25, 1993). © 1993, The Washington Post, reprinted with permission.

the director's category, and the youngest of any color—beating out Orson Welles's nomination at age twenty-five for *Citizen Kane*.

Singleton's new movie, *Poetic Justice*, which opened Friday, is a black urban romance, for which he snagged the princess of pop, Janet Jackson. She plays a hairdresser who writes poetry to ease the pain of the gangsta slaying of her boyfriend. The riveting lines she recites were penned by Maya Angelou, who was chosen by Bill Clinton to write his inaugural poem. Rapper Tupac Shakur plays the male lead.

Boyz N the Hood was a surprise success: Made for less than $6 million, it grossed almost $100 million (including overseas sales). Commercially—and critically—it may be a hard act to follow. But publicly, at least, Singleton seems to have no doubts about the new film (which cost approximately twice as much to make). It will, he confidently predicts, be another hit; it's "better [than *Boyz*]; I think the characters in this film are more complex."

Singleton is chuckling now, his mask beginning to crack a bit.

"All right? I'm having a measure of success. Little kids are starting to look at me and see alternate ways of living their life. So I'm an inspiration. . . . It's like they [tha police] try to tear down any black male who's trying to do anything. Anything they can find. Any little niche. . . .

"Look at Mike Tyson," he continues, now rolling comfortably on ground he's obviously covered before. "Mike Tyson is a political prisoner right now, you know, in Indiana."

Huh?

"Because, I mean, he was an inspiration for every young black kid in the ghetto, and they put him in jail and stuff. It's just another way of slapping every black man in the face. . . . I don't know if he was guilty of the crime or not. I mean, I don't want to get into the ramifications of that case and stuff, right?"

Well, yeah, except there are some awfully big ramifications for a lot of men and women out there who have been in similar situations.

"Yeah, I know. I know. It's a big issue, and it's an issue I plan to deal with in some of my other films, right? Because nobody has the right to violate anyone. But I'm just talking about—now I just want to deal with the fact that he's in jail now, okay?"

Well, okay. But can you really separate cause and effect?

"Oh boy," Singleton says. "Well, you want to talk about that case? . . . I know women who actually have been violated, and when I saw that woman [Tyson's accuser], like on TV, giving her side of the story, it wasn't like something bad had happened to her. . . . Being, like, a director, looking at people who act, I interpret human behavior constantly. And I just didn't think she was telling the truth. That's my honest opinion."

Is it true the ribs can tell the kick of a beast from a Lover's fist?
The bruised bones recorded well. The sudden shock, the
Hard impact. Then swollen lids . . .
Sorry eyes, spoke not of lost romance, but hurt.
Hate is often confused. Its limits are in zones beyond
itself. And Sadists will not learn that . . .
Love by nature, exacts a pain unequaled on the rack.

In *Poetic Justice*, love is a trip from L.A. to Oakland in a U.S. Mail truck. Two postal workers (played by Shakur and comedian Joe Torry) making the run bring along a couple of women (Jackson and Regina King) for the ride. Singleton has said that one of his influences was the Italian film director Federico Fellini, and *Justice* combines scenes of whimsy (an African festival near Big Sur, with a stage on which the Last Poets perform, suddenly appears) and reality (the breakup of Torry and King). It's a black fairy tale up there on the big screen, the likes of which have not been seen in these times.

"The black people survive in this movie," Singleton says of *Justice*, which he wrote, directed, and co-produced. "It's a love story with a happy ending."

Justice started out to be a film from a woman's point of view, as a counterbalance of sorts to *Boyz*. Singleton said he got the idea for the plot while he was shooting *Boyz* and began wondering what happens to the girlfriends of all the guys who get blown away in gang wars. However, in *Poetic Justice: Filmmaking South Central Style*, a book about the making of the film that Singleton wrote with Veronica Chambers, he concedes that the film ended up being primarily about Lucky, the postal worker played by Shakur.

"The more I look at this movie, the more I think it's about women, but it's still from a man's perspective," Singleton admits. "You still got the booty shots, the breast shots. . . . The fact is that I'm going to emphasize certain things in certain ways. I don't even know it until after I see it. It just comes from an innate part of who I am. . . . But you gotta admit, you've never seen so many black women in any movie in so many different sizes, shapes, and colors."

Perhaps so. But after a premiere screening of *Justice* ten days ago in Washington (a benefit for the acting troupe Voices From the Streets and the mentoring group Concerned Black Men), many people expressed dismay over the film's profanity. "I'm sick of all that cussing," said one middle-aged man, summing up the feelings of others in the audience.

"I've heard that," Singleton says. "But that's the mark of youth. When people are young, they can't articulate their feelings." So they curse.

There was also an element of gender-bashing in the film's dialogue that some found particularly offensive. One woman at the benefit screening screwed up her nose and said, "All those 'bitches' and 'hos.'" (The film even introduces a new anti-woman term—"yamp"— which evidently means "young tramp.")

"This wasn't the film to deal with that," Singleton says, moving on quickly, when asked about the politics of the sexes. Thoughts about the effects of such language on the many girls and boys who will see *Justice* are not articulated. Perhaps that's youth too.

In fact, Singleton is confident that, overall, women will like the film. "Specifically, black women," he says. "I don't think it'll be controversial. I don't think there's anything in here they don't know about. I don't set out to do controversial films, you know? I just set out to tell a good story, so that at the end of the day you can leave the theater and feel like you read a book or something, or you feel like you've been enlightened in some way."

He points to Spike Lee as more of a master of controversy, a "P.T. Barnum" of film, a "showman" who sparks social debate by shoving an issue in your face and forcing you to deal with it.

"My stuff just creeps up on you and bites you on your ass," Singleton says.

It's hot, and Singleton is dressed all in black, except for the rubber-soled cotton camouflage shoes he picked up while in Burkina Faso for an African film festival. He's a slight man with a gentle face, soft-looking facial hair, and hard features. The light is dim in the Washington restaurant where he's eating his chicken, but he still sports his dark glasses.

He made the unlikely choice early on of Janet Jackson to play Justice, the "round-the-way girl" lead character. He also decided early on to use Maya Angelou's poetry. And for months, fans and critics who follow his work closely have been twisting the concept around in their minds, trying to visualize the combination: ditsy diva vs. earth mother.

"Doesn't that seem interesting?" Singleton says buoyantly. "You're talking about the difference between sophisticates that know about Maya, and the whole mass population that doesn't know about Maya. After this movie, and what's happened this year [with Clinton], everyone will know about Maya, and hopefully this will spark a lot of other girls who like Janet Jackson to go and read Maya Angelou's poems. . . .

"And Janet is deeper than most people think. She just don't let everybody know what she thinks. People are like that. I don't either. You don't tell tha police everything."

He laughs. Right. Wasn't it Jackson who sang about "Control"?

Singleton says he settled on Angelou—after abandoning attempts to write his own verse—because he wanted poetry that had "some depth to it" without being "ultra-political or ultra-sexist or ultra-feminist."

"I just wanted it to be these, like, poems that everybody can get into," he says. "Maya's verse has a universal feel to it."

That's why, Singleton says, it was no surprise to him when Clinton asked Angelou to write an inaugural poem.

"We're two men from different backgrounds, going through difficult times," Singleton says. "I've been out of college two years and I'm still defining myself as a person, and Bill Clinton's been in office for six months and he's still defining himself as a leader of the Free World."

Clinton's showcasing of Angelou "was kind of a vindication," Singleton says, " 'cause a lot of people thought I was crazy for doing a movie about a poet."

Singleton's first step in making Jackson believable in the role of his poet— a "regular" sister—was to feed her waffles for three weeks to boost her weight by ten pounds.

"Her manager and all of them hated it," Singleton recalls. "I told her to have some fun. I told her to remember Robert De Niro in *Raging Bull*. . . . I just wanted her to look different. No makeup. Like Sophia Loren did in *Two Women*."

Next, he gave Jackson "home girl" lessons by having her hang out with young women who live the part. Some of them were hairdressers, whom Singleton considers "artists" and "professionals of the black community. . . . They can make more money than black men." He says they helped him write the script, offering tips on authentic dialogue and reality checks on the salon scene.

Jackson turned out to be a dream to direct, Singleton says. When she first came on the set, actress Tyra Ferrell, who plays the beauty salon owner, confronted her skeptically and asked whether she could be "hard." But in his book, Singleton says that the street isn't the only breeding ground for toughness: "I was telling Janet that in her character, being hard isn't just [a matter of] where you're from. There's a certain amount of pain and tragedy that Janet has been through that she can draw from. If I wasn't aware of this, I wouldn't have cast her."

Tupac Shakur—whose violent rap lyrics were recently (unsuccessfully) cited as a motivating force by a Texas man convicted of killing a state trooper— apparently was not as cooperative. He was often late getting to the set.

"I'm always looking for a young De Niro, and it always gets [expletive] up," Singleton says in his book. "I don't think a lot of young people respect what it takes to do great work. When you have things handed to you so easily, you don't respect it." (Shakur was fired from the film *Menace II Society* and is currently being sued for damages by its directors, Albert and Allen Hughes.)

Singleton was raised in south central L.A., shuttling between his father and mother, much like the lead character in *Boyz*. His parents, a financial planner and a pharmaceutical saleswoman, were stable achievers, also much like the parents of the *Boyz* protagonist, who is pulled back from the edge. And Singleton—like many African Americans regardless of their particular circumstances—came up with a constant awareness of the abyss that awaits those who lack a sure footing.

Singleton also grew up loving the movies, an affection his father shared and encouraged. So it was natural that Singleton chose to attend the University of Southern California's film school. He took what he said were the "hardest courses, honors classes, even though I wasn't an honor student in high school." That was his way of "getting more education for my buck, you know? And after some trial and error and getting some bad grades, I finally learned how to whip it."

Two years in a row, Singleton generated scripts—including an early version of *Boyz*—that won USC's Jack Nicholson Writing Award. The $8,000 prizes paid a nice percentage of his tuition, as well as bringing him to the attention of a major agency—Creative Artists—which took the unusual step of signing an untried, unknown student. (CAA's Bradford Smith says Singleton has "a singular vision. . . . It's not the community's vision, it's not Hollywood's vision. . . . That's what makes him different from the bumper crop.")

"I got in there on my brain and I got out of there on my brain and I got a job using my mind," Singleton says. "That's what my job is, you know, juxtaposing all these different things—camera, actor, sound, lighting, everything. I use my mind. My father has a saying: 'Work smarter, not harder.' And that's what I'm trying to do with my life."

In a time when kingdoms come.
Joy is brief as summer's fun.
Happiness, its race has run.
Then pain stalks in to plunder.

Singleton was in town again last weekend to appear at Black Entertainment Television's Teen Summit. It's part talk show, part showcase for entertainers such as Cultural Revolution, a group Singleton is producing as he experiments with the music business.

He talks to the teens about various writing techniques. Then he pulls a large black notebook from his backpack.

"This is one of the secrets of the trade," Singleton says, explaining that he has kept a journal since he was a boy. He writes in it every day, recording thoughts and bits of dialogue he overhears that he will someday use in a movie whose plot begins as a paragraph scribbled on the fly.

"Everybody has creative energy," Singleton says by way of encouragement to the young people. "It's just a matter of whether that energy is going . . . to be positive or negative."

It takes Singleton a while to get out of the BET studio, for he pauses to take a picture with everyone who asks, prescribes reading lists for aspiring young screenwriters and stops to banter with his band.

Once in his limo, completely calm even though his staff is frantic with worry that he won't make his flight, Singleton says: "If a person isn't articulate, then that creative energy is going to express itself in other ways. If you don't allow a person to have a creative outlet, then you've made that person dangerous." Or, as John Singleton once said, "If there's not more John Singletons, there's gonna be a lot more carjackings."

Boyz II Man

MARTHA SOUTHGATE/1993

I T ' S   A   S U N N Y May afternoon on the set of *Poetic Justice* and all's right with John Singleton's world. It's early enough in the day that the panic of trying to finish while the light is good has not yet set in. He's just been brought a fresh set of trade papers and he's comfortable in his director's chair. Only one thing is missing. He yells to his assistant: "David, get me a juice." Rather than heading for the snack-laden craft-services table, David reaches under the chair in which Singleton sits and pulls out a small cooler. He opens it to reveal an assortment of containers of a juice concoction called Capri Sun. After conferring briefly, David hands one to Singleton and replaces the cooler under his chair. Singleton returns calmly to his *Daily Variety* as though people have always been handing him things he could easily reach. They haven't.

John Singleton's life is riven with contradictions. On the one hand, he has a show-biz streak a mile wide. He can quote box office with the best of them; he writes on a top-of-the-line Apple PowerBook and owns a Nissan Pathfinder and 300ZX; and it was his idea, not the studio's, to cast superstar Janet Jackson as the lead in *Poetic Justice*. On the other hand, he still lives in Baldwin Hills, not far from South Central L.A., where he grew up. And though he doesn't hang out there anymore, he still thinks fondly of Crenshaw Boulevard, South Central's main drag—home, he says, of "sunny skies, palm trees, Crips and Bloods, and fine-ass girls in Hyundais." While he's a power player in one of the toughest games of all—one that only a few black men play—in many ways, he's still a kid, buying new comic books every Friday, playing Sega Genesis, hanging out at the Fox Hills Mall. He's only twenty-five, after all. He might just as easily be driving a Super-Shuttle van at LAX or working as a movie extra to earn money and free meals, both of

From *Premiere* (August 1993). Reprinted by permission of Martha Southgate.

which he's done. He's got one foot in the 'hood and one foot in Beverly Hills. That tension gives his films—and his life—an edge that few other filmmakers have. He plans to hang on to that toughness. It remains to be seen whether he'll be able to.

The story's been told a million times: how the cocky young Singleton had the most extraordinary directing debut of the past ten years, bursting out at twenty-two with a script called *Boyz N the Hood*, which he wrote at USC's Filmic Writing Program and insisted he be allowed to direct. Amazingly, he was. He went on to become the youngest person and the only African American ever nominated for a Best Director Oscar; the film, budgeted at only $5.7 million, grossed nearly $60 million (he says it's really $100 million in all markets but "they'll never admit it").

He worked on *Boyz* in relative anonymity, a brash college grad with a small budget. Not any longer. On *Justice*, media types were tripping over one another to get interviews. The budget, low by Hollywood standards at $13.5 million, was still more than double that of *Boyz*. And, of course, there was Miss Jackson. John Singleton had arrived.

He moves within the big time like an old pro. His friend Robert Thomas, who worked as a grip on both *Boyz* and *Justice* and roomed with Singleton in college, echoes the sentiments of many who know him when he says, "He's the same guy that he was when he was walking around USC with his Coke-bottle glasses on."

The glasses are still there, but they're no longer Coke-bottle thick. These days, Singleton is pretty cool. When he arrives this morning, he's driving his shiny new Pathfinder with a boomin' system blasting Arrested Development. He steps out and stops at the breakfast table to goof around with the crew members, looking more like a production assistant than the director. He's fairly thin and short and wears a baseball cap (sporting the comic strip character Black Panther), a black T-shirt, and little round sunglasses.

We're at Disney's Golden Oak Ranch, which served for many years as the setting for *Little House on the Prairie*. But now it's decked out as an Afrocentric festival with kente-cloth vendors and African-inspired knicknacks galore. The sound of drums fills the air and bright colors are everywhere. The scene will be familiar to many African-American viewers, less so to most white viewers. Singleton likes it that way. "Everybody makes movies about stuff you've seen before," he says. "This movie is all stuff we've never seen before."

Yes and no. As *The New Yorker*'s Terrence Rafferty pointed out in a review of *Boyz N the Hood*, "the young filmmaker's professionalism and precocious self-assurance sometimes work against his best instinct. Singleton's plot is disappointingly conventional; it obeys screenwriting-class rules." *Boyz N the Hood* is a heartfelt, powerful film, but it breaks no new ground in terms of storytell-ing or style; it's a skillful Hollywood debut. The script of *Poetic Justice* offers something of the same combination of hard-edged characters and show-biz smoothness. At heart, it's a boy-meets-girl story. Justice, the character Jackson plays, is a South-Central hairdresser scarred by a hard life and many losses. She finds solace in her work and her poetry (actually written by Maya Ange-lou). While on a trip up the California coast, she lets down her guard and falls in love with Lucky, a struggling post-office worker played by rapper Tupac Shakur. "*Poetic Justice* is much richer in its characters and its sexual politics," says producer Steve Nicolaides, who also produced *Boyz*. "Whether it will be as strong a film as *Boyz N the Hood*, I honestly don't know. It's not going to rock your guts in the third act. It's not going to make you angry."

Compounding any questions about the script are questions about the casting of Jackson in her first film role as the streetwise Justice. "What's next, Sylvester Stallone and Dolly Parton?" jokes Nicolaides. "But you know, once they see the movie, that won't be in anybody's mind. She's going to surprise a lot of people. It's really inspired casting because it's dangerous casting."

Singleton agrees. "When singers want to cross into something else like acting, they get a part as a singer. That shit is easy. But I came at her with another vibe, I said, 'I want you to be someone else. I want it so you can be considered a serious actress.'"

He worked hard with Jackson to give her credibility—assigning her films to watch (among them Vittorio De Sica's *Two Women* and Martin Scorsese's *Raging Bull*), having her spend a day doing hair in a South-Central beauty parlor (he says she didn't turn a head), asking her to gain weight (which she did), and introducing her to four woman friends of his who gave the sheltered Miss Jackson a crash course in Streetwise 101 (one of them taught her how to do hair too). Jackson remembers, "The day I met them, they all stayed over, and they ended up staying for two or three months. We hung out every single day."

To those who question her right to play the part, Jackson retorts. "People think that I've been given so much, growing up in Encino. But pain is pain. I've been through a lot in my life. It may not be in the same way, but it's still a pain you can feel. When you need to have that come across onscreen, you reach back to find that pain and put it up there."

Months Later, when *Justice* is near completion and Singleton is hard at work on a new script, he's asked if he's got any career jitters. Not a chance. "I've seen very few young filmmakers," he says, "who have come out in the last five or six years and consistently come up with good material, and I want to be part of a new renaissance in which every time I do a film, it's like a great novel, you know? I've studied the works of Steinbeck and Hemingway and stuff, and I want to do that in a filmic context."

This kind of braggadocio is typical of Singleton; it seems obnoxious out of context but is less so in person, perhaps because he veers back and forth between pompousness and charming boyishness like . . . well, like the very young man he is. He cares deeply about making good films, and he possesses an encyclopedic knowledge of the medium—but then he'll stop himself while holding forth on some complicated aspect of film editing to remember that he got a D in all this "technical stuff" at USC. Like a kid doing homework, he listens to music at earsplitting volume when he's working on a script—but it's the collected works of film scorer Ennio Morricone. He owns hundreds of laserdiscs and says casually of Laurence Fishburne, "He's my Toshiro Mifune." But then he'll suddenly switch gears and talk about his pet cat who died recently: "I loved that cat more than I love some people."

He *is* full of himself. But people who know him well say that he has always been this way. Hollywood may have amplified it, but it didn't start there. "From the first day I met him," says Nicolaides, "I always felt like John expected all of this to happen. I haven't seen any change in the deep, dark part of his soul. He's still the same intellectually aggressive, goofy, knucklehead, funny, loving, supportive, selfish kid that he always was.

"But he's got a little bit of an artist's attitude now," he adds. "He's sort of been hanging with the Spielbergs and the Coppolas, who are hopefully giving him 90 percent of their wisdom and 10 percent of their bile, but sometimes the quotient changes a little bit."

His mother, Shelia Ward-Johnson, says that she raised him to have few doubts. "I'm there to keep him as positive as possible," she says. "I always tried to put a lot of pride and strength in him."

John Daniel Singleton was born on January 6, 1968, in South Central Los Angeles. His father, Danny Singleton, and mother were in their teens and never wed. "John's father was not my enemy," says Ward-Johnson. "You don't have babies with the enemy." With that attitude to guide them, Singleton's parents worked out an informal shared custody arrangement much like the one that Tre, the protagonist of *Boyz N the Hood*, lived under: young John spent his early childhood with his mother and most of his high school years with his father. But the *Boyz* parallel goes only so far; the parent who appears to be the strongest presence in Singleton's life is his mother. They've always been a team. Ward-Johnson, now a sales rep for a pharmaceutical company, is a frequent visitor to his sets, talks with him about his scripts, and offers advice on matters large and small—for example, when he met with Maya Angelou to ask her if he could use her poetry and whether she'd play a small part in the film, Ward-Johnson suggested that he take her one red rose. He did. It worked like a charm.

"My son does not want me to be in the public eye," says Ward-Johnson. "But whatever he needs, I'll contribute. If I'm needed more, I will give more."

Contrary to popular belief, Singleton didn't spend all his growing-up years in the 'hood. He was bused to a predominantly white school in the Valley for one year—and hated it. "I had just never gone to school with anything other than black students," he says. "It was culture shock." His grades dropped, and he ended up transferring back to a series of schools nearer home. He says now of his migratory high school experience, "[It taught me to] never let my environment fuck with my self-esteem. I'm stronger because of it."

He gives his parents high praise for shepherding him through a hazardous childhood. "I saw a lot of creative people go down," he says. "People who could be greater filmmakers than me. People who could be great musicians, great novelists." When asked what allowed him to come out whole, he says simply, "My mother was a strong black woman; my father was a strong black man. Even though they never married, they made sure that I came up right."

Singleton, who is unmarried, became the father of a little girl last October, and he plans to make sure she comes up right—privately. "I'll just say this: I am a *very* good father. But I don't want crazy motherfuckers reading about my family and trying to come after them. I mean, hey, this is about the movie. This is not about me, you know?"

But Singleton *is* all about the movies. Thomas remembers that in the rowdy, boy-filled house they shared in college, Singleton would stay in his room watching movies for hours at a time. "John was the straitest-laced of all of us," he says. "I used to think he didn't know what having a good time was—but he was having a good time."

He has a good time on the set too, running things with a combination of goofiness and complete command. "I direct to protect my vision, but I love being in charge," he says. "How many black men do you know who can request that something be done and it gets done immediately? It's a kid's dream."

He's living out his dream by managing a crew of 150 people that is 50 percent black and 50 percent white—a level of integration almost unheard-of on a Hollywood set. He's also dealing with about 150 extras, 50 or so stalls and vendors, and the 16 members of the Ballet de Konman Kélé, an African-American dance troupe that performs traditional West African folk dances. Extras come up to him shyly offering pieces of paper to sign or asking to take Polaroid photos with him. He obliges everyone cheerfully.

As the dancers rehearse and the drums pound, Singleton alternates between looking into the monitor, laughing delightedly at his own inventiveness, and dancing around in front of the stage, his arms extended stiffly above him. Every once in a while, when a shot looks particularly good, he crows "That's *dope!*" to the skies. "I never thought about how romantic it is that Lucky and Justice fall in love among all these beats. It's very African." Like he didn't write the whole thing himself.

But every day on the set wasn't just another day in paradise. In fact, this production had to face issues of race and class far more than most movie sets ever do—just as Singleton has had to in order to navigate the business. For one thing, shooting continued straight through the L.A. riots.

There are reminders of the night Los Angeles burned all over the *Justice* set. A white crew member wears a T-shirt that proclaims L.A.: IT'S A RIOT in large block letters. Shorty, Singleton's six-foot-seven bodyguard/assistant, has the words NO JUSTICE, NO Ⓐ cut into his hair. A black crew member wears a shirt that reads GUILTY, GUILTY, GUILTY, GUILTY. The night the verdicts came down, *Justice* was shooting in Simi Valley, of all places. Singleton was on his way to the set when he heard the news from his Sony Watchman. In a fury, he wheeled off to the Simi Valley courthouse, where he tersely told TV cameras that the verdicts had lit the fuse to a bomb from which many people would feel the shrapnel.

But then he went on to the shoot. There was a $13.5 million movie waiting. "Emotionally, I was all messed up that night," he says. "We were watching TV, and I was worried my house was going to get burned up." His mother was also on the set that night. She remembers, "It was very painful for everyone. I was crying on the way over, but when I got there and everyone was sitting around the TV watching, I pulled John aside and told him, "That's too much negative energy. I wanted him to use his energy positively."

"I don't want to speak for all the whites on the crew," says director of photography Peter Lyons Collister, "but the racial thing became something I was aware of [during the riots]. Nothing specific happened. Things were just weird. That first night, John was watching a television constantly and was on the phone checking up on family and friends. The second night, I actually said to Steve [Nicolaides] that maybe we shouldn't keep working. We did end up giving people the option of not showing up for work if they were concerned about their families and stuff. But nobody stayed home. It turned out that everyone came in, but they brought their wives—and their dogs."

"A lot of people couldn't get back to their houses," says Nicolaides. "So at midnight, we're trying to find motel rooms in Simi Valley for fifty black people. It was weird. But we survived."

Not without some difficulty. Thomas, who is black, says the *Justice* was the most stressful job he has ever worked on, partly because of racial tensions that surfaced during and after the riots. "On *Poetic*, there weren't as many black people on the set as there were for *Boyz*," he says. "A lot of people were just showing up to get the pay-check. And there were a lot of people looking down on people, thinking that they weren't qualified to do their jobs."

Singleton acknowledges that there were tensions but says he didn't hear about them until after the shoot. "People kept stuff from me because I would have gone ballistic," he says. "I rarely ever blow my cool, but if I do, it's got to be something very serious." He also says it won't happen again. "I want to work with people who don't mind working with black people," he says. "They have to understand: if you work on one of my films, you will work with a lot of different kinds of people—black, white, Asian, whatever. If you can't hang, you got to go."

Singleton demands no less professionalism of himself. He despises interviews, but he's philosophical about it: "Gotta do what you gotta do to sell a picture." He doesn't let the studio mess with his writing, but he'll play the "let's take a meeting" game when he has to. He grins a little as he prepares for a talk with actor Brendan Fraser, hot off of *Encino Man* and *School Ties*. "Now the word is out that there's going to be white people in my next movie," he says, "so I've been meeting with a lot of white actors for that." And he hones his talent and ignores the naysayers, just the way he always has. "Some guy said after I made the first movie that I got it because I was black. They don't know anything about all the hours I spent in the computer room, learning how to write and everything, about all the journals I kept and the entries I had in them. It's not for them to even care about that, it's for me to care about it. If I got onto everything that everybody ever thought about me, then I wouldn't be doing what I'm doing now."

At the end of Singleton's sophomore year of college, the director of the writing program, Margaret Mehring, wrote an evaluation. "John has really blossomed as a writer, a filmmaker, and a person," it reads. "It is possible that he will receive the Nicholson scholarship next year. I hope so. He is very much alive, eager, and so full of hope and promise. He has charted his course and stuck to it. He recognized the need to learn screenwriting in order to do what he wants to do in production and has done so. I think that John will make some history, not just for black films but for films per se. I am so happy for him."

Staying the course and making some history. Those are still Singleton's goals. It was that way in college, and it's that way now. "Where I grew up, most people I went to elementary school with, a lot of those brothers, are not around anymore," he says. "So there ain't nothing that can scare me in this shit, know what I'm saying? I'm only twenty-five years old, and I got two movies under my belt, and I got another movie I'm going to do. So long as I don't get lazy and move to Bel-Air and get fat and get a white woman, then I'll be fine." And he probably will be. Hollywood is not John Singleton's enemy. You don't make movies with the enemy.

AFI Harold Lloyd Master Seminar

AMERICAN FILM INSTITUTE / 1995

MODERATOR: *It's a Hollywood story, a good one, and it's about a film school stu-*
dent who graduates and who gets a big agent writing a script that he convinces . . .
or the script convinces a major studio to put up the money to make. And then he con-
vinces the studio that he should direct that screenplay. He's only twenty-three years
old. Does this sound good? [Laughter] Yeah. And he goes out and . . . [directs] . . .
the movie, which not only becomes a commercial hit, but he is nominated for
an Oscar as Best Director and the screenplay as Best Screenplay. He doesn't win
because that would be just too unbelievable. [Laughter] But . . . well look, Rocky
didn't win in the first movie either, but there were five sequels. And my guess is that
our guest today will give us, maybe not sequels, but will go on. And please help me
welcome John Singleton.
[Applause]
JOHN SINGLETON: Thank you, thank you.

MODERATOR: *John, thank you for coming. If we can go to that part of your life,*
when Boyz N the Hood *was made and Columbia put up the money to make it and*
you wrote it and directed it. Can you tell us about all of that and how you made it
happen?
JOHN SINGLETON: Well, I wrote *Boyz N the Hood* in the late summer, early
fall of 1989. And I was a first semester senior and going to USC. It was cost-
ing me twenty thousand dollars a year that I didn't have, and I was trying
to figure out what I was going to do when I got out of school. I knew fairly
well that I wasn't going to get a job working in the film business right out of
school, so I planned to take this test in the L.A. School District and become

---

From the AFI Harold Lloyd Master Seminar with director John Singleton, 8 March 1995,
moderated by Ron Silverman. © 1995 American Film Institute. Reprinted with permission.

an elementary school teacher. In the meantime, I would write my screen-plays and try to figure out a way to get in the business . . . and if I couldn't get it, I'd raise the money myself to make the movie. I would depend on the relationships that I had formed, try to get Laurence to commit to the movie, or get Cube to commit, which I already had. (Then I'd find the money that way.)

I then started an internship with a company at Columbia Pictures. My job was to read script coverage and to read the scripts and do coverage on them. I would give my comments and synopsis on the scripts and I was reading a lot of bad ones. The head of my program, Karen Teischer, also the woman who hired me for the internship program, she read the two screenplays I'd written up to that time. In today's issue of *The Hollywood Reporter* it was reported that she's going over from Amblin to work with Peter Guber. One screenplay was called *Twighlight Time*, and the other was *Boyz N the Hood*. She said these are two good screenplays. I would always tell her, I'm a writer I'm a screen-writer, and that I wanted to direct. After she read them, she told me she knew a few agents. "I know an agent at William Morris and I know a couple people at CAA. Why don't you let me take your scripts around and talk to some people and see what comes of it." And I said, that was cool because in my mind, I had always planned to become an independent filmmaker. I was raised on the whole independent vision. I was thinking, I'm going to find my own money, it doesn't matter what these suits think. I'm going to make the films on my terms and do what I got to do. And so I really didn't seriously consider the studio system to be a viable option for me as a filmmaker.

So, nevertheless, she took my scripts, and she went to the two agencies. She set up two meetings with me: one with William Morris, and the other with CAA. The CAA meeting came first. So I was like, hey, you know maybe something will come of this. But I also took it with kind of a grain of salt since I had done this before. When I was a junior I had made the rounds with one screenplay that I got a couple of awards for, which was the first one. I met a couple of agents and they didn't want to sign me. This made me thick-skinned. So here I am, the second time around and I'm meeting with two of the largest agencies in Hollywood.

So I go into my meeting, I look at these people here, [Laughs] I immedi-ately have an attitude. I'm very skeptical about any of these people doing anything for me, because they've never met anybody like me. They don't know my kind of vibe. So I'm like, okay, tell me what's going on here. And my agent, the guy became my agent, his name is Bradford Smith. (He now works for me in my company. [Laughter] I hired him away from CAA. He's been my agent for four years.) He opens up and says, "My name is Brad

Smith and I just want to tell you I worked at the Yale Rep in drama and I worked on Broadway with August Wilson and Lloyd Richards on *Fences*, and I'd just like to say we want to sign you. I read your material, I think you have that flavor that reminds me very much of August Wilson." And anyone that really knows me knows that August Wilson is my idol. I mean, if there's any writer on earth that I really revere, it's him. And he got me there.

So being real cool about it, I said, oh, that's good you want to sign me. But inside I was like, yes, yes! [Laughter] Yes, because I didn't want to give it up, you know. I mean, the first thing you're supposed to do when they want to sign you is scream like you're on *Love Connection* [Laughter] or whatever. So, I just said, okay, that's nice. I went down the street to a pay phone and I called up Karen and said, "CAA wants to sign me, they want to sign me.

"She's like, "Great! Great!" And she says, "Do you want to meet with William Morris next week?"

I said, "No, I don't want to meet with William Morris, I'll sign with CAA."

And so it was really great for me because here I am a senior in college and I'm signed with the biggest agency in Hollywood. And up to that time I went to film school. I was one of only twenty black people in the program that had two thousand people. I always felt under siege because here were these kids, some of them had families that were in the business, and here I was, signed to a big agency. Although it was not really blatant, it was implied and I felt like people looked at me like, "What are you doing here?" you know? And this made me even more thick-skinned. Like a lot of people, you may not know me, but you think, oh, well he's an angry black man, but I'm not like that, you know, I've become kind of jaded for all the things that I've had to go through being a black man living in America, having people look at me, like, when I'm paying twenty-five thousand dollars a year in loans, saying "What are you doing here?" or constantly trying to say that there's no way that I would ever make films. So, it made me not so much angry, but more thick-skinned. It made me more skeptical. It felt like I was always on the defensive. So when I went to USC, a lot of people have said that I acted like I had a chip on my shoulder because I had to be ten times better than anybody going to the school. I had to be better. I studied film for eight, maybe ten years before I even went to college. So I went to school trying to be just a guy, being friends with everybody. But then there were people who would act like I was nobody because I was a black person going to film school. So after a while, instead of being cool with everybody, I was like fuck all y'all. Excuse my French but, after a while, after just trying to be very amiable and trying to be human about it, and be like, hey, we're all in film school, let's get together, let's talk about movies. Let's do this. But then having people diss me. After a while, I just got real thick-skinned. So, getting signed by CAA was like, the shackles were off. There's nothing y'all can tell me now. There's nothing that cannot be accomplished. There's nothing that I cannot do.

So, fine, I get signed by an agency now. So what am I going to do? I get signed by this agency, I don't have a job anymore. I stopped working because I started getting awards for my screenplays and I was able to pay my tuition and I would get a little bit of money here and there. So I decided to devote myself to trying to figure out what I was going to do after I got out of school. And so my agent told me I wasn't eating right. He told me that I had to get a job or something. He says, "Well, I'll tell you what I'll do. I'll try to schedule you meetings with people. You know, I'll try to get you as many meetings in a week as possible, so you can meet people. And preferably . . . we'll try to make them lunch meetings so we'll get them [Laughter] to take you to lunch and you'll eat."

And I said, "That's cool, because all I need is [Laughter] one meal a day."

So the first meeting I had, I thought I was totally big Willie. My first meeting was with Jasmine Guy. And she was on *Different World*, at the time! I was [Laughs] in the middle of USC campus, and they would say, "Hey, what's up, John, how you doing?"

I'd say, "You want to know what I'm doing today?" [Laughter] And I would just say, "Yeah, I'm going to a meeting with Jasmine Guy."

So the first meeting was with Jasmine Guy. Then I met all these other people. And what I would do is I would talk to them about the screenplays that I had and the work that they would possibly want to contract me to write, because at the time, I was just going out as a writer. I would always pitch them this little movie about three friends growing up in South Central L.A. and people would always say, "Well, let me have it, let me have it."

And I'd say, "No, you can't have it."

And they'd say, "Why can't I have it?"

"Because I'm going to direct it," you know.

And they said, "Oh, okay."

So, after a while, the word started to get around about me. You know, everything in this town, in any business, is all about marketing. So, in doing this, I created kind of like an aura for myself. And I had no track record. All I had was two screenplays that weren't set up anywhere. So I created an aura about myself where I was like a hot young filmmaker out of USC. I hadn't made one film. I had written screenplays. I hadn't made any films yet, but it was like the whole aura of this somebody at USC and, you know, it started to get around. And then the title of the script started getting around. I had a meeting with a guy by the name of Stan Lathan who was working for Russell Simmons. This really sparked things for me. Russell Simmons was putting together an entertainment company, he was thinking about getting a deal with Columbia Pictures. Stan Lathan read the script, he loved the script. Unbeknownst to me, I think he wanted to direct it himself. So he gave it to Russell. Stan tried to get Russell to read it. So Russell and I had breakfast at the Mondrian. And I was like, hey, another free meal for me! [Laughter] So we're sitting across the table and Stan is like "You got to read this . . ." pitching the script. Russell's sitting there like, he's big New York and I'm all L.A. 'ed out. That's my whole thing, West Coast, you know, so anybody East Coast I'm always like, no, it's about the West Coast. See, it's a hip hop kind of thing.

So he's like [Laughter], "You're supposed to pitch me the story."

I said, "I don't need to pitch this story. This is not *Krush Groove*, you know. [Laughter] This is about drive. This is about growing up where you hear helicopters every night over your house, and you hear automatic gunfire in the distance. It's about L.A., you know."

And he just looked at him like who is this? But you know, what? I felt that I had to be who I was. I looked at all the other people that I knew that got a few meetings, and they really took a back seat to whoever they were meeting with, which would put them in a lower position so that person always is going to act like you're smaller. So I decided to be big on him because he was that kind of dude. So he's like, "Alright, I'll read it." No, no, no, no. The reason I caught him was because I told him about some scenes, like having cars going by and you hear boom boom boom boom boom, hearing the music coming out of the cars. That's when he sat up and he says, "You know, I got an album coming out by L.L. Cool J. And it's called 'The Booming System.' I know what you mean now." [Laughter]

And so that kind of got him. He got on, like, the MGM Grand airline that existed at the time, and he read the script. All this was going on, and then one day while I was hanging out with my friends he called down from the plane. He said he'd read the script and that it was the greatest script he'd ever read in his life. He said he was negotiating with people like Stephanie Allain at Columbia Pictures and he was hanging out with Jon Peters and a lot of other people. He said, "I swear, this is the first movie I want to produce," you know? So here's Russell Simmons who has a company that pulls in at least fifteen to twenty million dollars a year on his own through Sony with music. And he's making a film deal. And he says it's the greatest script they ever read, by an intern. So they're, like, "Where's this script? We need the script. Let's find this script." While this was happening, CAA submitted it to Orion at the same time as Columbia. But at Orion a reader gave it bad coverage.

MODERATOR: *Bad coverage?*

JOHN SINGLETON: Said I had no talent. Said that I tried too hard to capture the vernacular of the street. I have a copy of the coverage at my house. I have the coverage from Orion and I have the coverage from Columbia. Coverage from Orion says I have no talent, says that the dialogue was bland, says that it just really degrades the whole script. And the coverage from Columbia says in the hands of a good director, this could be a very great film. So, you know who I went with. You know the story. [Laughter] Now, everyone's going crazy trying to get the script, and I think there's a million stories right now as to how the film got made, because everyone at the studio takes credit for it. The people I did the internship with take credit for it, even though they read it before but they didn't want me to direct it, they didn't really want to do it. Everybody takes credit for it. Stephanie reads the script and she says this is great, this needs to be made. She goes to Frank Price and tells him about it. They decide to do what's called a weekend read with the Columbia group. After the group reads it, they said it was alright. They don't really want to do it. So she goes over to Peter Guber's and Jon Peters's companies, and tells them that this has to be done. Stacey Snider also read it and said it was great. It's so convoluted now, who was responsible for what. So Peters says let's do it. We'll do it for six million dollars, it won't cost us much. And if it doesn't work we'll just shoot it to video.

MODERATOR: *Now, excuse me. At that point, you had made it clear that you were going to direct this movie and they knew that?*

JOHN SINGLETON: Yeah, yeah, I told my agent if Columbia wants to do it, I want to direct it. I don't care who's . . . twenty-five people were involved, I don't care. You know, Cube has an album coming out, real soon he's going solo with NWA, I'm going to have Cube, I got Fish, I'm going to make it on my own, I don't care. So he said, okay, I'll support you on this, but I think he was kind of skeptical.

So I get a meeting with Frank Price. And I go into my meeting. And I guess I didn't know any better how to act or how to dress in those meetings. I'm a poor film student. I have, like, some shorts on and a Public Enemy shirt. I had a very small wardrobe at the time. Had about three pairs of shoes and about five pairs of jeans, all with holes in them, and T-shirts. Basically, jeans and T-shirts. When you're in school, that's what you have. So I go into my meeting with them, and they say, "Hey this is a great script and everybody wants to do this." And, "We understand you want to direct."

And I said, "Yes, I want to direct this." Frank Price, Michael Nathanson, and Stephanie Allain were in the room. I said, "Well, I can't conceive of anybody else directing this."

And then they said, "Why?"

And I said, "Because this is the movie that me and my friends talked about, sitting on the porch just kicking it, watching life go by. And when we would go to the movies, we'd talk about how whacked the movies were, and this is the movie that we would want to see."

And they said, "Well, what if we just want to pay you the money and have you go."

I said, "Well, you can't have the movie. I got to do it myself." You know. And I said, "Hey, it's not going to cost that much. Instead of getting real helicopters, we'll do the helicopters with sound and light. You have the xenon light go past and then you add the sound, you know, and it'll be a helicopter." Bottom line is money. Six million dollars is a drop in the bucket for them. So, they decided to do the movie.

And at the time, I was just graduating from USC and I had applied to film school for the fall, to graduate school. And it's funny because they had a reluctance to accept me in the graduate school because I didn't have a B average. I had a 3.3 average, you're supposed to have at least a 900 on the GRE. I had a 910. I had a teacher that was trying to get me in. I finally got an acceptance letter while I was in preproduction on my movie. [Laughter] So I call up USC and I say, "I'm not going to be able to go to grad school," real happy, you know. [Laughter] But there was a guy there, I think his name was Peter, he was working in the office. And I said, "I can't go to grad school, man."

He says, "Why?"

I said, "Because I'm working on a movie."

And he said, "Oh really? What you doing?"

I said, "I'm directing."

He's like, "Yeah, right." [Laughter] I said, okay. And that was it. And so instead of going to grad school that fall I directed my first feature film. And that's how I got my start. [Laughs]

But before that, you know . . . . that's all in a nutshell. But you've got to understand, that before writing those screenplays and doing all of those things, all through school I had done internships and I was a PA with several different companies. And I did my grunt work, and it just got me so pissed off, it just made me feel like hell, I got to write my own material, you know. I got to . . . nobody's going to give me a script to direct. Nobody's going to give me something that is very soulful and that has heart in it, you know. And then say, here, we'll pay you X amount of dollars to do this. It's not going to happen like that. I learned at an early age that I was going to have to take my career into my own hands and control my own destiny as a filmmaker. So.

MODERATOR: *What about now? Are you . . .*

JOHN SINGLETON: It's the same thing. I mean here I am. I've made . . . I think the movies that I made for Columbia Pictures for the last three years; I've made over a hundred million dollars; about a hundred twenty-something million dollars. But nobody's handing me a script. It doesn't even happen like that. It only happens like that with the actors. And directors for hire. I've learned now that I'm really not a hired gun. A hired gun is somebody, you get a script and say, well, who can we get to direct this? And then that person fits the prototype of comedy director, dramatic director, or whatever type of director. I don't fit those molds. The films that I feel I make are more character-based in nature and come from real life. They're films about people not just plots. I think the Hollywood conception is to make films about plots, and there's only seven different stories in the world that have been told. And they all have been told at any one time. But for me, I believe that there are so many different people in the world that if you take those different people and then you let them tell the story, you get something totally new. You see?

MODERATOR: *When you acknowledge that at USC, your response to the way that people treated you was to become a bit hardened.*

JOHN SINGLETON: Yes.

MODERATOR: *Now, you show them, you make this film, this film goes out, and it's a commercial hit. You're nominated for two Academy Awards. How did you handle all that? Going into your next project? Were you a different person at that point than when you got to Columbia?*

JOHN SINGLETON: I think I stayed grounded. I used all of what happened to me at USC when the success started coming. I used all those skills I learned, to just let stuff fly over my back. I used that when the cameras are there and I'm meeting people like Spielberg and like Coppola and, they see my films and they like them. I use that, and I say, oh, that's good, but I have to come with another movie. That's all I would say to myself. I'd say, but I'm just starting out. I got to come with another. I've done three movies, but I feel like, right now, at my age, I'm just now supposed to be finding out what I'm doing with my life. I'm only twenty-seven. So I'm just now supposed to be figuring out what to do with my life in general.

MODERATOR: *Have you figured it out?*

JOHN SINGLETON: No. [Laughter] But I'm trying to figure it out. I mean, like films for me, I'm just trying to find the next great thing to do in terms of how to go to the next level of experience in filmmaking for me. I'm still very much a film student. I mean, whereas before I had plenty of time to watch films, to watch different types of films, now it's like I'm inundated with all these other things that try to distract me from what is at the core and the soul of who I am, you see? Because I'm the kind of person that will sit up and kick it and read speeches of Malcolm X, and at the same time plug in, later on that day, like a Sunday, plug in a Truffaut film. But now it's like I have very limited time on my hands, you know, so I have to make the best use of it. It's all about managing it, I guess.

MODERATOR: *Who has a question?*

Q: *What kind of deal did you sign initially with Columbia? Because, I don't know, did they also produce* Poetic Justice?
JOHN SINGLETON: Yeah, they financed *Poetic Justice.*

Q: *They gave you some kind of multi-picture deal and said we're going to . . .*
JOHN SINGLETON: Well, they said that with *Boyz* they wanted to have me stay there for three years after the movie was over with. And it was something that even at the outset I wanted to fight. I don't want to stay here. What if the movie doesn't do well? Well, if the movie doesn't do well, then you have a deal here at the studio. I said, well, what if it does do well? Well, if it does do well, we don't want you to go somewhere else and make a movie. So, from 1991 to 1994, I was locked in an exclusive kind of deal with them. Whereas I couldn't do anything anywhere else, you know. And after *Boyz*, I did have a few offers. I could have done *What's Love Got to Do with It?* I would have made it more gritty [Laughter] instead of candy-coated. But then it became what's called a non-exclusive first look deal, where they can have a first look at whatever I do. So, now I'm in this first look deal for the next year. But that doesn't mean I can't take films to other studios. Yes?

Q: *Was the Columbus University in the film based on any real university?*
JOHN SINGLETON: Well, at its base, it was USC, for those of you that know USC. I think it serves as a model for any private university in America. All knowledge is to be questioned. Especially when it comes from one set point of view.

MODERATOR: *Do you shoot mostly on location? Have you done studio work as well?*
JOHN SINGLETON: I've worked on soundstages a lot. I mean, you know, a lot. But I really prefer to be on location. I think it's a different vibe. There are cer-

tain types of films that serve better to be shot on stages, and then there's other films that, you know, are much better suited to be shot in the real world.

Q: *What kind of things did you do before the first film to prepare yourself to direct actors? Did you do any kind of homework or how did you deal with the actors?*

JOHN SINGLETON: Well, I had taken acting classes while I was at USC, and interestingly enough, around the time I was taking acting class, I started messing around as an actor. You know, just like, showing up for a casting call, for commercials and things like that. If I get a commercial, I'll get a little bit of change. So I got a Burger King commercial when I was in school. It paid me, like, six thousand dollars over the course of eight months. So I had these checks coming in. And that helped me as a director to learn how to communicate with actors. Because creating a rapport with actors is all about communication. And that communication can be verbal or it can be non-verbal. Depending on how close you are with your actors. Just before I started shooting *Boyz N the Hood*, I also took acting classes. While I was in preproduction, I was taking acting classes and I was doing scene studies, and I was an actor with these other actors who did not know that I was a director. To those actors, I was John. I told them I worked at UPS, and that "I'm really thinking about doing something in the film business, you know." I was acting in an acting class. It was so much fun too. People tell me I should act. [Laughter] I was just going and doing that kind of stuff, and they thought that was good.

There's a funny story behind that. There was a kid in my acting class who read for *Boyz N the Hood*. The school was down the street from my office for *Boyz*. He came to read for one of the roles, and I was sitting in the office. When he came in to read, he says, "Oh, man, hey, how you doing, John?"

I said, "Yeah, how you doing, Ross?"

So he says, "So I'm reading for this, are you reading for something?"

I said, "No, man, I'm working here."

And he said, "You got a job here?"

I said, "Yeah."

He asked, "What you doing?"

I said, "I'm doing something behind the scenes," you know. [Laughter]

And he's, like, "Oh wow, that's good. I'm supposed to read for Jackie Brown today."

I said, "That's good."

He says, "I'm supposed to get a chance to meet the director."

I said, "That's good."

So I go upstairs and he comes in and shakes everybody's hand. He shakes the producer, Steve Nicolaides' hand, Jackie Brown's hand, and he turns to see me, and he's like, this is the director? And he's like, ooooooh! Because he had known me as an actor, you know. And it threw him off guard. So he's trying to read, but he kept messing up the lines. He just couldn't concentrate, because it threw him off guard.

But I'd highly recommend to any of you that are considering directing and even writing to take some acting classes. This whole business that we're in in terms of filmmaking, I can boil it all down to the art of communication. Of human communication. Of communicating ideas and stories to people. You know? And anything that you can do that sparks you creatively, in terms of telling a story, you should do. Whether it's going to see some comedy and studying comedians and seeing how certain comedians tell stories. Seeing how an old man will sit up on the corner and just talk. You should be watching all those different aspects of human life to see how a story is told. I get a lot of creative energy from just sitting up and watching old nature shows; just watching animals do what they do and hunt and screw each other. It may sound funny but it's just life. If you get to the point where you can look at life and draw upon it in a creative way, it makes you a better story teller because it's all about interpretation.

Q: *Can you go through the genesis of* Higher Learning? *You know, where did you get the idea and how did it change as it went through the various stages?*
JOHN SINGLETON: Well, *Higher Learning,* I had the idea when I was still in film school. And it changed over the course of four years. I'd have an idea in the back of my mind and I'd write a couple of lines down. Or write about the kind of characters that I wanted to deal with. I thought after *Boyz* and *Poetic* I wanted to do something totally different that would take it kind of out of the urban mode. It's like I don't need to research anything having to do with urban experience because I can draw upon personal experience. So, I figured I wanted to do something very different and deal with different characters. I started to compose this story about these three freshmen coming into school, being very naive, not knowing who they were in the world, and they would either find out or they would become parts of different groups and then you would see their experience through one semester. That's just a whole slice of life thing. And after a while, with what happened in 1992 with the L.A. riot, I started thinking, well, I got to really do something that really speaks to this whole repression that America has about talking about

anything having to do with conflict, whether or not it be racial, sexual, or class distinctions. I wanted to start dealing with subjects like that. So, that's where *Higher Learning* came in. And it was a hard movie to get made because I'm dealing with some different kind of issues here, and to a person at a studio they see a script and it has the brothers, with their presence on campus, it has a lesbian relationship, and skinheads and all this stuff, and it's like, this is not commercial. You know, automatically. I'm like you don't know what's commercial. My attitude is if everyone else stays very conformist in their ways and modes of looking towards film, this will be commercial because it'll be so radical. There won't be anything like it. So I wrote the script and I tried to make sure that all the characters were metaphors for a certain part of America. Like Kristin serves that whole view of the girl that's from an upper middle class family that now has had that downturn in the '90s. I figured her family really prospered well in the late '70s and all through the '80s, until the aerospace industry fell out, and then she had to go to college and face the real world. And Malik, he's like a metaphor for the black man in America that always got to run, feeling under siege from forces—how can I say this?—overt and covert, you know. And Remy is a guy who's a middle American dude who comes from a dysfunctional kind of family. He can't really socialize with people. Probably was made fun of and picked on. Maybe was a kind of loner in high school. And he's going to do what he's going to do at the end of the movie anyway. You know, regardless of going into this group or not, he's going to do what he's going to do.

MODERATOR: *Did you feel he was a metaphor for the racial problems in this country today? Or do you think it was exaggerated . . .*

JOHN SINGLETON: I feel that he's a mixture . . . he's a really good character and he's not accepted by the fraternity guys. He's not accepted by society, and that's a class thing. He's not accepted by the brothers, that's a racial thing. And then he gets in with the skinheads and he thinks that he has a group to belong to, and he ultimately is not accepted by them, you see? So the whole movie is a comment on individuality and how individuality is not defined by what group you belong to, it's defined by what you have inside. And I like the fact that I got away with not tying it all up at the end. At the end of the movie, you don't know what Malik's going to do. You don't know if he's going to stay in school or if he's going to just go and do whatever. You don't know what's going to happen to Kristin. Is she going to be with a man or is she going to be with a woman? And that's how life is, you know? I mean, I like that whole thing where not every film has to be tied up with a neat little ribbon.

Q: *Did you ever get overwhelmed by the content that you're bringing together all in one film? Did you ever feel like the things you were . . . you know, the three pieces that you were juggling . . .*

JOHN SINGLETON: No, not at all. I just wanted to get into each one to a certain level. I knew that I couldn't have it with a whole lot of dialogue expounding upon each with any one of these groups. It'd be too heavy and everything. I knew I had to just show certain things in a visual way. Like Remy feeling like he's surrounded by all these ethnic people. And so he shows these ill feelings in his engineering class with the looks. He sees the black dude to his right and he sees the Asian guy to his left. He sees an Asian girl up in front of him, and he sees an Indian guy and he's at the back of the class. So it's a metaphor for that whole supposedly angst that some white men in America have now, with being surrounded by everybody. Remember *Time* magazine a year and a half ago had this thing, when *Falling Down* came out on white male bashing with Michael Douglas? And it was so laughable, because there was all this white male angst. There was no acknowledgment of how everybody else had been kicked around over the centuries. So, I was speaking to that whole issue. I feel it's very intelligent to look at race in the sense that it's not just about color, it's also about classicism. A lot of people don't really want to get into the whole issue about how to kill racism? But whenever they bring up a discussion of how to kill racism, they never bring up the subject of killing white supremacy to kill racism. Racism was founded, also, as an economic concern. You have to have a population of people to keep down in a certain way, psychologically and physically, so that one can make a lot of money. That's the point. It pervades every aspect of American culture because we live in a very capitalist culture. I'm going to finish this right now, before we get any other film questions. I don't want to leave this hanging. I'd like for you to hear me out clearly. Like I said, whenever anyone talks about killing racism, they never bring up the subject of if you kill white supremacy, then you kill racism. You may not think that we live in a country that is white supremacist in nature. Or when you hear white supremacy, you think I'm speaking of Nazism or whatever. It's on different levels. It's an institutionalized belief that if you are not white, male, and rich, you shouldn't be here. You can be white and male and not rich, and on a lower level. But they've made it complex in the sense that over the centuries is that they've made white people feel that just because of the color of their skin, they should feel that they are better than other people, regardless of class. That's why in the South, you had prosperous black people after slavery trying to get their own thing going, or trying to grow their own food, trying to do business amongst themselves. And then you have people who did not have enough money, who did not have anything to say. Well how can I be less than a nigger? If you're a nigger how can a nigger be less than a white man? What is that? If someone's trying to work and pay their dues and has honest intentions of making their own way and then because of the color of their skin you're going to say that they're less than human and try to keep them down as human. A lot of people don't understand that that's the way that blacks and Chinese and everyone else who's come to this country has had to live over centuries. And it's been enforced through laws. Not through just people, but through laws to keep people down. That's what I'm trying to address in *Higher Learning*, in the sense that all of this is institutionalized. And it's not just race, class is mixed up in it as well. If you're going to be smart about it, you can't deal with racism and then divorce it from class. Especially being an American. So that's my soapbox on that. We could talk about movies the rest of the day. [Laughter] Because I don't want anybody to think that I'm only saying this because I'm black. Like I told you before, I'm thick-skinned about doing things like this. I have to do all these interviews and the first thing they see is a black man, not a filmmaker. And I get this whole attitude when people interview me, that just for the fact I'm black, they don't like the fact that I'm doing movies. So then it makes me angry, and so I treat them like I'm angry. It's not that I am, it's just that I'm very insightful and I say certain things that people don't generally come out and talk about. And I think that if you're afraid to talk about certain things, then there's something wrong with you. So, I'm just being real.

Q: *In* Higher Learning, *you're saying the characters also serve as metaphors, and you have the Omar Epps character, who is the freshman who is naive and he's come to learn, he's come to gain experience through this process, and he's being influenced by Ice Cube and he's being influenced by Tyra. I get the sense you're trying to shape him or . . . interaction with them.*
JOHN SINGLETON: Everybody's trying to shape him.

Q: *His interactions? Yeah, also with Larry Fishburne. His interactions with these three people help to shape and define his attitude, his outlook on how he is perceived in this community. So, what does the death of Tyra represent? Or symbolize? What is he . . . how are we to gain from that?*
JOHN SINGLETON: It's not to gain anything from that. She's the light of his life. She's the most positive thing in his life so to take that away from him is the most devastating thing that could happen to him in his young life, and trying to find his way. So he has nothing to gain from that. And at the end of the story, he's still very empty. It's like there's a piece that's cut out of him.

Q: *But of all the people at the concert, why does she die?*
JOHN SINGLETON: Other people die, but they die off screen. [Laughs] The innocent die, you know? That's the last person you would expect to die.

Q: *I was wondering because you were talking about metaphors if there's a reasons behind it. That's cool.*

MODERATOR: *You said that* Higher Learning *was a tough one to get made. What process did you have to go through with the studio to get it made?*
JOHN SINGLETON: Oh, that's such a long story. I had to do everything but threaten to get physically violent . . . [Laughter]

MODERATOR: *That worked?*
JOHN SINGLETON: Yeah, it actually worked. I'm an artist and I've made a lot of money, so they're going to, at the end of the day make the movie. We can kick and scream but if it makes money I'm going to get my way. I feel that I'll ride this out as long as I can. If I start asking too much about what they think, then they try to get their way. So I have to be very decisive on what I want. This is the way I want it, this is the way it has to be, no questions. There comes a point when you work with people that, after a while, you get real comfortable and you think that they're your buddies. But they have an agenda too. It's not necessarily evil or bad, but it's their job to give their opinion. So in *Higher Learning*, everything that was suggested to me I refuted, and I made it a point to refute it, because I said anything that they suggest, I have to do opposite of what they suggest to make it good. There were so many scenes in this movie. I can't name one scene that they did not want me to take out of the movie. From the three-way love scene to Fudge talking about the American flag, I mean, everything. After a while, I had to make a call to CAA to tell them to tell these people to don't call me anymore or come around me. I would act like if they came to my cutting room I'd have a gun. I had to act like that just to preserve my vision. It's a marvel that anything halfway decent gets made. I think if I didn't have to go through that then the film would be even better than it is now. I mean, it's a good film, but when working under siege like that all of the time it's harder to pump out a great film.

MODERATOR: *Did it have any champion at Columbia?*
JOHN SINGLETON: There was a point where they were even afraid to release it, like it was so radical. And now looking at it, I say it's not that radical. I want to get more radical. I want to really shake people up in the sense that it's so true that they cannot deny its power. I like things that are based in fact. That's the way I look at life. I try to do films that make people come out

of the theater and see something in real life and say, damn, that's like in the movie. Then they think about me and they think about my movies and then put it into context. But it's like there's a machine that tries to keep you from doing that and it's that machine's job to keep you from doing it.

MODERATOR: *Are you working on some stories now that you think will shake them up more than they have been?*

JOHN SINGLETON: Oh yeah, yeah, definitely. I'm not at liberty to talk about anything right now. I pride myself on being a man of action and not of words. There are filmmakers who come to these conferences and they talk and they love to hear themselves talk. But I like to go and sit with my Power-book and work on my script and work with writers and bounce ideas around. That's my job. It's not my job to get up here and talk about myself.

MODERATOR: *We're glad you're here.*

Q: *I just wondered, how did the budget change for* Higher Learning, *and how did you feel about your technique as a director relative to the first time?*

JOHN SINGLETON: Change? Change from the first one to the second one? Well, the first film I did was made for six million dollars, and this film was made for just over twenty. And I just think that this film is a bigger film than either of the other two films, in the sense that there are more characters involved, there are different types of scenes. There were points in shooting it where it became a drama with two white girls and a movie with some brothers on campus, and then a sports movie on track. Week to week the movie would change. It was fun shooting it, because it allowed me to become even more technically proficient in different ways in which to shoot a film. There are certain ways that you shoot a dramatic scene with two actors, and there's other ways that you shoot films that are visceral. The track scene is a visceral montage with no dialogue, whereas the scenes in the classroom are not. You have to figure out ways in which to keep the dialogue going; keeping a scene that has a lot of dialogue going visually. I try to study a lot of different works and since I'm a young director, I didn't shoot a lot of footage. I'm cutting my teeth, learning how to shoot films as I'm doing it. So, I tried not to make the mistakes that I see a lot of other young directors make, where you know that they're directing the movie. There are certain points where you want to be imperceptible. I would block out my scenes and think about that in mind. What is the underlying theme or point I'm trying to get across in this scene, and how can I most visually show this? How can I use my skills as a director in terms of camera, in terms of acting, in terms of sound, to get the point of this scene across? These are some of the things I think about when I'm going through the script and I'm breaking it down on every scene, and I'm shooting it.

Q: *This is a question, probably, first for John Singleton the writer, and then the director to answer, I guess, if you can separate the voices. I found that when I'm writing, the more I try and have characters represent something, either a class or an entire sector of people, or a type of person, the more I put that in thematically, the less their individuality as a human being or the degree to which an audience will connect with a character is there. You know, the more they represent something the less they are a real person. And I was wondering how you, first as a writer, and how you as a director communicating with actors, found that balance when making this film? I mean, how did you approach dialogue that was supposed to be representational of a whole ideology?*

JOHN SINGLETON: Well, what you do is you try to find people actors that represent that ideology. And then the actors have something that's special within themselves that is very unique to them as people, that is very much the character. And that's what I did in *Higher Learning*. The actors that I hired were a shade away from the characters that they played. It's not very much work for an actor to be that character. I think the person that had to make the biggest leap in *Higher Learning* was Michael Rapaport, because . . . Michael is from New York, he grew up around a lot of brothers, he's Jewish, and he's cool. And I'm wanting him to play a skinhead from Idaho. It's out of my love for him as a person that he was able to do that, and because he's close to me. So we could think about all these ways to make this guy not a bad person. He's the dude that kids used to smack the towel at in PE. We would sit up and think about things that make this guy kind of crazy, but really he's just a quiet kid who went bad. If you notice in the movie, he's always moving. He's always moving from side to side, he can't stay still. Anybody notice that? So we would find these little things that would add to this guy's character. But I do like to hire people that are really close to the role. Or what's really interesting is to find a role in which an actor, the same thing that's going on in the movie is going on in that actor's life. Because once you get that then, like I said in the beginning of this conversation, it's all about human communication. And directing, writing, acting, singing, anything that is creative, is therapeutic. Being able to express yourself creatively is very therapeutic and it's very cleansing to the soul to get something off your chest. It's like, for all those who have been to a black church, and hear the gospel and people getting out of their seats and raising their hands, that's therapeutic. And so what you do as an artist is a reflection of who you are as a person. No matter how hard you try to get away from it, no matter how many times you say this is not necessarily me; it is you. Whatever you're doing that is coming from your mind, that's coming from being spoken, that are your thoughts on paper, it's who you are. So I try to, when making my actors a part of my films, I try to make them a part of that process, and I keep that in mind.

Q: *On the flip side of that, for your production team, do you usually work with the same people? Do you feel like you have certain people that can create the kinds of things that you're going . . .*
JOHN SINGLETON: I try to work with some of the same people, but I work mostly with different people on different projects. The crew for *Higher Learning* was very interestingly mixed in terms of race, sex, sexual orientation, religion, etc. When I worked on *Boyz N the Hood* it had a 94 to 96 percent crew that was all black, because that's what I preferred at the time. We were shooting in my neighborhood and I wanted people that were comfortable. There has to be a lot of love, and I don't want anybody working on the movie that wouldn't do this for free. When you have that kind of atmosphere on a set, when you have a crew that's with you, it's like an army, it's like a family. And that always shows up on film, no matter how good people say the crew and the director is, the whole vibe behind the scene shows up on film. And it affects the actors too. On *Poetic Justice*, I had a mixture. I had a mixture of about, about sixty-forty. But the L.A. riot broke out and it created a whole schism within the crew. Here you had some rednecks on the Teamsters. This was a big thing, and I'm trying to shoot the movie and not even hearing that all this shit is going on because if I hear about this, I'm not going to think about the movie. My producer knew I would fire everybody and say give me some folks that can work with black people. So that was kept away from me and there was this tension behind the scenes that I didn't even know about.

So with *Higher Learning*, which was not like *Poetic Justice*, in that it is controversial, racially charged, class charged, sexually charged, and I have all these different types of people working on it. I have blacks, I have whites, I have Hispanics, I have gays, I have straights, everybody on this crew. So all these different people working together on this hardass movie where they're saying nigger this and white boy that and Jewish this. Then everybody behind the scenes, because of working on something so hard, we're seeing these scenes, and we're talking about them while we're shooting them, we all come together as a family, you see? Because we're about being very, very real with the subject matter that we're dealing with. My first AD is an Israeli

Jew. And he and I are talking about that whole method in which people are trying to use scapegoats between blacks and Jews. We're talking about that and we're dealing with the different subjects all in this film, and everyone behind the scenes is talking about it. And, we all really got along. It was very, very beautiful. And on the last night of shooting, about four-thirty in the morning, I called the crew together and we did the last shot and I just told everybody how much I loved them and how much the film for me was kind of like a purging. Looking back on the film I'd say it was a purging of something that I had to get off my chest and that was in my soul about angst. I never knew that there were so many different types of people that I could be close to and be friends with, because of what had been put upon me and how I felt I had to act to save my self-esteem.

It was a very beautiful experience working with those people. I just think that even in your student productions, you should always try to work with people who really feel it. You have to question yourself. "Do I really feel it?" And what is it that you feel, and why is it that you're doing what you're doing? It's something I deal with every time. If you look at it, I've only really been in the film business for less than four and a half years now, and I'm making a pretty good living. But I figure that I never want to do a film just to do it. I never want to do something just because I need this big paycheck this year. It's got to be because I want to spend nine months to a year of my life working on something that has some meaning to it. I don't give a care whether or not I make a film that makes a hundred million dollars or two hundred million dollars. That's not really that important, you see. What's important is to work on something that has some meaning, that has some lasting value, that makes a statement of where I am personally, where I am as a person, what I'm passionate about. I live by that and I die by that. That's the kind of person I want to be in terms of being a filmmaker.

MODERATOR: *Since you write, produce, and direct your films, is there somebody around you or a number of people around you that get involved with you creatively that you listen to?*

JOHN SINGLETON: Yeah. Oh, yeah, yeah. I have plenty of people around me that their jobs are not to say yes to me, are to challenge me, not negatively, but as an advocate and to take the other perspective. I have to have that. I can't have people there that always say, yeah, John, yeah, John. Or yeah, you're right all the time. I don't get anywhere creatively like that. I need somebody to say no. And why no? Well, no because of this and no because of that. And I can either agree or disagree. It's great that way.

Q: *Now that you're at the studio, how much time do you have to develop your projects. You said you're working on . . .*

JOHN SINGLETON: I'm working on several projects right now. I'm working with other writers on films, which is very fun, because it's like we can sit and talk about different ways to do the film, and I see myself, and it's funny . . . I see myself telling writers to do things that I haven't done because I've been too lazy to do them. But since I'm telling them to do and then they're doing it, things are turning out better than if I would have done it myself.

MODERATOR: *Can you give us an example?*

JOHN SINGLETON: For instance, I have a writer that I'm working with right now, that I tell, I don't want you to write one word of this screenplay or write any more of this outline until you write character sketches. I need you to sit and think for a couple of days and really for us to talk about these characters. Why is this woman like this? Why does this man do this? How does he feel like this, about his wife after this? You know, give them that. Give them that meat. So I'm talking about characters because I know that this guy's really good with plot, so I want him to really have my characters defined, so that when I get my actors six to eight months from now, they don't go over the script and say, oh gosh, wow, this character doesn't have enough meat, there's not enough meat here. I'm putting all that in, in advance. And before the outline is done, you think about the people. Because for me it's like the people are what drive the story forward not the plot. I mean, the plot can be as fantastical as possible, but if you're not with that character it's just not there. You should try to think about ways to make that person really complex.

Q: *I just wanted to start by saying* Boyz N the Hood *really touched me because it's a hard core reality that I don't always like to think about but that is very existent in L.A. and throughout the nation. And* Higher Learning *really touched me because I could relate to a lot of different experiences, especially Omar Epps's character in the movie. And I wanted to ask you, I know you said that the story, you have to do something that you truly believe in, but what else? What drives you to make the films that you do?*

JOHN SINGLETON: It's like me having a conversation with you all. Making a film, for me, is like conversation with me. You know. That's it. That's what drives me.

MODERATOR: *Have you met August Wilson?*

JOHN SINGLETON: Yes, I spent last weekend with him. (Laughs)

MODERATOR: *Last weekend? Really.*

JOHN SINGLETON: He's like Chekov to me. [Laughter] What's beautiful about him is that he's so in tune with African-American culture, and he's very much in the tradition of the oral tradition of African story-telling. Telling the story verbally. Our language is a special language because we take languages and make them our own. He really has a flair for the language of African Americans and it's just something that I really have a large amount of affection for. You know Zora Neale Hurston. How many of you are familiar with Zora Neale Hurston's work? She was a novelist during the early part of this century and she was a black woman. She wrote great novels but she was largely ignored because she was a woman and because she had a flair for the black vernacular at a time when we had these bourgeoisie men that were pretty much the head of the Renaissance that were acting like they didn't want to hear black people talking that old Southern dialect. But that's very special because here are people who are creating their own language. It's like an anthropological lesson. And August is very much in that tradition. I told him I wished he was my grandfather because I could talk to him about stories and language and playwriting. You know, he's writing another play right now that just premiered, I think in Chicago, called *Seven Guitars*, that's going to start touring. And I'm thinking I'm going to hang out while the actors are working and see how theater works, seeing how a play changes, where actors are really like taking it and making it their own, and looking how another writer works.

I think I'm at a period in my life where I've made three movies and I have other stories that I want to tell. Hollywood is very much a machine that thrives on creativity. Don't let anybody ever tell you that there's no place for you here in this business, because there is a place for you. Hollywood needs you, it needs new talent. It's a big machine that thrives and grows and sustains itself on young, new blood. But at the same time, it can be very . . . how can I say it? It can be very debilitating, because it steals your soul. And part of the challenge for me is how to keep my soul. How to stay successful but at the same time not play myself and keep my soul. And so, I'm at a point where I'm in a soul regenerating state, where I feel I have to go do other things so that I can be creative, so that I can tell stories, you know. If you look at the arc of any filmmaker's career, they go through periods where they're really real creative, real spurts, and then there's a creative downturn. And you can look at their lives and see where they're doing it just to be doing it. But when they're really passionate about something and they're really just going with it, they're busting their ass just to really get this film made because it's something that they really feel, that's when it doesn't matter how much money it makes. Doesn't matter period. There was something behind the motive of making this film, just a film. I just hope that every film that I do, that I can sustain that, that I can do it because it's something that I'm really passionate about.

MODERATOR: *On that very important note, let us say thank you, John Singleton. Thank you for coming.*
[Applause]

Ashes and Embers

GARY DAUPHIN/1996

LAKE COUNTY, FLORIDA—A few miles away from the live-action entertainment complexes of Walt Disney World and Universal Studios Theme Park, director John Singleton and producer Jon Peters have built the set for *Rosewood*, replicating several houses that once stood in and around a small black logging town in Florida that was burned by a white mob seventy-three years ago. The remains of the actual Rosewood lie several hours to the South in Levy County, and those who've made the pilgrimage report that it's not much to look at. Today it's a place of mud patches, roaming dogs, and the occasional junked car or boat, the wary, all-white residents watching from behind screened windows. There's little to indicate that it was the site of an atrocity, although the black folks who've been there say that it's not a good idea for some to linger after dark.

I don't go see the real Rosewood myself while I'm in Florida. It's been odd enough coming to the duplicate, with it's black extras hanging nonchalantly from safety nooses during setups, the white extras milling around craft services tables smoking or juicing up on caffeine until it's time for the lynch mob to be made up. I don't know what I'd learn from seeing the town itself except that there are still plenty of angry white people living in swamps. Seeing how black people remember is much more interesting to me.

With *Rosewood*, a young black director from L.A. is trying to shoot and edit together two hours of black memory, applying the tools of Hollywood moviemaking to the ephemera of old tax records, family photographs, and yellowed newspaper clippings. All of it harkens back to the week of New Year's 1923, during which survivors huddled in the surrounding swamps and watched their homes go up in smoke, their fathers strung from trees, and

From the *Village Voice* (May 21, 1996). Reprinted by permission of Gary Dauphin.

their mothers shot and dumped in mass graves, which the State of Florida has, to this day, yet to locate. Decades passed before anyone who could actually remember it would even speak of Rosewood above a whisper, but since the late '80s, there have been an official apology from the state for its inaction, reparations to survivors, token restitution of property, a book, and of course this movie. All these amends hope to restore a bit of the Rosewood that was lost, making the movies unique among mediums: where else can you honor a place by burning it down a second time?

On the main Rosewood set, a large clearing in the woods, the crew has been doing night shoots out here for the last month and a half, with six-day-a-week vampire schedules of 8 P.M. to 8 A.M. By the time I arrive on set at 10 one Saturday night, the mosquitoes are already out in force and members of the crew are clapping the air around them, one grip occasionally holding up his blood-flecked hands and wondering aloud whose blood it might be—white lead Jon Voight's, perhaps? The only building burning is the one-story Prince Hall Mason Lodge, and that just barely: Controlled jets of gas-powered flame shoot out from the windows, and between shots, p.a.'s douse the building with high-powered hoses, steam and spray rising up into the sky.

The set took three months to build, production designer Paul Sylbert using local architectural models as well as the memories of Rosewood survivors. Off to the north is a road leading to the set for Sumner, Rosewood's neighboring white town. It was there that on the morning of New Year's Day 1923, a white woman named Fannie Taylor was found in her home beaten, bruised, and screaming that she'd been assaulted by a black man.

The lynch mob never found their rapist, but turn a few paces southeast on set and you'll find the remains of the Carrier House, already burned to the ground when I arrive. A white posse congregated there four days after New Year's, when word reached Sumner that armed black men were massing inside. In fact, it was just the aged and younger members of the Carrier family, all brought together for safety by Sylvester Carrier (played in the film by Don Cheadle). The posse demanded Sylvester come out with his hands up anyway, taking potshots at the house and killing Sylvester's mother Sarah (played by Esther Rolle). It was at that moment that Rosewood went from a horribly typical tale of Southern "justice" victimizing blacks to a suitably heroic tale of black male resistance. Sylvester Carrier, holed up by himself with kids in the attic and his mother dying at his feet, returned fire on the white men outside. His self-defense precipitated a bloodbath: about 1,500 white men would converge on Rosewood soon after, and a week later there would be no Rosewood at all.

Turn away from the Carrier House and you'll spy the back door of John Wrigth's home, which is the setting for the scene now being filmed. Wright was Rosewood's only white resident, owner of a general store. His two-story house (the finest in town, it was said, and certainly the finest here) was the only structure left standing once the destruction of Rosewood was complete, a good thing considering that Wright had hidden a number of black women and children inside. In this shot, Ving Rhames's character, Mann, is trying to get an older couple into the safety of Wright's home, Wright being played in the film by Jon Voight. I get to watch Singleton direct them for some time before I'm introduced to him. Once quitely run rehearsals and lighting are taken care of, Singleton plants himself behind video monitors, hunching close and shaking an excited finger at the video whenever he gets the shot he wants. He seems very relaxed in a slightly sleepless kind of way, and watching him you'd have a hard time telling that this is the biggest motion picture he's ever worked on.

Like *Boyz N the Hood* (and *The Color Purple*), *Rosewood* is a Jon Peters production, but for Singleton it's the first time he's ever worked as a hired gun; the project was already in development when he was attached to it, and the script already written by a white writer, Greg Poirer. *Rosewood*'s budget was described to me by associate producer Tracy Barone as "well below the industry norm," but it's certainly more money than Singleton has ever had to play with, between $20 and $30 million. As he leads his crew (a little more than a third of them back by my count) through another take, industry concerns seem as far removed from here as Hollywood itself.

In contrast to the talkative Voigt, Rhames is a large but quietly contained presence. If he and Singleton share a particular bond from both being black men, it isn't apparent from watching: Both are friendly and professional but during downtime Rhames keeps to himself, moving off to the fringes of the set, a prop cigar kept smoking in his hand. When I wander off to where Rhames had earlier taken one of his solitary smokes, I find what's left of the Carrier House—a charred rocking chair on the ruin of a porch, mattresses and bedsprings piled up on what look likes a collapsed ceiling. Even burnt and broken, the place has a dignity to it, the conflicting reports and final unknowables of what transpired inside averaging out to a solemnity a contemporary watcher can link up with anything from the Warsaw Ghetro Uprising to the bombing of the MOVE headquarters in Philadelphia.

Ving Rhames says the challenge of *Rosewood* for him was getting into the historical mind-set of his largely fictionalized character. "At the time of the massacre, there were large numbers of black men who were WWI vets, so I have to account for the mentality of black men wanting to put on a uniform and fight in Europe and then coming home to Jim Crow. You can't tell me when they came for their families here in Rosewood only Sylvester stood up."

It's a role Rhames figures he's particularly suited for. "Some of the actors who were considered for the part were going to be physically . . . more palatable to certain audiences than me. I mean, I'm a quote-unquote big, shaven-head nigger, where someone like a Denzel Washington is physically more acceptable to white America. You think of Ving Rhames and you think of Marcellus in *Pulp Fiction* being a bad motherfucker. I may not even be that in real life, but that's what people see."

The walks to the Carrier House show, though, that even a big, shaven-head nigger can be affected by the sight of black homes burning and black men hanging. "There had been something very eerie about this project," he says, his voice going a little tentative. "A stillness to it, not so much in terms of us suddenly being there with them in Rosewood but as if the ancestors have been here with us, watching us. It's hard to explain, but we've definitely felt it on the set, or at least I have."

I ask whether he'll have to do some special decompressing after this. He laughs. I've worked a year straight without any time off so I need to go somewhere *in general* and as far away as possible, so I can replenish myself physically, mentally, and spiritually."

A long vacation. Where?

"Bali. My wife has the tickets."

The next night of shooting there are no black actors on set. Flame bars are setup just about everywhere, and a posse led by Michael Rooker, best known as Henry the Serial Killer, is approaching the Wright house, wanting to know if they've got any nigras holed up in there. Lynchings were always carnivalesque for the white participants and that's certainly the case here. Rooker runs around making whooping noises and cackling his every comment in character to an appreciative crew, his voice hoarse from the yelling he does in the scene. Two posse members are having what looks like a tobacco-spiting contest while Jon Voight and a member of the crew engage in a mock-serious discussion about one of John Wright's lines.

"I think," says Voight, "the line should really be 'What do you all pecker-heads want?'"

"No one uses 'pecker*head*' around here," answers a voice from the crush around the camera. "It's pecker*wood*.'"

"Historically speaking, 'peckerhead' is what the people around here would've said." Voight goes on in some detail until it's obvious he's not joking and that line changes are being discussed, at which point Singleton's head jerks away from the footage he's been reviewing.

"'Peckerwood,' alright?" he yells, spoiling the white boys' debate. I get to sit down and talk to him while all this swirls in the background.

"What really sparked my interest in this project," he begins, waving a hand at the lounging lynch mob, "was meeting the survivors of this incident. They were all in their seventies and early eighties, people like Minnie Lee Langley and Wilson Hall and Arnett Goins, and I sat there and interviewed them about their experiences as children being chased in the swamps right after New Year's. It was so horrifying, I just felt it was a story that really needed to be told."

Did you have worries about working on a film you hadn't written?

"Not about that. There *was* a time when I was preparing this movie last December when I was going to walk away from it because of the money thing. I felt it was a real important movie, but it looked like the studio was trying to make it for less than we thought it should be made, to lessen the scope of it.

"Then in December one of the survivors, Minnie Lee Langley, passed away and I went to her funeral and listened to family members and people who had been in her life and it was a really humbling experience. Because I met the woman, I interviewed her. She was the one on the *60 Minutes* episode about Rosewood who tells Ed Bradley when he asks if she had any advice for the young children: 'Never live in a place where there's a whole lot of white people, where you're surrounded, because if something happens, you'll be the first to go.' Going to the funeral gave me the strength to fight for my vision and what I felt the scope of this picture should be."

He shrugs a little. "And somehow we prevailed with the studio. Now everybody's on our side. I'm not a very religious person but there's a lot of spirituality in the picture, in it and around it."

When Singleton talks, his manner and his words are all so distinctly urban I wonder if he's undergone any culture shock here. Lake Country is a long way from South Central.

"A little. For a long time I've had a large amount of reservations about the Southern portion of the United States because I felt that a lot of the horror and despair that our people experienced was situated in the South. Growing up in the West, basically my attitude was just 'F the South. I'll never do a movie there, I don't want to have anything to do with it. Meeting these people, and doing this film, helped me deal with that attitude. Now I want to do a lot of films in the South because I think it's something people need to talk about."

Does being from L.A. allow you to bring a different perspective to the South?

Singleton laughs. "What I'm bringing to this film is a *youthful* perspective. If I was fifteen or twenty years older, *Rosewood* would probably look more like a documentary. I'm doing this for people in my age range and the audience I've had. The older people maybe they'll come, maybe they won't I'm twenty-eight. I want people my age to come. I want this to be a date movie. I've got romance, I've got action, I'm counting off the times that one of my lead characters get his and kills a couple of crackers. 'Cause I know the brothers on the street ain't gonna sit through a whole movie where there's a whole bunch of black people getting killed and no black folks are fighting back, you know what I mean?"

I do know what he means, but I wonder if aiming for it means compromising in other areas.

He shrugs. "This is still a down-home kind of picture. The thing, too, is: I look at the arc of my pictures and this is probably my first adult movie. The other pictures, well, I started making pictures when I was twenty-one, twenty-two [he really laughs here], and they made a lot of money basically because I was writing from the same perspective as the people who were going to the movies. The first three were coming-of-age, coming-of-consciousness pictures because I was going through that. But this movie, I've matured and I think the work reflects it. I've gotten out of the whole ghetto-movie thing. Hopefully *Rosewood* will get the *Boyz N the Hood* monkey off my back."

I tell him it sounds like Hollywood has been getting him down.

"I had to get away from L.A. I was born and bred in L.A. and I'm starting to not be able to stand it. There's so much strife there and everybody's so pretentious about whose got whatever car and how you dress. I've never really been a part of that. I look down on it. I remember after I did my first movie I got a huge amount of money from the studio. It was these three white men—'course they all were white—and they handed me a check for, like, a large amount of money, okay? Large. And they were all waiting in there to see how I would react to it, like: this nigger's gonna come in here and he's gonna jump up and down and say I'm gonna buy me a Mercedes!' Another studio executive, a black woman, said everybody had a bet on what kind of car I was gonna buy. So you know what I did? I didn't buy a car. They handed me a check and I said: When's the next one coming? I'm really a practical kind of person when it comes to that stuff. That's why I never fit into the hotsy totsy L.A. mentality."

How do you go from there to a rural, God-fearing mentality like Rosewood's?

"It's all natural. Even the wildest and craziest black man has some kind of faith. I mean look at Tupac, look at how much he talks about God. Brothers in jail? First thing they do is move toward religion. They either become Muslims or Christians. So I think if you're born in this country and you're black with all the shit you have to go through, you're gonna get some faith, because otherwise you're gonna commit suicide or murder somebody.

"I've had moments on the set where I just walk off and I just sit and think: Man . . . I think about where I'm from and what I've been through and now I'm here. I feel very blessed and very lucky because at any one moment I could have walked around a corner and my life could have had a very different path. I could've not be accepted to college and probably would've . . . I don't know. I wasn't planning to go to school unless I was going to be in film school.

"I'm wandering right now; my home is wherever I'm at. I really just want to make motion pictures that interest me. On one hand I feel real, real lucky and everything, then on another hand I feel like: Fuck it. I've earned the right to work on this level. There's a lot of irony down here. Here I am directing this big-ass film in Florida and if I play my CDs too loud in my apartment they call the cops on me. If I play Wynton Marsalis they call the cops. It's a trip. I've never been this far away from home in my life for so long. I've been here six months, and I've been out here, out in the woods, catching snakes. I have a five-footer I caught and keep in my apartment, but I always forget to videotape it when it eats. . . ."

He laughs, reaches over, and gives me a playful slap on the knee before pointing out at the swamp. "There's nothing like this."

Arnett Doctor, son of Rosewood survivor, says, "I choose to think that God was preparing me for all this," this being everything from his work on the restitution bill to *Rosewood*. "And I know that God isn't something that media correspondents really want to hear about. The fact is that since a very early age, everyone that has been significantly impacted by Rosewood—survivors, legislators, and lawyers—their paths and my paths have crossed. That isn't a coincidence."

I ask him if it isn't hard to think about something like faith when all these people were killed, but he tells me that I've missed the point entirely. "The reason we're *here now* is because people had faith. You may not agree, but I believe that on one of those nights in 1923, someone black fell to their knees and called out to God to save them. It took Him seventy years to hear them but He did, because if He hadn't, none of us would be here."

I tell him I think seventy years is a long time to wait, but Arnett Doctor just smiles. "Fear of the Lord is the beginning of wisdom; later come understanding," he says. "You call the Lord whatever you want, but there has to be a point where you admit there are certain burdens you can't bear alone." The smile goes a little wry then. "People who were born and raised in the cities often can't understand a thing like that."

I don't know what I'll think of that idea back in the city, or even in the theater when *Rosewood* opens in late 1996, but driving through the fog, I think for just a moment I can see Arnett Doctor's point. I think John Single-ton can too, especially when he walks a few yards off his set and into the wet, ancient green of the Florida swamp.

Dredging in the Deep South

JORDAN LEVIN/1996

THE RACCOON is a little shy, peering out from high in the tree, then squirreling his way down to sniff tentatively closer to director John Single-ton, who—rapt, smiling, coaxing—is holding out a bit of food. He is sitting in the central Florida woods just northwest of Orlando, for the moment ig-noring the ticks and the chiggers and the mosquitoes and the rattlesnakes, as well as the cast and crew assembled for the night shoot.

"Hey, Arnett!" Singleton calls. "Look at this!"

He is addressing Arnett Doctor, whose mother was burned out of the small black town of Rosewood, Florida, in the real-life version of the story Single-ton has come here to film. "I do believe this is changing him," Doctor whis-pers. Then, grinning, he calls back, "That's some good eating there, John!" The raccoon seems to get the message and scurries back up the tree.

Singleton grimaces. "Eating!" he says with a shudder.

"I love it here," Singleton says later. "All the wildlife. If you were here in the daytime, you could see the spring—it's crystal-clear—and you can see snap-ping turtles." He reclines in the seat of his dark green Toyota Land Cruiser. It's almost midnight in the second-to-last week of shooting on *Rosewood*, the end of a month of night shoots, and Singleton is tired. His voice is so low it almost disappears.

"Yeah, it's all been like a camping trip," he says sarcastically.

Tackling this story of racism gone burning wild in the heart of the South has been considerably more than a nature excursion for him. "I had a very deep—I wouldn't call it fear—but a deep contempt for the South," Singleton continues, "because I felt that so much of the horror and evil that black people have faced in this country is rooted here. I thought, 'I'll never make

From the *Los Angeles Times* (June 30, 1996). Reprinted by permission of Jordan Levin.

a movie in the South. Fuck the South.' So in some ways this is my way of dealing with the whole thing."

In the first week of 1923, Rosewood was attacked and burned by a white lynch mob after a white woman in the neighboring town of Sumner claimed a black drifter had attacked her. Rosewood's residents, many of them prosperous, independent property owners, fled homeless into the swamps.

The incident made headlines across the country. "Many Die in Florida Race War," said the *Miami Daily Metropolis*. "Kill Six in Florida," announced the *New York Times*. But then it dropped out of history as completely as the town itself disappeared from the landscape; as with a hidden cancer or a childhood rape, the survivors—traumatized, fearful, and enraged—kept silent.

Then, in 1982, a *St. Petersburg Times* reporter dug up the story. Doctor, whose mother, Philomena, was one of those who fled, pulled survivors and descendants together for a reparations lawsuit that led the Florida Legislature to award them $ 2.1 million in 1994. That same year, producer Jon Peters saw a story about the town on CBS's *60 Minutes*, contacted Doctor and bought the rights. Now Warner Bros. and Singleton are putting a Hollywood spotlight onto what was once a horrifying secret.

One of Doctor's distant cousins is playing his mother as a child, and Singleton is feeding raccoons in the woods, digging for the wellsprings of racism. There's a spine-tingling sense of history hovering over this movie, as if the ghosts of Rosewood are peering hopefully around the palmettos.

Everyone involved, from stars to production assistants, seems to sense that gaze from the past, to believe that they're involved in something important, something real. "I feel that we are witnesses, almost like survivors are witnesses, because of the depth of our identification with this thing," says Jon Voight, who plays John Wright, the storekeeper who was the town's only white resident. "Obviously we could never stand in the same shoes. But in some way, because we've chosen to immerse ourselves in this story, we have that feeling."

Which is a weighty one. Doctor—a gentle-voiced, dignified man of fifty-four who has devoted most of his life to Rosewood and who serves as an executive consultant on the film—says that when Singleton came to Florida to meet with the dozen or so elderly survivors, one of them told him: "Son, you were chosen to do this movie by God. So don't try to take anything from it or add a whole lot to it. Just do the movie. It'll take care of itself."

Singleton lowers his eyes and exhales at the memory of that moment. "I just took a deep breath," he says. "I was proud about it. After meeting the survivors, it was a lock. I definitely wanted to make the movie."

Tracy Barone, the film's executive producer and president of Peters Entertainment, thinks that had a profound effect on Singleton. "When you hear these people and witness what they go through emotionally in order to re-create the story, it's a very powerful experience," she says by phone from Los Angeles. "I think that cemented something in him that was greater than just the telling of this movie. It was a commitment to these people."

One of the most chilling aspects of the Rosewood saga is the way public knowledge of the incident was buried. For decades the survivors refused to talk about what had happened. "They had an intense fear of repercussions," Doctor says. And with good reason, given that no one from the sheriff up to the governor tried to stop the weeklong attack, and racism in central Florida made life dangerous for blacks well through the '60s.

But underlying guilt and a reluctance to acknowledge such a flagrant piece of racism's violent history also kept it hidden. "I have been talking about Rosewood all my life and only in the last ten years has anyone of the opposite race shown any real interest," Doctor says. "In fact, when I would talk about it earlier, people did not want to hear about it. They thought I was pointing a finger at them."

He sees the movie as the final vindicating step in a series redressing all those years of silence: the *St. Petersburg Times* article; the legislative award, which engendered national news coverage; Michael D'Orso's book *Like Judgment Day: The Ruin and Redemption of a Town Called Rosewood,* which came out this spring; and now a big-budget Hollywood film that should plaster the incident all over America's consciousness.

"History has told us that unless you address an inequity, it is bound to repeat itself," Doctor says solemnly. "Because if you allow something like this to pass, then what you are saying in essence is justice is not constant. And whatever was wrong in 1923 in Rosewood is wrong in 1996."

Rosewood was filmed about two hours from the site of the original town, now covered by swamp and scrubwoods. Driving away from the commercial billboard blare around Orlando to the set, you pass into another world; trailers and ambling shacks under spreading oaks dripping moss, open fields with horses and beef cattle behind barbed wire and cedar fences, woods of tall scruffy pines and sharp-leaved palmettos.

It's dense, eerie, musky Southern country. It was often inhospitable for the film crew. Nighttime temperatures dropped into the thirties and forties while the actors huddled in the woods or slogged through swamps. There were clouds of mosquitoes, and the crew taped up their pant legs to keep chiggers and ticks from burrowing under their skin. An assistant director was bitten by a rattlesnake and spent the night in a hospital.

As grueling as this was physically, it was even more so emotionally. The script sticks closely to the actual events, which are dramatic and often horrendous: There is a standoff in which Sylvester Carrier (Arnett Doctor's uncle, played by Don Cheadle) holds off a white mob surrounding his home and family. Voight's character, Wright, bands with two brothers to bring in a train in the middle of the night to carry out the women and children. The elderly Sarah Carrier, played by Esther Rolle, is killed by men she nursed in childhood. One man is shot and dismembered in front of the local sheriff, and a crippled elderly man is forced to dig his own grave. All of it really happened.

"The most powerful thing this movie has going for it is that it's true," screenwriter Greg Poirier says. "So it was really important to stick as closely as possible to the real thing, so people don't have that out of saying, 'Oh, they made a lot of it up, it wasn't that bad.'"

A former theater director (this is his first major screenplay), Poirier used hours of interviews with Rosewood survivors, contemporary newspaper accounts, and a two-hundred-plus-page report commissioned by the Florida legislature in writing the script. In fact, Poirier says, the reality was so grim they had to tone it down.

"At least the violence I'm showing has a point," Singleton says. "Only a few people in this movie get killed on screen, but it's real, it's emotional violence. You feel it."

Rosewood is a stretch in more ways than one for the twenty-eight-year-old director. *Boyz N the Hood*, *Poetic Justice*, and *Higher Learning* were all urban contemporary films closely linked to his own experience. In this movie, he's had to deal with a drama far removed from his own time and place. And with eighty-four speaking parts, hundreds of extras, houses burning, and horses chasing trains, it's also the most logistically complex film he's ever made.

Singleton is aware of this, and if there's some youthful bravado when he talks about how the large scale allows him to see "the clarity of my vision," the reach into the past also seems to have genuinely inspired and excited him.

"I wanted to make it as cinematic as possible, like an epic, so you get a sense of what life in the 1920s was like," he says. "It's very fun to create a whole world, an entire time and place."

On this April night, he's shooting a scene with Ving Rhames, who plays a black World War I veteran named Mann who drifts through town, falls in love with a schoolteacher named Scrappie, played by Elise Neal, and becomes a reluctant hero as he is caught up in events. Mann has returned to Rosewood after the attack to find some fifteen children hiding in the bushes with Scrappie.

A camera on a huge crane hovers through the trees, the crew scrambles through the prickly underbrush with smoke machines and cables, while the actors keep ducking in front of a space heater. Singleton mutters about time and working with the kids (happily rambunctious locals, only a few of them professional actors) but he seems happy with what he's getting.

"Yeah, that's good, that's good," he says, stooped over a monitor, bringing his fist down rhythmically as the camera pans slowly from one tearful face to the next. "Boom! Boom! That's it!"

Around 3 A.M. he takes a full five minutes with Neal—who is a bit awed at working with actors such as Rhames (*Pulp Fiction, Striptease*) and Voight in her first major film role—about a tiny detail of the scene. "Now here I've been making you look beautiful through this whole movie," he whispers, coaxing, even seductive. "Why won't you just trust me on this a little bit?"

Neal and many of the African American actors have made some profound and disturbing connections in working on this film. "Being brought up in Memphis, I saw a whole lot of racism, in ways that maybe people in L.A. or New York don't understand," says Neal, adding that her grandparents told stories like *Rosewood*'s. "I didn't have to reach too far to imagine what the people in Sumner were saying about us in Rosewood."

"It's real funny to see how far we've come and how far we haven't come," says Cheadle, who was Denzel Washington's manic sidekick Mouse in *Devil in a Blue Dress*. "This is not that long ago. In Kansas, my mom used to be able to go to the amusement park one day out of every year. It was called Nigger Day. But my grandfather would never let them go. They didn't know till they were much older that this is what it was called, they just knew he wouldn't let them go, and they thought he was the meanest man around. But my mother said, 'He would rather us hate him than know that America hated us that much.'"

The fact that the burning of black churches across the South should be in the news in the months before *Rosewood* opens might seem terribly ironic. But when asked about it recently, Singleton says it doesn't surprise him. "We live in the same country that existed seventy-three years ago. I don't see any irony in it at all. If white men are still burning down churches in the South on a regular basis, then I don't really think things have changed that much."

Singleton believes that the similarity between current headlines and the historical events shown in *Rosewood* could increase the film's impact.

"I think that enlightened people will make a connection," he says. "And I think there are other people who just don't want to hear it. . . . They definitely don't want to think about the horror of what came before, and of the fact that what came before is evident now also."

Rosewood ventures into uncomfortable territory by showing a piece of inhumanity not in Germany, South Africa, or Bosnia, but in our own history. "It is very easy for Americans to look at a film like *Schindler's List*," says Rhames, an imposing man with a subterranean voice. "But this is something that's at home. Malcolm said the chickens have come home to roost, and this film has some of that. I think it's really gonna force Americans to look at America in a light that we've tried to ignore."

But this is not just a tale of racist whites vs. victimized blacks. Rhames's character, Mann, one of the few non-historical roles in the film, is an amalgamation of contemporary accounts of newly militant black WWI veterans and of the real Sylvester (nicknamed Man), an independent, strongwilled man who demanded respect to a degree that seems extraordinary for the time. For Singleton, Mann and Sylvester represent "a spectrum of black man in American history who black people know of, but who never really get anything to do in American cinema. Strong black men who have honor and dignity and fight for what's right."

But if Mann and Sylvester are the film's heroes, it is Voight's character Wright, along with the white Bryce brothers, who also help save the women and children. "In telling the story we have tried . . . to not only re-create it as truthfully as possible, but to present it in a balanced light," Barone says. "The ultimate message is a hopeful one."

Hollywood can bring an aggrandizing self-consciousness to a subject like racism, but it can also bring attention to serious issues that they might never get otherwise. *Schindler's List* and *JFK* are two obvious examples. "It's *Batman* joins *Rosewood*," Peters says. "We make movies that make millions of dollars, so when we focus on *Rosewood* it's suddenly a story that has enormous power."

Peters says he is talking to ABC's Ted Koppel about doing a televised town meeting on *Rosewood* when the film is released in the fall, and he is clearly counting on controversy to bring people into the theaters.

But there also seems to be a healthy dose of sincerity at work.

"I hope this movie will inspire people to be curious and investigate our history," Cheadle says. "We seem to be in a resurgence of racism and xenophobia and conflict right now. I think if you understand why, you're better able to deal with it."

"We haven't really been able to truly acknowledge or make amends for this part of our past," Voight says. "And maybe this movie will move us to that. I mean, we're talking about a movie, and nothing but a movie. But that's the prayer."

It's 7 A.M., and Singleton is as quick and intent as he was at 10 P.M., maybe more so, because he's about to lose the cold, white morning light and at

7:30 everyone goes into overtime. He wants to get one last shot in, showing Voight walking down the road, then panning down to show Akosua Busia, who plays Wright's mistress Jewel, lying raped and dead in the bushes.

"The audience will be going, 'Look! Look!,' but he won't see her," Singleton says excitedly. "This is one of those scenes the studio has been trying to get me not to do, because of budget, so I've been basically stealing shots. These are the important ones, the ironic ones, they hit home. So I've been doing them all anyway."

The volume of his voice doesn't rise but the intensity does. "I think maybe the movie will bear the brunt of a lot of people—like the people around here—who will say, 'Why you bringing that up? Why you talking about this?' But why not? If you don't talk about it, then it could happen again and again and again. It's more than why not. It's like the Holocaust. Because you can never forget."

He settles down slightly. "Everyone's going to have a different reaction to the film, black people, white people. But it's a truly American story. And on the other hand it's a human story. It's the same deal."

John Singleton Searches for
Justice in *Rosewood*

JAY CARR/1997

I T ' S   O N E   T H I N G for Americans to watch *Schindler's List*, or films about the wars in Bosnia and Chechnya. Horrible as those stories are, they didn't happen here, and distance can provide a certain insulation. But there's no way Americans can distance themselves from John Singleton's *Rosewood*, opening Friday. The epic film depicts the weeklong systematic torching of a black town by a white mob in central Florida in 1923, as the governor and a local sheriff stood by. Almost as bad as the atrocity itself was the silence that surrounded it for decades. Then, in 1982, a St. Petersburg Times reporter brought to light the story that had until then existed only as oral history.

In 1994, the Florida legislature awarded $2.1 million in reparations to the surviving families. A TV special attracted Hollywood interest. Which is how Singleton, who grew up in South Central Los Angeles and made his mark with the autobiographical *Boyz N the Hood*, found himself learning from the locals how to dodge rattlesnakes, endure mosquitoes, and tape the legs of his trousers to prevent tick and chigger bites in the swamps during the shoot. The filming, a lot of which was done at night, took place two hours from the ghost town, where the only house left standing belonged to Rosewood's sole white family, that of a shopkeeper played by Jon Voight.

"The only time I had been to the South was when I had driven there years ago on a trip to visit relatives in South Carolina with my uncle and my cousin," Singleton says, stretching out on an East Side hotel sofa after a day of interviews and a photo shoot. "Everything I had heard about the South was pretty much bad for black people. A lot of the evil that black people have

From the *Boston Globe* (February 16, 1997). Reprinted by permission.

faced in this country is rooted there. I remember thinking, 'I'll never make a movie in the South.' But then I met Arnette Doctor, who comes from one of the families involved. His mother, Philomena, was eleven years old at the time. She's in the film. He spent his life digging into the story. He was the one who initiated the court case.

"There was a lot of silence from the black families, partly because they were afraid of repercussions, partly because there was a sense of shame about being victimized. But, after the court case, they were more willing to talk. I met some of the survivors and I was humbled. I felt very strongly about their testimony, about the things they told me had happened to them. I couldn't help but get involved and make this movie. I felt like here's a story that had existed for seventy years, and people were trying to deny it had happened. I felt like me being a young man with the ability to make motion pictures, I had the responsibility to go and do it."

Rosewood proved an arduous and logistically complicated shoot, especially for a director whose three previous works were urban contemporary films. "It wasn't like going to summer camp," says Singleton, smiling wryly. "In a way, making this movie has helped me get over my problems with the South. You know, I met a lot of white people, too, who were only one generation removed from this massacre. They were crackers. They call themselves crackers. And I had to direct them. Me. I had to interact with these people for seven months. We had a lot of crackers on the crew. Dozens. And tons of extras. We all got along. They respected me and helped me make the movie."

Some whites, Singleton says, have questioned the need to make *Rosewood*. But not the Floridians who worked on the film. "They were happy to have a black man directing them," Singleton says. "We were the ones who brought jobs. In the movie, the white shopkeeper makes money off the town of black people. Now we had a whole town of shopkeepers making money off us. I guess I was the shopkeeper. But then the racism in that incident had an economic basis. At the time, a lot of people migrated to the area—whites, blacks, Hispanics. They were vying for employment in the lumber and turpentine business. You had a whole lot of economic tension.

"So here you had Rosewood, which was a prosperous black town, and you have Sumner, four miles up the road, a company town with the white people there not doing too well, living in tract housing. And so you're sitting on a powder keg. You had a lot of whites thinking, 'Well, if I'm not better than the nigger, what am I better than?' That's why we have the scene where the white man is incensed that a black man not only owns a piano, but teaches music. And so the powder keg got lit when a white woman named Fanny Taylor, who was having an affair with another man, said she got beaten up by a black man, when in actuality it was her white lover. The white people of Sumner hated the black people of Rosewood because of their prosperity."

One difficulty, Singleton says, arose from a need to find something positive in the black response. This led to re-creations of historical characters (and amalgams of them) being augmented by an invented figure played by Ving Rhames and inspired by returning black Army veterans of World War I, who had discharge bonuses in their pockets and a newfound pride that led them to stand up to racism. In the film, Rhames is at the forefront of some payback as he heroically leads survivors out of Rosewood to Gainesville aboard a rescue train put at their disposal by two white railroading brothers who actually existed—as did the shopkeeper played by Voight in ways that make his exploitative ways clear, but also allow for a certain sympathy to blacks.

Perhaps as a psychological necessity, Singleton has gone for his next project to a lighter chapter in black history: *Shaft*, the black private eye series starring Richard Roundtree, invented by a white man, Ernest Tidyman, and begun in 1971 by one of Singleton's directorial role models, Gordon Parks. "It won't be a remake," Singleton says. "It'll be a continuation. Contemporary. *Shaft* wasn't blaxploitation. All that black exploitation stuff came after *Shaft*. You know, *Shaft* was a detective story. At its core it was respectful. We don't know who'll star yet. But whoever it is, whoever puts on that leather coat and walks through Times Square, is going to be a star."

If there's a hint of the pitchman in Singleton's talk about his next project, it isn't accidental. He's the first to admit that he had to sell himself hard to a film world where the list of black filmmakers pretty much began and ended with Spike Lee, another of Singleton's role models—although Lee might have been left wondering about this when they met in 1990. "I met him two weeks before I started film school. And I said, 'Hey man, I like your movies. I'm starting film school in two weeks. Watch out for me!'" Hollywood loves this kind of talk, and Singleton realized it when he began working his way through the University of Southern California as a crew member on film shoots.

He was encouraged by his family, he says, since the days when as a nine-year-old, he began making animated notepad drawings, which he describes as flip books influenced by *Star Wars*. "It was so visceral," Singleton says. Later, he adds, Coppola, Spielberg, Welles, Huston, Capra, and Kurosawa entered his field of vision. "I remember taking junior college classes in cinematography so I could have access to their equipment," he says. "And my mother would just take my film down to the lab. She was happy to do it because I told her Steven Spielberg's mother took his film down to the lab for him when he was a kid. I had to dig, man. I was at film school, doing all type of internships, you know. I didn't have family in the business, you know, at all. I had to learn by doing.

"And so by the time I graduated in 1990 from USC, I already had representation with CAA, the top agency in Hollywood, and I was in pre-production for my first feature film, *Boyz N the Hood*. I caught lightning in a bottle. But I went after it. Talked. Pitched myself, you know? Talked a lot of crap. That's what you do in Hollywood. But once I had an opportunity to direct a movie, you know, to be getting $6 million to do my first movie, I backed it up. How autobiographical was it? Very autobiographical. At twelve years old, I was really unruly. Living with my father as the adolescent in the film does made me more of a disciplined man. My father, named Furious Styles in the film and played by Laurence Fishburne, started making me take out the trash and wash the dishes and have responsibilities, you know? I love my mother, but if I lived with my mother, I would never have become the man that I am now, you know?"

Chains of causality are strange things. Because Singleton's father made him shape up, a shocking piece of history long muted and now perhaps within reach of closure will be emblazoned across the public consciousness with the kind of large-scale imprint only Hollywood can muster. Not, Singleton quickly makes clear, that Rosewood is now to be quietly tucked away in the past. "If you don't talk about it, it can happen again and again," he says. "It's like the Holocaust. You can never forget. Look at all those church bombings. Look at Susan Smith. She used a black man as a scapegoat for murdering her children. Look at that guy in Boston who murdered his wife and said a black guy in Roxbury did it. Everybody, every black face, was a suspect. Everyone was guilty."

Stirring Up Old Terrors Unforgotten

BERNARD WEINRAUB/1997

JOHN SINGLETON SAID he would never forget Minnie Lee Langley's fear and courage as she told him about the murderous rage she had witnessed as a child more than seventy years ago in Rosewood, Florida.

Mr. Singleton, the twenty-nine-year-old director of such films as *Boyz N the Hood* and *Poetic Justice*, said the financial and emotional pressures of making his newest movie, *Rosewood*, had left him so drained that he might have walked away from the project except for the memory of Miss Langley.

The film, which opens on Friday, deals with the slayings of a group of blacks in the Gulf Coast mill town of Rosewood, Florida, in 1923 by whites from neighboring Sumner. The rampage was set off by a white woman's false accusation that she had been assaulted by a black stranger. Within days Rosewood had been burned to the ground.

"There were times I wanted to quit," Mr. Singleton said. "I knew I had to honor this subject. I knew I couldn't make a bad movie. But this was so daunting. And there were fights with the studio about money and wanting to make this a big movie. And I wanted to quit. I was, like, I don't want to do this. And then Minnie Lee Langley passed away."

Ms. Langley, who died just before filming began early last year, was nine when the terror took place. "She told me how she hid in the marshes with the other black kids as the white posse hunted them like animals," Mr. Singleton, seated in a restaurant in Santa Monica, said the other day. "Here was a woman in her mid-eighties and you could see the fear and trepidation that she still had. And she was brave. She testified as an elderly woman in front of the State Legislature, which took tremendous courage on her part.

"I went to her funeral and that gave me energy, because all these people were there talking about her courage, and I thought, I've got to keep going here. I've got to do it, just do it, and fight to do it, because this story should be told."

The slayings in predominantly black Rosewood, which are still surrounded by some mystery, were virtually unknown until 1982, when Gary Moore, a reporter for the *St. Petersburg Times*, began working on an article about the area. He noted that there were no black residents and asked why.

Soon, with the help of old newspaper clippings and interviews, he tracked down survivors of the killings, many of them ashamed that they had been victimized and still afraid that their lives might be threatened.

At least six blacks and two whites were killed in the rampage. Black families fled through the swamps as the prosperous town was burned to the ground. Mr. Singleton said he believed the number of dead was probably far higher.

Three years ago the Florida Legislature offered reparations to the survivors of Rosewood and their families. Two months ago a documentary about Rosewood, produced by ABC News and the Discovery Channel, was broadcast on Discovery.

Mr. Singleton's film, written by Gregory Poirier and based loosely on the facts, stars Ving Rhames as a black World War I veteran who comes to Rosewood to start a new life and Jon Voight as the lone white shopkeeper in town who helps black women and children flee.

Mr. Singleton said he had spoken to about five survivors of the violence who were, of course, young children at the time. "They remembered it vividly and they're still frightened," he said.

Throughout the making of *Rosewood*, Mr. Singleton pressed Warner Brothers for more money. Jon Peters, the producer, admitted that he as well as Warner Brothers were nervous about the box-office prospects for the movie, which cost about $28 million.

"It's the riskiest film I've ever done," said Mr. Peters, who, with a former partner, Peter Guber, produced such movies as *Batman* and *Rainman*. "If it's not sold right, it'll do nothing. Hopefully people will embrace it."

By all accounts the film would probably not have been made without Mr. Peters's involvement and his clout with Warner Brothers, which in recent years has focused on big action-adventures and comedies. He acquired the rights to the Rosewood survivors' stories after seeing television news reports about the Florida Legislature's decision and seeing a segment about the killings on *60 Minutes*.

"What appealed to me was that these people had no voice, there were no grave sites, no records, very little about what happened," he said. "It was a chance to make a contemporary movie. I didn't want to make a popcorn movie."

Though Warner Brothers is nervous about the commercial prospects for the bleak movie, which was trimmed to 2 hours and 20 minutes from 3 hours, Mr. Peters noted that Gerald Levin, the chairman of Time Warner, showed *Rosewood* to members of Congress last week.

It was an unusual gesture. "It's seen, I hope, as an important movie," said Mr. Peters, who has gained a reputation as one of Hollywood's more flamboyant producers. "And for me, it's an opportunity to do something good." Mr. Singleton said that in making *Rosewood*, he had been especially influenced by Steven Spielberg's *Schindler's List.* Mr. Singleton went so far as to enlist John Williams, who composed the music for the Spielberg film, to write the score for *Rosewood.*

"I loved the way Spielberg structured his scenes and the way he used music and how he didn't make his antagonists one-dimensional," he said. "Even the Ralph Fiennes Nazi character was deeper, three-dimensional. And I didn't want to make the white characters all fire-breathing racists and the black characters holier-than-thou, just singing in church and not shooting back when they're shot at."

Surprisingly, Mr. Singleton said that finding actors, black or white, for *Rosewood* was not especially easy. "Black and white actors were afraid because of the subject matter and because we didn't have a whole lot of money," he said. "On the whole, people in this town don't like to make too much of a wave and are not inclined to do anything of depth."

Mr. Singleton grew up in a middle-class home in south-central Los Angeles, and attended the University of Southern California Film School. His debut film at the age of twenty-three, *Boyz N the Hood,* earned him the distinction of being the youngest person—and the first African American—ever nominated for an Academy Award as best director. Since that film he has been offered numerous scripts, many without racial themes.

"My greatest fear is winding up a hack—you know, 'Let me read twenty-five scripts and see if something interests me,'" he said. "I have to find something that I have in my heart and soul that I want to spend two years on, usually with a lot of angst."

He said that the depiction of blacks in films remained troubling, and that some of the fault rested with black filmmakers. "It's commerce, everything is commerce," he said. "I mean there are black filmmakers trying to get paid just like white filmmakers. And not everybody comes to the table in a certain way in which they feel they have a responsibility to do anything except make a profit."

For his next film, Mr. Singleton is planning a remake of *Shaft*, about the suave black private eye in New York. There were three successful *Shaft* films, starring Richard Roundtree, from 1971 to 1973.

"I want to get away from real people, real events, real tragedy," Mr. Singleton said with a smile. "That's been a very heavy responsibility."

Can Ya Dig It?

GLENN WHIPP/2000

WHEN DIRECTOR Gordon Parks made *Shaft* twenty-nine years ago, sexual and political revolutions were in the air. African-American audiences embraced Richard Roundtree's smooth private detective as a hero unlike any they had ever seen in a movie theater. Here was a black man who dressed, talked, and acted the way they did—or at least, wished they did in their coolest moments.

"He was doing all those things that John Wayne and Audie Murphy and Errol Flynn did; he was the guy who could walk through a hail of bullets, kill all the bad guys, and save the girl," says Samuel L. Jackson. "And that was a revelation. All of a sudden, here was somebody I could emulate instead of look at and not care about."

In the new version of *Shaft*, which opens Friday, Jackson is John Shaft, the nephew of the original John Shaft. (Roundtree has a cameo in the movie.) But while Roundtree's character was, to quote the opening words from Isaac Hayes's Oscar-winning theme song, "the black private dick that's a sex machine to all the chicks," Jackson's Shaft, a cop, seems to enjoy violence more than he does sex. More on that later.

The new *Shaft* has its share of racial politics, too, but they're nothing compared to the maneuverings that were happening behind the camera. Jackson and director John Singleton (*Boyz N the Hood*) clashed with producer Scott Rudin on just about everything—the screenplay's language, its action sequences, and its dearth of love scenes.

"Different times call for a different hero," Jackson says. "Richard was fighting against the Man and the system. This Shaft embraces and enjoys his violent side. Unfortunately, he never seems to sleep, so we can't see him

---

From the *Los Angeles Daily News* (June 11, 2000). Reprinted by permission.

in bed with anybody. I guess we live in more politically correct times these days."

The question, then, is why make another *Shaft*? Jackson didn't have an answer when Singleton sent him the script two years ago. In fact, the fifty-one-year-old actor couldn't even see himself playing Shaft, whom he pictured as a young, virile man.

"But then, when I look in the mirror these days, I don't see what I thought I would see when I got to be fifty-one years old," Jackson says. "When my grandfather's brothers were fifty, I knew they were fifty. Most of my daughter's friends would not look at me and say, 'That man is fifty years old.'"

Singleton saw Jackson as perfect because "Shaft is a (trash) talking character and everyone goes to Sam's movies to hear him talk (trash)."

Roundtree cites Jackson's vocabulary as one dramatic difference between the two Shafts. "Sam's pretty good at saying (the mother of all cuss words) and saying it with conviction."

Jackson also has an aura of cool about him, and Singleton believed that attitude is "90 percent" of a *Shaft* film.

"My biggest fear was making a square version of 'Shaft,'" Singleton says. "And that's what most of the big fights between me and the studio were about. I could not afford for this movie to be square. We don't have any big special effects, so it had to be about how cool these characters are."

Problems arose when Rudin (who declined comment for this story) hired novelist-screenwriter Richard Price (*Clockers*) to rewrite the script that Singleton had completed with Shane Salerno. Singleton admits that Price helped flesh out the movie's police story. But the director balked when Rudin told him to shoot the script exactly as it was written, and he had a willing ally in Jackson.

"I told (Scott) point blank that I refused to say that white man's lines," Jackson says, referring to Price. "I'd do it my way and then poor John would have Scott Rudin breathing in his ear demanding that he make me say the lines they'd paid so much money for."

Adds Singleton: "Price didn't have a clue about the attitude of 'Shaft.' He took out all the flavorful dialogue. He just didn't get it. His pop culture references were stuff like 'Bulldog Drummond.' Now what does that have to do with John Shaft?"

Another source of conflict was over Shaft's sexual escapades—or the surprising lack of such encounters. Roundtree, who made three *Shaft* movies and appeared in a short-lived television series based on the character, says he missed the sensual aspect of Shaft's screen persona and believes the studio made a "mistake" in not developing it.

He's not alone in that regard. Says Singleton: "If it was my choice, he'd be kicking (butt), then he'd have a love scene, then he'd be kicking more (butt) and then he'd be saying, 'C'mon, baby, give me some sugar.' But times have changed. We're living in an even more puritanical society than we were thirty years ago. So it's OK for Shaft to bash somebody's head in, but to show him (having sex), well, that would offend women, I guess."

Jackson lost that battle, but on other clashes he refused to budge. Jackson not only disliked Price's dialogue, but thought his action scenes lacked logic and believability. Rudin wanted the sequences shot the way Price wrote them. Singleton wanted to film the scenes the way he wrote them. Eventually, Rudin asked for a compromise and requested the scenes be shot both ways. But Jackson wasn't going for that, either.

"If we shot it his way, then his way will end up in the movie and not mine," Jackson says. "I wanted to be faithful to what I think the *Shaft* movie is, so I'm not going to get bullied or allow whoever else is being bullied into doing something that I don't want to do just to defuse something. I don't have to defuse anything. In the end, I'm the one that's up there on the screen. Nobody's going to be saying Scott Rudin really (messed) up this time. They're going to say Sam Jackson did. And I'm not going to let that happen."

Remarkably, both Jackson and Singleton seem interested in the possibility of a *Shaft* sequel, even though that would mean working with Rudin again.

"There were times when I wanted to choke Scott, and there were times when I wanted to give him a hug," Singleton says. "Bottom line: He's the best producer in the business, man. He's the Irving Thalberg of our age. I learned a lot—like always have everything in your contract before the movie starts."

Jackson isn't as complimentary, but he's resigned to the current arrangement, if only because making a sequel would probably mean that he and Roundtree would enjoy much more screen time together.

"The response to him is still amazing, and rightfully so," Jackson says. "It just shows what an impact he had on us. And hopefully there will be somebody who sees this movie that will sit up a bit prouder or walk out of that theater with a bigger smile because we were the hero and we won and they can have somebody to relate to. Maybe they'll think, 'I can go out and buy a coat like that and maybe get a girl.'

"Because that's all we wanted to do after we saw *Shaft*," Jackson continues. "We wanted to go out and get the girl—put my Afro out, put my leather on, put my turtleneck on and say, 'Hey, baby, how ya doing?' Can you dig it? Right on."

Who's the Man?

STEVE DALY / 2000

H E R E M E M B E R S reading that *Boogie Nights* star Don Cheadle might play the part. He also recalls talk of Wesley Snipes. But when a script for a new take on the 1971 blaxploitation hit *Shaft* first crossed his desk in late 1998, Samuel L. Jackson—the man who's so far made his biggest box office scores by partnering with flinty white costars (including John Travolta in *Pulp Fiction*, Bruce Willis in *Die Hard with a Vengeance*, and Tommy Lee Jones in *Rules of Engagement*)—says it didn't occur to him that this might be his shot at solo, above-the-title billing on a major summer movie.

"Well, what character do they want me to read for?" Jackson recalls thinking.

He conjures the moment as he cocks his head and leans his six-foot-three frame back into an overstuffed chair in a sunny Paramount Pictures screening-room annex. Decked out in a resplendent black suit, lavender shirt, and slightly lighter lavender silk tie, his skin smooth and glowy enough to make Cate Blanchett look epidermally challenged, the fifty-one-year-old star radiates so much charisma that it's hard to take his aw-shucks declaration completely seriously. And as Jackson warms to the subject of how he went on to help shape Shaft, he soon sounds a lot less self-effacing and a lot more ticked off. It takes only a few minutes' conversation to see why: The picture went through so many rethinks, rewrites, multiple-option takes, and rerecorded lines of dialogue—upon each of which Jackson cast a cold, critical eye before agreeing to them—it could have been called Shift.

"I'm reading it," says Jackson of the initial script he saw, which was in good part the work of novelist and screenwriter Richard Price. "And I'm sitting there going, Oh, well, this is not happening. 'Cause this John Shaft is a cop. He's on the police force. And I'm goin', What part of that song do they

---

From *Entertainment Weekly* (June 16, 2000). Reprinted by permission of Time, Inc.

not understand? Song says, 'Black private dick who's a sex machine to all the chicks.' Script says he's a cop. And there's no sex. I was like, What's wrong with this picture?"

That's a question Jackson kept asking himself—and his collaborators—straight through the production, according to lots of folks involved in giving the detective an update. The star constantly questioned the dialogue, the plot permutations, and the editing decisions in the $50 million-range action flick (a modest sticker price by current summer-movie standards, but high by comparison with the original *Shaft*'s indie origins). And Jackson wasn't the only one raising hackles. Conflicting visions about how multiculturally, politically, and sexually correct this Shaft should be began to surface from the first exploratory meetings.

Typically, the sides were split by race. In one corner, there was Jackson and his thirty-two-year-old director, John Singleton, who'd made *Boyz N the Hood* at twenty-two and become the youngest Oscar-nominated helmer in history. In the other stood producer Scott Rudin (the manic mind behind *The First Wives Club, In & Out, Clueless*, and the Addams Family flicks, among dozens of other credits) and primary scriptwriter Price (best known for his novel *Clockers* and the script for *Sea of Love*, in which Jackson had a bit part a decade ago). Despite a variety of beefs and bouts, the disagreements often shared a thrust: Where does a white producer employing a white scriptwriter get off telling two brothers how to angle a story about John Shaft?

Jackson says that quite a few lines and situations that Rudin and Price came up with prompted him to protest, "But you're not black." He flatly rejected as "offensive" one of Price's rewrites of a much-debated Shaft-gets-it-on scene that would have required him to respond to a girlfriend's complaint that he won't take her out for dinner by tossing a candy bar at her. The scene never did get filmed, though it wound up in very truncated form under the opening credits with a body double subbing for Jackson. And one proposed hateful remark especially rankled him. "We were going to have some lines where [a white] character said, 'Brother comes in here like a lump of coal in a snowbank,'" he says, referring to the movie's opening white-on-black murder scene. "Just to make sure that the audience knows [they're witnessing] a race crime. I'm goin', What the f--- is that? And I'm supposed to make some smartass retort that, you know, plays the race card like ta-daaaa?"

The lines never made it into the final print. But the rancor over this and other dialogue and script battles festered long after the material was scrapped. "It was very evident," says Christian Bale, who follows up *American Psycho* with a turn as the bigoted young murderer whom Jackson's character spends much of the picture tailing. "Nobody tried to conceal that [there was tension] on this movie. But I think that everybody has their own way of working. And some people work better when there's pressure and arguments."

Relations weren't helped when a *New York Daily News* article appeared in August 1999, shortly before shooting began on locations in and around Manhattan, claiming that Rudin and Singleton were at odds over the dearth of minority hires on the movie. In fact, while Singleton's costume-designing alum Ruth Carter was on board (she was Oscar-nominated for *Amistad*), much of the rest of the technical crew—the cinematographer, the production designer, the editor—were all white. Rudin says he heard plenty of complaints about it from other African Americans in the movie and Broadway communities he moves in. "There were a lot of times where I thought, I'm not the right person to be doing this," he says.

"Scott has a certain system," Singleton says. "He likes to hire people that have worked on twenty-five other Scott Rudin films. And they're the top of the line in their craft. Everybody's been nominated for Oscars. Some of them are black and some of them aren't. But there were black crew people I could have hired that had worked on some of Scott's films that didn't want to work on the film." Why not? "'Cause they knew it was hell to work on a Scott Rudin film!" As for the passed-over professionals who sounded off to journalists, Singleton sympathizes, but still dismisses them as "disgruntled."

The director paints his own exasperations on *Shaft* with a broader brush. "There were times making this movie," he says, "that I wanted to give Scott Rudin a hug. And there were times I wanted to choke him."

When he first pitched the idea of resurrecting *Shaft* in the mid-1990s, John Singleton thought it would be a pretty simple, low-budget, funky affair. "I was interested in a nouveau Samuel Arkoff version of *Shaft*," he says, referring to the famous exploitation-film producer, "with chicks raising their breasts and everything." Singleton also wanted to bring back the actor who'd originated the character, Richard Roundtree—who spent time wandering in the badlands of made-for-video movies after making two satisfyingly pulpy *Shaft* sequels by 1973, then watching *Shaft* flounder as a TV series—as the older, wiser parent to a brash, new, hip John Junior.

But MGM, the studio that controlled the story rights, wasn't digging it. "They didn't even want to finance it for $25 million," says Singleton. "They were like, 'Oh, this is just a black movie.' But they were kind enough to say, 'If you can set it up somewhere else, we'll let you take it.'"

Provided, of course, that the other interested party paid off several million dollars of development costs that MGM calculated it had sunk into Singleton's early proposals. The director shopped around the update concept, but reports that "nobody in town got it. They had silly conceptions of what *Shaft* meant to people. Probably most of them had never seen *Shaft*. They probably just knew the music."

Singleton knew every scene. And he remembered the huge impact the first movie had on him when he saw it at the tender age of three on a double bill with *The Chinese Connection*. "*Shaft* is the paradigm for everything that came after it," he enthuses. "You wouldn't have seen John Travolta walking in Brooklyn at the beginning of *Saturday Night Fever* without Shaft walking [in Times Square] first."

The sight of a confident, sexually aggressive, unapologetic black man calling everybody "cat" and "brother"—"the first one ever shown with a mustache, which had always been too intimidating," says Roundtree proudly—was dynamite to black audiences, and to lots of white moviegoers, too. It was *Shaft* that decisively kicked off the blaxploitation genre, in the process goosing the manufacture of dozens of imitators, not to mention such white-urban-rage milestones as *Dirty Harry* (which followed *Shaft*'s summer 1971 debut in December) and 1974's *Death Wish*, with Charles Bronson. But Hollywood execs were not impressed by Singleton's passion. That is, not until Scott Rudin called one day out of the blue to say that Paramount Pictures might be interested.

Rudin, a prolific producer of serious dramas (*Searching for Bobby Fischer*, *Angela's Ashes*) and light comedies as well as Broadway fare (he just collected a Tony for *Copenhagen*), seemed a highly unlikely shepherd. But he felt he smelled a potential hit. "Quentin Tarantino had made this kind of style cool again," Rudin reasons. "To me it was something that could be updated without a lot of difficulty."

But difficulty, to paraphrase that other hipster Austin Powers, turned out to be Shaft's middle name. Things went well initially, as Rudin laid down his typically strong hand in script and casting matters. Among the first changes: lose the father-son story concept. "It made you feel like you were watching *Young Indiana Jones*," sniffs Rudin. Overruled, too, were Singleton's early thoughts of casting Don Cheadle, whom he'd directed in the racial-conflict historical drama *Rosewood* (1997) and who had done an early script reading with impressive panache. Explains Rudin, "It was always going to have to be a star if it was going to be a big, down-the-middle, Hollywood movie."

Jackson was the obvious choice. Soon after he came aboard, the father-son dynamic became an uncle-nephew link, and Roundtree agreed to return in an older, wiser version of his original role. "I wanted to pass the baton after thirty years," says Roundtree, still suave at fifty-seven. "Maybe now [the fans] will be looking at somebody else as that character. It will take some of the pressure off me. Good God, if I have to stand there and listen to people recite the lines once more, like I've never heard them before . . . They're coming from a great place in their hearts. But they don't have any idea how many times I've heard those damn lines."

Jackson began to wonder just how he'd accrue some of those instant catchphrases after Rudin hired Richard Price to rework Singleton's earlier drafts (which another writer, Shane Salerno, had also taken a pass at). Price had come through for Rudin on Ron Howard's *Ransom*, and the producer was sure he could "turn around a situation that was in trouble" again. Unfortunately, Jackson strongly objected to Price's conception of the new John Shaft as a career cop, insisting that the character quit the force early in the movie. (He got his way.) "Richard writes great cop stories," gripes Jackson. "That's what he writes, you know? He was trying to be comfortable in what he does."

Counters Rudin: "I don't know how to make a movie in which a black man is walking the streets of Manhattan shooting people on sight. In Giuliani's New York, how is that man getting from Brooklyn to Queens to Manhattan alive?" Rudin also pooh-poohs some of Jackson's complaints as a reflex action. "Sam objects to everything," he says. "He's great in the movie, and I can't imagine anyone else having played it, but I also wouldn't give up Richard Price's contribution to it for anything. If you asked me who is the unsung hero of this movie, I would say it's Richard Price." (What Price would say is unclear; the author's agent did not respond to requests for comment for this story.)

Putting aside Price's more controversial contributions, everybody who made *Shaft* agrees on his one dazzling success: his invention of a self-important Dominican drug lord named Peoples Hernandez. He enters the plot after Bale's murdering thug as a seemingly secondary villain, but soon hijacks the movie. That's largely thanks to the impression made by Jeffrey Wright, the star of *Basquiat* and a Tony award winner for playing a flamboyant gay nurse in *Angels in America*: Perestroika. He got the part when John Leguizamo dropped out to star as Toulouse-Lautrec in Baz Luhrmann's musical *Moulin Rouge*, costarring Nicole Kidman. Rudin says Leguizamo "did the movie a gigantic favor."

So much so, in fact, that Wright's performance helped exacerbate some story problems. "Early on, everybody said, 'Jeffrey's wonderful, we must have more of him,'" says *Shaft*'s veddy British editor John Bloom (an Academy Award winner for *Gandhi*). "But when you have two villains, you've made life difficult for yourself." So when push came to shove in the editing room, Wright's scenes stayed in—while Roundtree and Bale got the you-know-what. A subplot with Roundtree backing up Jackson's character as a decoy was dropped as redundant, says Bloom. And Bale was especially disappointed to see his big fistfight sequence with Jackson on an airport runway—the scene that was one of the main reasons he took the villain role in the first place—land on the cutting-room floor, since Peoples's showdowns with Shaft had, as Jackson puts it, "become the story."

Rudin, Singleton, and Jackson all bemoan the decision to give Roundtree less to do. But Rudin says Paramount execs pressured him to make Jackson the sole savior at the tale's end, forcing the curtailment of plans to give Roundtree a bigger tribute. Says Jackson of the jockeying: "I wasn't producing. I was just, you know, I was a hired hand. I was doing what I could do. Trying to keep as much of my stuff intact as I possibly could, so I couldn't worry about his."

Jackson wasn't the only one hanging on to his script pages for dear life at times. There was the day that Rudin arrived for the filming of a scene set in a snooty Upper East Side nightclub and declared to Singleton, "These extras don't look WASPish. They look like they're from the Weehawken mall. We're not shooting tonight." Singleton felt Rudin was "absolutely right," and applauded Rudin's insistence that the entire scene be re-prepared and shot weeks later—but the sharp introduction to the spend-and-fix mentality threw him. "I'm used to working in low-budget films where you say, 'S---, I'm going to make the best of it.'"

Singleton experienced another culture clash when gossip-page buzz began that some people on the set found the director entirely too enthusiastic about auditioning as many beautiful young ladies as possible for scenes set at Shaft's fave hangout, Harlem's Lenox Lounge—and lingered with them in his trailer. (To this complaint, Jackson replies, "John's single, so what's the problem?")

Singleton says he's both "flattered" and "mad" at these slaps from "pissed-off" women on the set. "It was true I looked over sexy extras," he says. "But I wasn't screwing two of them in the trailer and running the crew at the same time. I mean goddamn, you know? Give me some professional f---ing consideration. Nobody thinks about the fact that every image of the film I had to think out in advance to save us time and money, and that it's written out and everything. And that I know exactly how many shots, or think in advance of how many shots I want to do for the day."

Astonishingly, given the tales they freely tell about their frustrations, the producer-director-star team behind the new *Shaft* say they'd be delighted to see the movie become a new franchise—and to team up again for another chapter.

Says Rudin, "I've had a lot of experience on movies like this where they're a bear in the making and you come out the other end and you don't remember it was a bear." Would he bring Singleton back? "I can't imagine why he wouldn't do it," the producer says.

Singleton first plans to reenter *Boyz N the Hood* territory with a follow-up story, *Baby Boy*. (Possible lead: Ving Rhames.) But that doesn't mean he isn't already thinking sequels. "It will always be me," he declares. "I'm the one who originated it, I'm not going to end up letting somebody else do it. I'd like to take the characters to Jamaica. I like that whole volatile way Jamaica is. If I was going to do something next, the villain wouldn't be Dominican, he'd be Jamaican."

Jackson is all in favor of moving the character to a warmer climate, since he shivered his way through this wintry production's New York locations. "But then again," he says, "you can't wear leather when it's really hot. Maybe Shaft could be in linen. In the Caribbean? In Hawaii?" He ponders the thought—and stomps on it. "Naaaaah. It's gotta be cold. Gotta be leather."

Sounds like the crossfire over *Shaft 2* is heating up already.

The Shafting of John Singleton

ERICH LEON HARRIS / 2000

IN AN INDUSTRY that feeds on its young, few first-time moviemakers survive to make a second or third film. *Shaft* marks John Singleton's fifth outing, one that many are calling his return to form. The early buzz is that an innovative release of the *Shaft* trailer on the Internet has executives rethinking film marketing; the studio's hope is that surging website hits and high scoring test screenings will herald a summer blockbuster . . .

Singleton has had to do a lot of growing up in the nine years since *Boyz N the Hood* made him a household name and garnered him Oscar nominations for best original screenplay and best director. The media had crowned him Spikes heir apparent, and the boffo box office receipts endeared him to Hollywood's powerbrokers. But in the years and movies that followed, *Poetic Justice* (1993), *Higher Learning* (1994), and *Rosewood* (1996), Singleton watched his box office momentum slow to a grinding halt. At the same time that many critics spoke to his artistic growth, his maturing film grammar and visual storytelling skills, he struggled to repeat his early success with audiences.

Regarding what *Shaft* means to John Singleton, a well-known Hollywood producer said recently, "To be well-reviewed is great, but baby this is show business, not show art. Singleton needs a hit like a crack head. Once you've had a taste, success is very addictive."

John Singleton was in great spirits on the day of this interview. He'd just returned from a fishing trip after putting the finishing touches on his new movie. He was outspoken, candid, and brimming with confidence of a moviemaker who believes he's got a surefire hit in the can.

From *MovieMaker Magazine* (July 2000). Reprinted courtesy of *MovieMaker Magazine* (www.moviemaker.com).

ERICH LEON HARRIS (MM):   *Every moviemaker who has met or worked with you seems to have plenty to say, but the consensus is that no one really knows you. Your enigmatic style has some calling you the Howard Hughes of film.*

JOHN SINGLETON (JS):   I'm the Howard Hughes of film? [*Laughs*] I guess there's a similarity because I like to spend a lot of time traveling when I'm not making films. I'm in one state one day, another state the next, on the other side of the world next week. I was in the Bahamas last weekend. Fifty miles out in the middle of the ocean, fishing.

MM: *Does fishing help you to get your head together?*

JS: Yeah.

MM: *Is your much-anticipated new movie,* Shaft, *a remake of the classic?*

JS: It's not a remake. It's the next in the *Shaft* series.

MM: *What drew you to the material?*

JS: I really wanted to do something that was basically a fun movie, because I've gotten this punch of being a so-called controversial filmmaker. I really don't think that anything I do is controversial. I just think that I think differently from most people who make movies.

MM: *How is your thought process or POV different?*

JS: Well, I'm a young, virile black man [chuckles]—you know what I'm saying?—who is very much in tune with myself. I'm not trying to be anything other than who I am. That sets me apart from anybody who is not black, and it sets me apart from most other black men. There's nobody like me making films.

MM: *I went to your web site,* Shaft-themovie.com, *and saw the trailer. The look of this film, judging by the trailer, is quite a bit slicker than your other work. Is that fair to say?*

JS: Yeah, it is slicker in the sense that I've had more toys to play with on this film than I've ever had before. But I only use technology in the service of telling the story. I don't try to use equipment just for the sake of doing a fancy shot. I never try to do that.

MM: *Never? You're never just flexing your muscles?*

JS: If I'm flexing as a director, you as a viewer shouldn't be aware of it. I'm not one of those directors who says, "Look at this! This is going to be a fly shot!" Now everybody is going to be looking at how fly the shot is. No! People are going to be watching this movie and the fly shot just passes by. Because people are engrossed in the story. I call this "The Big Dick Director Theory."

MM: *Please expand on your Big Dick theory.*

JS: Some directors try to swing wide and show how fly a shot they can take, or how long a master shot they can make. Just to show off how big their dick is. But if the shot is not called for, you know that they've got a little dick. They're not using the technology in the service of telling a story. A fancy shot just for the sake of a fancy shot is nothing. But a fly shot in service of a story is the flyest thing a director can do.

MM: *Tell us the story behind* Shaft. *What's it about?*

JS: Basically it's like this: the movie's about a bad motherfucker that dresses well, kicks ass, and gets all the women. That's what it's about. Of course, you get all that old plot shit about a murder case and a witness he needs to find to save because a rich white kid is trying to kill her, as are some Dominican drug dealers, but that's just plot shit.

MM: *Sam Jackson plays Shaft's nephew, is that it?*

JS: Yeah, Sam plays the new Shaft. He's his nephew, but Richard Roundtree plays Shaft.

MM: *The role of Shaft was the most coveted in a long time. Were actors calling your house, calling your mother's house, and slipping headshots in the pizza box, vying for your attention?*

JS: Yeah, almost every black actor wanted to read for the role. Stars read for the role. Because they say if the movie is successful there's going to be a series.

MM: *What were the factors in you choosing Sam?*

JS: Because Sam's a bad motherfucker. He can talk shit, and everybody loves it.

MM: *What does the success of this picture mean for you and your career? What are your hopes and expectations?*

JS: Hopefully this film will be very successful commercially. Not to say that I haven't enjoyed box office successes before. Matter of fact, every picture that I've done, outside *Rosewood*, has grossed way more than its cost.

MM: *How important was it for you to come do something as commercially viable as* Shaft *on the heels of* Rosewood?

JS: Very important. It adds to my longevity as a filmmaker. This business is all about the money.

MM: *Are you all about the money?*

JS: Not from my perspective. If that were true, I would never have made a *Rosewood*. But from the people who put up the money's perspective, it's all about money. The reason *Shaft* got made is that the studio thinks it's going make a hell of a lot of money; that everyone will want to see it.

MM: *Did* Rosewood *disappoint you, in terms of its box office receipts or the critical reaction?*
JS: I wasn't disappointed because of the box office. It came at a point in my career that I felt that I could make *Rosewood* and not care if it made money or not. That was the reason I made it. It was good to be able to make that movie and not be concerned about whether or not it was going to make money.

MM: *When you look back to the start of your career, did you expect to come out the way you did with all of the hype that* Boyz *created?*
JS: When I was in college, I always told people that I wanted to come out the way a first round draft choice would. That's what I set out to do. I wanted to come out hard, but in a film sense. I feel like I accomplished that. I was like Muhammed Ali, in terms of movies. I said I was going to come out and kick some ass, and now my thing is just to knock motherfuckers out with every movie.

MM: *In the foreword of your book on* Poetic Justice, *Spike Lee basically warns you that the press blew you up, and now you had better get your skills together, because they're going to come after you.*
JS: It didn't matter what I did after the success of *Boyz N the Hood*, they would come after me. But that doesn't concern me. I specifically began to make films because I had something to say to anyone who wanted to hear it. Basically, I felt that mine would be a predominantly black audience, so I speak in that voice. And anybody else who was cool and who was interested would go and see it. But the films were so successful that a lot of other people went to go see those films.

MM: *Wasn't Spike Lee one of your mentors early on?*
JS: Very much so. I knew Spike from the moment I went into film school. I met him when I was eighteen and I stepped to him outside of a movie theater and told him that I was going to make movies, too, and I was going to come out hard. You know how LA guys are, we like to be on full, all the time. [laughs] I came at him like that.

MM: *You got started as an intern at Columbia Pictures, right?*
JS: Yeah. I went from being an intern to being a director in less than six months.

MM: *Are you an anomaly or do you think anyone can do it?*

JS: I don't think anyone can do it. When you're a filmmaker, you have to live, breathe, eat, and shit movies; to be *really* involved in the process. If you want to be a filmmaker, that's what it takes. You have to do it at the expense of having a social life or anything else. You have to have the love of being a storyteller. That's what I honed in going to school, but I had it before I even went to film school.

MM: *Nobody does it alone. Who were some of your early supporters?*
JS: Basically my mother and father. My mother and father never married, but they both have been very supportive of me. My mother taught me how to sneak into movies. We'd go to the multiplex and we'd see three movies in a day. My father was very encouraging. He would tell me that I could be whatever I wanted to be.

MM: *At what point did you know that this is what you wanted to be doing?*
JS: I knew from when I was a kid, because I would always make these little animated movies. Whenever I could get my hands on a camera I'd shoot stuff. I didn't even come from a middle class background. We lived in apartments for the first fifteen years of my life.

MM: *What part of LA did you grow up in?*
JS: In the bottoms, over on Lawrence Street in Inglewood, then on Vermont and 101st, in the "Hoovers," if you know what that means. So that's where I come from. In order to do this it had to be a Kamikaze mission. Everyone else around me wanted to play ball, if they had any ambition at all. It wasn't even about being a filmmaker. I had to lock myself down and stay focused. This is off the track a little, but it's funny how cats are flaunting their ghetto stripes now. Especially in the music business. They have all of this new money and are claiming how they love the ghetto and love living in the ghetto. Let me tell you something: Niggas from the ghettos don't want to be in the ghetto! That's why I can say I'm truly from the ghetto. Because when I was in the ghetto, all I wanted was to get the fuck out! But I couldn't get. All I could do was lock myself up in the library, or maybe catch the bus with my friends up to Westwood or Hollywood. Then I'd see a whole other world. People who know will really know.

MM: *Your films speak to a generation of young black people, many of whom probably want to follow in your path. What advice do you have for the seeds trying to find the light?*
JS: I tell them to learn how to write a script. It all starts on the page. And to make a commitment and live it. It takes a lot to write a movie and even more to direct. You'd better have discipline.

MM: *It seems a young black moviemaker has to learn to write, direct, produce, and sometimes distribute his work and then it had better make money. Is that too much pressure?*

JS: No. I think everybody has that pressure no matter what race they are. You could be a white boy from the valley and make a movie, but if it doesn't make any money, you won't get another job.

MM: *You came out with a class of moviemakers that nobody hears from anymore. To what do you owe your growing longevity?*

JS: My persistence, and I'm a ghetto brother that's made it in this business. I survived a whole other world, so Hollywood ain't shit to me.

MM: *In this year two thousand, are you where you wanted to be?*

JS: I have a career. I'm an established name now. I'm not the new kid on the block anymore. I'm not the Johnny-come-lately. I am a filmmaker and I still have a long way to go. In some ways, I think I've had it relatively easy, once I got my foot in the door.

MM: *Easy in what respects?*

JS: I really haven't had to go through the whole struggle of trying to get my foot in the door. I came out of USC, they gave me $6 million to make my movie and left me alone. I made it the way I wanted to make it without anyone fucking with me, and it came out good and made a lot of money. So that helped me do all of these other films.

MM: *What are you most proud of?*

JS: That I still have my soul.

MM: *What's the biggest misconception about you?*

JS: That I'm this fire-breathing black militant director. Actually, I think that I'm quite humorous. I've got jokes for days.

MM: *Could we explore a bit more of your process toward writing? Earlier, your attitude seemed almost cavalier, but we know that writing is one of your stronger skills.*

JS: My approach to writing is such that I don't just sit down to write. I have to be inspired. I write in bursts. I never just sit down to do it, because I'll get bored. I have to just think of something, like while walking down the street and a great idea comes to me. Then I put it in my journal and I may not come back to it for six months before I put it in a script.

MM: *You build from your main character first, or is it story?*

JS: Character always. I let character dictate the story.

MM: *You've never talked much about your Oscar experience. It must have been the high point of an eighteen-month cycle that started after* Boyz *was released.*

JS: Yeah, I guess you could call it that. It was cool. But the day after, I started rehearsals on *Poetic Justice*, I wasn't thinking on it all the next day. Like, 'Aw man, I didn't get an Oscar last night.' I was with Janet Jackson and Tupac, working on the next movie. I wasn't even thinking about it.

MM: *When he was nominated, Samuel L. Jackson told me, "I'm not going to be a party to this 'It's just an honor to be nominated' bullshit. If I'm in a contest, then damn it, I want to win!" But you were relieved?*

JS: [laughs] That's Sam. I was kind of relieved. Just think: Who wants to win an Oscar at twenty-three years old for his first movie, you know? Everything I did after that, they'd say, 'well he didn't get an Oscar for this, he didn't get nominated for that.' Hey, I didn't kiss anyone's ass to get recognized. I wasn't one of those cheese-eating Negroes, saying 'please recognize me.' I was this kid from the ghetto and I had a take-Hollywood-by-storm attitude. Fuck all the old guard, I'm going to be the new rabble-rouser on the scene. Then I get nominated for two Oscars. The next year, my friend Janet Jackson gets nominated for best song. So in my first two movies, there are three Oscar nods. I feel good about that.

MM: *Is this just ghetto bravado, or is there a more reflective side that you're downplaying?*

JS: Maybe you should talk to the people around me who know me.

MM: *I'm asking you. Presumably you're the one who knows you best.*

JS: I'm not putting on a show for you. The way I talk to you is the way I am. If you talk to people around me who've known me for years, they'll tell you. I like to shake things up. I like to show people things they wouldn't believe they'd see in a movie. It's more interesting.

MM: *How much does the public's opinion influence your work, if at all?*

JS: I guess in the end it does, if I consider myself the public. Everyone would tell me, when they passed me in the street, that I should make another *Boyz N the Hood*. So for many years I tried to get away from doing something urban. I felt that I didn't want or need to do something set in the ghetto. But now I want to make the most ghetto movie that I ever made. Something filled with ghetto poetry, though. Soulful. The kind of ghetto I'm talking about is the feeling you get when you were six or seven years old and your mother would sing along with Marvin Gaye records while you were eating hot links. Only someone from the ghetto could know that feeling. You didn't have any money, but you were happy. I want to bring that feeling to the masses.

MM: *You've explored moments of that ghetto poetry in Boyz, and you definitely were working at it Poetic Justice. Why didn't you write those poems?*
JS: I couldn't write it. I tried to, but I just couldn't get into that girl's head. I thought it would be interesting to use Dr. Angelou's poetry.

MM: *Do you think that her poems made your scenario uneven?*
JS: I don't know. The script wasn't perfect. I wrote it real quick. I had to get another fucking movie made.

MM: *Why did you have to get a movie made?*
JS: Because I didn't want to sit resting on my laurels. I didn't want to be that guy three years later talking about one movie.

MM: *Was being around Spike and watching him release a movie every eighteen months creating an urgency within you?*
JS: No. I'm not trying to be like that. He really gets it out there. For me, it doesn't matter if it's perfect, it's important to get the work done. Not every film is going to be perfect. It's funny, and who's to say it's right or wrong, but I elected to not have that film be too violent.

MM: *Is that because you took some hits that Boyz was violent?*
JS: Yeah, but *Boyz* wasn't that violent. In my films, at least up until now, I've never had violence that was gratuitous. It was always a character point when someone got their ass whipped or got killed,

MM: *How does the violence play in Shaft?*
JS: Oh, there's gratuitous violence in *Shaft*. [laughs] This is my biggest commercial film, so there's going to be gratuitous violence, and spontaneous ass-whippings. It's Shaft, and if he wants to kick some ass, there's going to be an ass-kicking.

MM: *Many people think that you've experienced a fall from grace of sort, since your box office receipts haven't equaled that of your first film.*
JS: I don't think so. *Boyz N the Hood was* successful in a number of firsts, because it was a youth-oriented film, it became a crossover hit because people were interested in that world. I think that my work has been maturing since then instead of trying to make the same movie again and again.

MM: *In what specific ways do you feel like you've grown?*
JS: I've just grown as a filmmaker. Look at the way I tell a story, as opposed to the way I told a story ten years ago.

MM: *You say that after* Boyz, *the suits were telling you that you could do anything that you wanted to do. Did that change after* Rosewood?
JS: No. I did *Shaft*.

MM: Shaft *was no trouble to set up?*
JS: No.

MM: *So was your absence, or perceived absence, just bullshit?*
JS: What absence?

MM: *What year did* Rosewood *come out, 1996? Four years ago?*
JS: Yeah, but *Shaft* was supposed to be made years ago at MGM, but MGM didn't have the money. I just took it over to Paramount and now it's coming out next month.

MM: *A successful producer friend said that success is addictive, once you've had a taste, and John Singleton needs another hit like a crackhead might. True?*
JS: [Laughs] If you look at my batting average, since this is about grosses of my films, *Shafts* could tank and I'd still be making another movie. Of course, it won't tank. Shit, we're talking about *Shaft*.

MM: *Could you have made* Shaft *on your second outing instead of your fifth?*
JS: I think so. I'm all about stepping up to the plate. I've been doing this since I was twenty-two. Now I'm thirty-two I'm just now getting my steam up. I'm really going to kick ass in a few years.

MM: *So what's next? When are you coming home?*
JS: Soon. We'll be setting up offices off of Degnan Ave, but I was there last weekend. We played pool off of Crenshaw and then went down to the strip club in Gardena.

MM: *How was the talent in Gardena?*
JS: Extraordinary. Angels with baby faces and greasy booties! [laughs] I loved it! Be sure to print that part.

A Difficult Coming of Age

PATRICK GOLDSTEIN/2001

JOHN SINGLETON is standing out on the sidewalk, admiring a row of palm trees that stretches down the block, out to the horizon. The moon is peeking through the palm fronds and, perhaps because film directors see things filtered through the gauzy eye of artistic intentions, the humble street just off Vernon Avenue and Crenshaw Boulevard, with its gnarled backyard orange trees, seems to glisten with all the serenity of picture-postcard Los Angeles.

"It looks just like Beverly Hills," Singleton says.

Back in his old neighborhood, the thirty-three-year-old director is feeling expansive as he sets up the last shot of the night for *Baby Boy*, which Sony Pictures will release June 29, almost ten years to the day after *Boyz N the Hood*, his celebrated debut film. At Singleton's side is Big Cat, a former Rolling 60s Crips O.G. (original gangster) who serves as the director's "gangologist," counseling lead actors Tyrese and Omar Gooding in the walk and talk of authentic gangbangers.

As someone who has just marked the first anniversary of release from his latest stretch in prison, Big Cat sees things with a little less picture-postcard glow. Looking up at the palm trees, he alertly points out a crime helicopter circling overhead. "I don't know, John," he says. "I think we're a long way from Beverly Hills."

If Singleton weren't so young, you'd call *Baby Boy* his comeback film. His last movie, *Shaft*, was a commercial hit, but it got mixed reviews and was firmly under the control of producer Scott Rudin, who publicly feuded with Singleton, as did Samuel L. Jackson, the film's star. Before *Shaft*, Singleton had made three personal films, all with black casts and subjects, but none had the overwhelming critical and commercial impact of *Boyz*.

With this film, Singleton wanted to look inward, to make a movie that would capture the intimate moments between black men and women that are rarely visible on screen. He envisions *Baby Boy* as a coming-of-age story, much like *The Graduate* or *Saturday Night Fever* but with a black man as the hero of the story. His hero is considerably different from *The Graduate's* Benjamin Braddock: Jody is a twenty-year-old weed-smoking hustler who has two babies with different women but lives at home with his mother and her O.G. boyfriend, spending most of his time in his room, playing with remote-control lowrider model cars. Singleton sees the movie as his version of Marvin Gaye's "What's Goin' On," a soul-searching look at a lost generation of young black men.

"The hardest thing to do is shock black folk," he says one day. "But this movie is going to be strong." As he says that last word, he mimes a punch to the stomach. "Somebody at the studio said this movie is misogynistic. I know the black bourgeoisie are going to hate it. But I'm not celebrating ignorance, like rappers bragging about not knowing how to read. I'm just being honest—I'm not wrapping things up in an easy package. For me, this movie is like watching the soul of a black man on screen. It may be dysfunctional, but it's real."

Having read the script and watched Singleton at work last month, I can safely say that *Baby Boy* will shock more than just black folk. In an era in which Hollywood has produced a steady stream of cozy, feel-good movies, *Baby Boy's* raw, unsettling portrait of violent young black men who've been raised by single mothers could provoke enough debate to knock Eminem off the op-ed pages for a while. It's certainly a bracing departure from dramas like *The Legend of Bagger Vance* and *Family Man*, in which black characters have largely been on hand, as critic Ernest Hardy put it, to play "spiritual mammy to white folk."

If any one moment captures the mood of *Baby Boy*, it's a scene in which Jody has sex with his girlfriend Yvette. As they moan with passion, they growl at each other: "I love you, I hate you. I love you, I hate you. . . ."

One day Singleton shows me the movie's opening sequence, which displays Jody, naked except for his gang tattoos, curled up in a pool of fluid like a baby in a womb. "This is a movie about a generation of young black men who haven't grown up," he explains. "They've all been raised by women, so they're always trying to show how much of a man they are, when what they really are is baby boys."

Singleton sees Jody and his friends as young lions on the Serengeti, except "they're going around the Crenshaw Mall, checking out the sixteen-year-old girls. They're trying to define and defend their manhood at the same time, from their women, the white world, and themselves. In their neighborhood, you're not a man until you're a killer. You look at me the wrong way—bam! I'm not putting a good or bad [judgment] on it. It's the way it is. We kill, we make babies, we try to survive."

Singleton grew up in South Central too, but unlike his friends, he wanted to be Steven Spielberg, not Magic Johnson or *Scarface*'s Tony Montana. Singleton went to the USC film school, where it was obvious he was a special talent. He remains obsessed with movies; after spending all day shooting his film, you could find him at 3 A.M. in his production office screening room, watching *Crouching Tiger, Hidden Dragon* or *Billy Elliot*.

He was only twenty-three when he made *Boyz*, which earned him an Oscar nomination and helped launch the careers of *Boyz* actors Cuba Gooding Jr., Ice Cube, Nia Long, Angela Bassett, and Morris Chestnut. In many ways *Baby Boy*, which completed shooting earlier this month, is *Boyz N the Hood* revisited a decade later. The set has a familial feel; the largely black crew includes about fifteen people who worked with Singleton a decade ago on *Boyz*.

The movie is cast largely with newcomers like Tyrese, the charismatic MTV veejay who plays Jody, and Omar Gooding, Cuba's brother, who plays Jody's friend Sweetpea. Its best-known actors are Ving Rhames, who plays Melvin, Jody's mother's O.G. boyfriend, and rap star Snoop Dogg, who plays Rodney, Yvette's just-out-of-prison old boyfriend. The script almost didn't get made because most studios found it too violent and disturbing. Eventually Singleton took it to Sony, where studio Chairman Amy Pascal, an original supporter of *Boyz*, agreed to do the film for $14 million.

Singleton says he couldn't have made the movie until now: "I'd never been anywhere, never done anything except go to school. I'm grown now. I couldn't have written this without being a father. It made me a better director and a better person."

When he began writing the script, Singleton questioned various friends, male and female, about their relationships. He says he was struck by a common dysfunctional nature, especially by how much control women had over the purse strings in black households. "There's no Cinderella thing in the black community," Singleton explains. "It's the women who take care of the man. They have all the disposable income—the cars, TVs, clothes. With young men, there's this pimp thing . . . , but the women have the real power."

Although the story is clearly told from a man's point of view, its themes may resonate with women too. The movie hit especially close to home for Michelle Richards, a veteran actress who was a "character" coach for the less experienced cast members. "You see stories like this everywhere," she says. "For a lot of young black men, their only power is either having a child or having a gun. Women are very emotional beings, so they raise these young men to go out into a world that is afraid of them, and the men end up being volatile and emotional like their mothers, except that the emotion comes out in bravado and gunshots." Richards thinks that the movie will cause a furious debate in the black community. "But John is showing the truth. This movie is a mirror. It's saying, 'Is this who you want to be?'"

Singleton insists that the film is more personal than strictly autobiographical. Still, Singleton and Jody do have something in common. The director, who was married once for five months, has fathered five children with four women. All but one were born out of wedlock. Singleton says he has joint custody of all five kids and provides them with financial support. The two eldest girls have small parts in the movie. He acknowledges that some of the film echoes his various relationships: "The drama of maintaining a relationship with someone you had kids with, but didn't live with, that's definitely in the movie."

Singleton blames his failed relationships on his celebrity status, saying that after he became a film director, women "were all after me; it was my success that made me attractive. Let's face it, women have an instinct to nest and men have an instinct to spawn."

When pressed on the issue, he reconsiders a bit. "A lot of the responsibility is on my end. I was selfish and I didn't know what I was doing. But having children is a choice, and it takes two people to make that choice. It's a matter of the heart, not the brain, so it's not easy to judge."

It's not so easy to judge the young hustlers in his new film either. Like a lot of younger artists today—and certainly Eminem comes to mind again—Singleton won't spell out what he's saying about their behavior, insisting that we interpret it for ourselves. The only thing that seems clear is that Singleton sees Jody as a kindred spirit, whose humanity is as real as his scars and tattoos.

"Jody is me if I never went to college or never got out of the neighborhood," he says. "He's my friends and cousins and millions of young black people. You know, one day my mother was watching me shoot a scene and she said, 'All you're doing is playing in the neighborhood again, except now you've got a camera to play with.'"

Singleton Returns to the Hood for *Baby Boy*

JOSHUA MOONEY/2001

I N 1 9 9 1, director John Singleton made history. He was a twenty-three-year-old African-American filmmaker whose first film, *Boyz N the Hood*, was a raw but poetic look at life in the gang-infested streets of South Central Los Angeles, where Singleton had grown up. *Boyz N the Hood* earned Singleton Oscar nominations for best director and best screenplay. He was the first African American, and the youngest person, ever to do so.

But Singleton then experienced a sophomore slump. His next two films, *Poetic Justice* and *Higher Learning*, were neither commercial nor critical successes. In 1997 he made the historical drama *Rosewood*, which explored violence against a black community in Florida in the 1920s. Last year, Singleton directed the big-budget remake of *Shaft*, the classic urban action-thriller from the 1970s. *Shaft*, a success at the box office, was a problem-plagued production. There was ongoing strife between Singleton, star Samuel L. Jackson, producer Scott Rudin, and screenwriter Richard Price.

Now, ten years after *Boyz N the Hood*, Singleton, thirty-three, has returned to his roots with his sixth film, *Baby Boy*, an urban drama with dark comic overtones set in South Central. "During *Shaft*, I was always thinking about doing this film," Singleton says. "I just wanted to do something close to home and personal. Shooting in my neighborhood with people I know. Directing people who are like family to me. This film is born out of my organic desire to really do something within the community."

Shooting the $65 million *Shaft* in New York was clearly not a joyous experience for Singleton. Particularly irksome were his ongoing struggles with Rudin, who had hired Price to do rewrites on the film, which led to

From the Nielsen Entertainment News Wire (June 21, 2001). © 2001-2007 Nielsen Business Media, Inc.

confrontations with Jackson. At times, it seemed everyone was at war with everyone else. Jackson went so far as to criticize the inexperience of his director in interviews last summer.

A year later, Singleton says the conflicts were blown out of proportion. Singleton says he and Jackson worked on improving the screenplay and found themselves at odds with Price (who is white). "Basically, Richard Price wouldn't take any of our notes, for whatever reason," Singleton says curtly. "Anybody who's so obstinate to believe that they know more about black culture than two hip black men is an idiot."

Overall, Singleton maintains a positive, if detached, attitude towards *Shaft*. "The film is what it is," he says. "It was a hit, and that's cool and everything. But I personally didn't feel satisfied as an artist. I wanted to do a film that would basically be personal but commercial at the same time."

Baby Boy is a very personal, very human drama. It tells the story of Jody, a twenty-year-old black man who is having trouble growing up. He still lives at home with his mother and can't hold a steady job. He's managed to father two children with two different teen-age girls, and he struggles to maintain ongoing relationships with the women and children in his life. He also has to contend with a volatile male friend who is even less ready for real-world responsibilities. He's being shadowed by a dangerous thug recently released from jail. And his mother's new boyfriend is making life at home increasingly difficult.

Singleton says he was inspired to tell Jody's story after visits to the Crenshaw Mall, one of the social hubs of South Central L.A. "I'd be setting up at the mall, watching these cats walk around the mall rubbing their chests, talking to these fifteen-, sixteen-year-old girls," he says. "Those guys in their twenties are the ones that foster all these teen-age pregnancies. So I just figured, damn, I want to tell a story about a guy like that."

Singleton is confident *Baby Boy* will be a commercial success, but he hasn't shied away from taking chances with the film. It's full of raw, authentically coarse language and scenes of intense sexuality, violence, and drug use. "It's realistic, but actually hyper-realistic," Singleton says. "I pride myself on taking pains to pay attention to the minor details, the nuances of a scene. Because even if people don't notice it, they feel it."

There is plenty to notice and feel in *Baby Boy*. Much in this film won't go down easily and will no doubt anger and upset some filmgoers. Which is just fine with Singleton. "That's cool," he says casually. "This movie isn't for everyone. It's just for the real, cool, hip people who would get it. It's basically like a rap album on film. It's bold and brash and audacious, and either you're feelin' it or you ain't."

In telling Jody's story, Singleton is intentionally addressing broader social and political issues about life as a young black American in the twenty-first century. He agrees that the film will no doubt be critiqued on these larger levels as well, and he's looking forward to that. "I believe in making films people want to see but that challenge an audience to think," he says. "I don't think enough commercial cinema does that."

All the major characters in *Baby Boy* are complicated, flawed individuals. Jody (Tyrese Gibson) is irresponsible and immature, drifting easily into petty crime. His girlfriend Yvette (Taraji Henson) leaves her young son with a drug-smoking, violent ex-con (rap star Snoop Dogg). Jody's mother, Juanita (AJ Johnson), has a new boyfriend (Ving Rhames), a former gangster now living a relatively clean life, who takes pride in the fact that he was once a killer.

Singleton says his characters' imperfections were crucial to the story. "I figured they had to have as many flaws as strengths, to really live and resonate with an audience. But that's what makes this [film] more interesting than anything that's out. We go for broke with no apologies."

Singleton says he'd originally intended to cast his friend Tupac Shakur, the rap star, in the role of Jody. (Shakur had starred in Singleton's second film, *Poetic Justice*.) But before the film could go into production, Shakur was murdered, a victim of gang-related violence. The murder had a profound effect on the director. "Sent my whole life into a tailspin," he says, shaking his head. "When you have somebody that passes in that way, you start thinking about your own mortality."

The director says he worried he'd never find an actor with "the heart and soul" necessary to play Jody. Then he met Tyrese Gibson, a young musician, model, and MTV VJ. Gibson auditioned for the role and won it.

"Tyrese became a real actor off this film," Singleton says with enthusiasm. Like Singleton, Gibson is a native of South Central. "I knew he was from Watts," Singleton says, "and I figured if he was from Watts and survived all that, then he can do anything."

From *Boyz* to *Boy*

GLENN WHIPP/2001

TEN YEARS AGO, filmmaker John Singleton made *Boyz N the Hood* and won commercial success and critical acclaim for his tough, plainspoken portrait of the tenuous nature of friendship and family in South Central Los Angeles. It was to be the first movie in a planned South Central trilogy. Singleton finished the second film, *Poetic Justice*, in 1993.

So why has it taken eight years to complete the trilogy?

The answer can be seen in the bedroom of Jody, the main character in Singleton's new South Central movie, *Baby Boy*. Jody (played by r&b singer and MTV personality Tyrese Gibson) is twenty years old and has fathered two children with two different women, but he still lives at home with his mother. Jody doesn't have a job, takes little to no responsibility for his offspring and spends much of his time alone in his bedroom, meticulously putting together model cars underneath a looming mural of rapper Tupac Shakur.

It's Singleton's riff on *The Great Gatsby's* eyes of T.J. Eckleberg, the figure that looked down from a giant billboard in F. Scott Fitzgerald's classic novel, observing and silently judging the actions of the book's characters. It's also Singleton's way of saying that if Jody doesn't get his act together, he could wind up dead just like Shakur.

"Pac was a Jody," Singleton says of the rapper, whom he directed in *Poetic Justice*. "He was a baby boy. You couldn't tell him anything."

Shakur was shot and eventually died from wounds suffered in a drive-by shooting near the Las Vegas Strip in September 1996. Several weeks before the incident, Singleton had run into Shakur at the Crenshaw Mall in Baldwin Hills and told him that he wanted him for his next movie, *Baby Boy*. Shakur

From the *Los Angeles Daily News* (June 29, 2001). Reprinted by permission of the *Los Angeles Daily News*.

had been signed to play the lead in Singleton's 1995 film, *Higher Learning*, before an arrest and jail time kept him from the project. Singleton was anxious to work with the rap star again, and the feeling was mutual.

"I was like, 'I've got the movie we're going to do together,'" Singleton remembers. "And he says, 'I'm with it.' And a few weeks later, he's dead. So I put the movie on the shelf. I figured no one is going to have enough heart and soul and ability to do it like Pac could. And no one did–until Tyrese came along."

In coming back to his old neighborhood, Singleton is returning to what he does best—surveying and commenting on the actions of mostly young, mostly impoverished African Americans. Unlike *Gatsby's* Eckleberg, there's nothing silent about Singleton's observations, and his movies' audaciousness have often upset various segments of the African-American community.

"The people that have the most problem with me are the conservative black people who look down on the people in the 'hood and think, 'Why do you have to show this?'" Singleton says. "And I don't really give a care about that. The only thing that can come out of telling the truth is some kind of change."

Baby Boy takes its name from the expression Singleton and others have used to describe young black men who thoughtlessly father children, but live off their mothers without giving a thought to looking for a job. Says the director: "They've all been raised by women, so they're always trying to show how much of a man they are when they really are baby boys. They have nothing going for them."

Adds Ving Rhames, who plays an ex-con elder statesman in the film: "We've got all these black families where the mother is trying to be both Mom and Dad. And that's just not the natural order of things. It's very hard for a woman to teach a boy how to become a man. So you end up with all these young men, growing up and not taking any responsibilities. It's killing black families. You definitely see that in this film."

But you see a lot more than that. While *Baby Boy* features a healthy dose of Singleton's Afro-centric political sentiments, the movie has plenty of character-driven comedy and a highly charged sexuality. The prominence given to the characters' love lives is no coincidence following Singleton's battles with producers and Paramount studio executives last summer while making *Shaft* with Samuel L. Jackson.

"I took all the sexual repression from that movie and put it into this film," Singleton jokes. "I'm still amazed that you could have a movie about the black private dick that's a sex machine to all the chicks and people wouldn't want him to have sex."

As for his new movie's humor, Singleton is equally outspoken. "It's ironic humor, like the kind of stuff Woody Allen writes," Singleton says. "You look at all these movies with black talent and it's all slapstick. It's sitcom stuff. My movie is funny as hell, but it's not a sitcom movie. It's ironic humor. You find the joke in what they're saying."

Obviously, Singleton isn't a man suffering from a crisis of confidence, even though his first movie, *Boyz N the Hood*, remains his most successful. It's easy to look at *Baby Boy* and view it as a retreat back to familiar turf after failed attempts to venture beyond South Central (*Higher Learning* and 1997's *Rosewood* both failed to find much of an audience), but Singleton says that, like Allen and Martin Scorsese, he's just returning to the neighborhood he knows.

While growing up, Singleton split time between his mother's apartment in Inglewood and his father's place at 101st and Vermont, the heart of South Central L.A. After a childhood spent taking the No. 204 bus from Vermont to Hollywood to see movies at the old theaters like the Chinese, Egyptian, and Cinerama dome, Singleton decided to become a director because he saw that "that was the person in charge." He wound up going to film school at USC, not far from where he spent much of his childhood.

"I went to school in my neighborhood where I was one of the only black people and people looked at me like, 'What the hell are you doing here?'" Singleton says. "It was an animosity. I was just so different. What gave me strength was that I was raised to be proud of who I was and where I was from. I hate it when black filmmakers say, 'I'm not a black filmmaker.' Look at everything that's cool about this country. It comes from black people. Why would you even go there?"

If the quality of Singleton's films has often failed to match his ambition and bravado, he has undeniably developed a consistent track record for discovering and fostering new talent. *Boyz* introduced Cuba Gooding Jr., Ice Cube, and Nia Long. *Poetic Justice* contains singer Janet Jackson's lone feature turn, and Don Cheadle won his first starring role in *Rosewood*. With *Baby Boy*, it's Tyrese Gibson's turn to make movie audiences' acquaintance.

"He's from Watts and he's got a lot of flavor and he's just one shade removed from the actual character," Singleton says of Gibson. "All he needed to do was get comfortable working in front of twenty-five people every day for four months."

Gibson, who is quite good in the film, admits making *Baby Boy* was a "humbling experience," adding that he often had trouble remembering his lines. Observes co-star Rhames: "He's got a lot of raw talent. He needs to cultivate it and take some acting classes."

Word, though, is already out about Gibson's performance. Denzel Washington is considering him for the lead of *The Antwone Fisher Story*, the true story of an embittered sailor who, through psychotherapy, comes to understand the roots of his rage and begins a search for the family that abandoned him. Washington will make his directorial debut with the movie.

On the day of a recent interview, Gibson was supposed to audition for Washington, but he begged off, saying he wasn't ready. Singleton was providing counsel.

"Tyrese is special," Singleton says. "I wasn't sure I was ever going to make *Baby Boy* until I met him. That's when I knew he could step into Tupac's shoes. And those are some big shoes to fill, you know?"

Rocking the Cradle

KRISTAL BRENT ZOOK/2001

W HEN   JOHN   SINGLETON—then a "bookworm" twenty-one-year-old film-school student, by his own description—made *Boyz N the Hood*, his saga about growing up in south-central Los Angeles, he was instantly catapulted into fame and fortune. Made for $6 million, *Boyz* eventually grossed more than $56 million in the United States, and it garnered rave reviews. Because of it, Singleton became, in 1992, the first African American and the youngest filmmaker to receive an Academy Award nomination for Best Director (plus a nod for Best Screenplay).

This week came Part 3 of what he calls his "hood trilogy" (1993's *Poetic Justice*, with Janet Jackson and Tupac Shakur, was number two), and in it Singleton returns to a signature theme: the cycle of doom that perpetually threatens to engulf the unwed black matriarch and her children.

Baby Boy opens with the disconcerting, hallucinatory image of a grown man surrounded by blood vessels, membranes, and fetal liquids. The umbilical cord still intact, he rests, at peace, inside his mother's womb. Juxtaposed is the undeniably manly voice of the character, played by Tyrese Gibson.

"There's this psychologist," his voice-over begins. "A lady named Dr. Frances Cress Welsing. She says . . . the black man is a baby. A not yet fully formed being, who has not yet realized his full potential." (Welsing, an African American, writes in her book *The Isis Papers* that this process happens "unconsciously" in response to the black mother's fear for her son's fate.)

Cut to an abortion clinic.

Now the same man, Jody, is assisting his grieving girlfriend into a car. This is not the first pregnancy to be terminated by the couple, and Yvette (Taraji P. Henson) and Jody are already raising a young son. Right after depositing

From the *Washington Post* (June 30, 2001). Reprinted by permission of Kristal Brent Zook.

"baby mama" number one in her apartment, Jody again takes to the streets, this time to visit baby mama number two across town.

Baby boy's final stop is his mother's home, to his own room (decorated with images of the late Shakur and a former Singleton flame, model Tyra Banks). Here Jody retreats into a favorite pastime: tinkering with low-rider model cars. Clearly, the film implies, it is time for Jody, twenty years old and unemployed, to grow up.

But Singleton is not a message man, he insists. "I hate that whole thing of being this guy who always has to—like I'm sticking a message down your throat," he says. "I'm not that guy at all. . . . Basically I'm here to like, you know, entertain people. And if they find something in it, then cool."

He continues: "When I made *Boyz N the Hood*, I was just really cathartically writing something about the way I grew up. And it's so funny because now every time I make a film, it has to have some kind of social commentary. That was never my original intention. My goal [with *Baby Boy*] was to try to make a film that was kind of like a rap album: audacious, young, brash . . . funky."

Singleton does acknowledge, however, that he makes "personal" films about subjects close to his heart. Economic empowerment and self-reliance, for example, is a favorite theme. (In *Baby Boy*, he even makes a cameo appearance as a video-selling entrepreneur.) But the central subject matter of this, his sixth film, is dysfunction, a word Singleton uses often when discussing the movie.

"You get stuck in a mentality," offers Omar Gooding, who plays Jody's friend Sweet Pea (Cuba Gooding Jr., who made his feature film debut in *Boyz*, is the actor's older brother), "and you have females who allow you to live off them." One of them being the baby boy's own mama.

On the one hand, Singleton pokes fun at Jody's predicament. Picture muscular Gibson tearing through town on a souped-up bicycle, for example, after Yvette in her car. But Singleton also seems intent on justifying how the baby boy came to be. "Black women are acting out of the dysfunction of a racist society that attempts to emasculate the black man," he explains. "Black people as a whole are . . . fighting more than they're communicating, [while] the women have to bear the burden for the whole community. They have to take care of the children, they have to work and take care of their men. . . . Some women give in to the whole dysfunction of that and say, 'Hey, you know, that's my man. I'm gonna roll with it.'"

Ving Rhames, who also stars in *Baby Boy*, says the film "deals with what I call psychological slavery. Because I can look at way back in the day [when the] white slave master'd get the big black buck and say: 'Look. Here's ten slave women. I want you to sleep with them, get them all pregnant. I'll give you a chicken for every baby you produce. You don't have to father that kid. You don't have to nurture the kid.' Jump to 2001, black men having babies, and where's the black man?"

Boyz N the Hood angered some feminist critics, who argued that the film demonized, yet again, the black matriarch. For many, it was a bitter reminder of the "Moynihan Report," issued in 1965 by then-Assistant Secretary of Labor Daniel Patrick Moynihan, a document that many in the black community saw (despite Moynihan's stated intent) as blaming low-income single mothers for the chaotic state of African American families. In *Boyz*, Angela Bassett's character is chastised by Laurence Fishburne's for not letting go of her baby boy. Another early prototype of the baby mama railed at her ten-year-old son: "You ain't [expletive]. You ain't gonna amount to [expletive]." And in one scene a neglected toddler wanders into the street while her mother peddles sexual favors for drugs.

Matriarchal blame is even more apparent in *Baby Boy*.

"In Jody's case," explains Henson, who plays Yvette, "his brother died, so. . . all of [his mother's] energies went into him. He was spoiled. He didn't have to be aware of anybody else. Because that's how Miss Juanita set his life up for him."

"These are babies having babies," says Adrienne-Joi Johnson, who researched her part as Juanita by talking to teenage mothers. "We're dealing with what happens now that they're growing up together . . . and trying to raise each other actually, with no guidance."

Henson, a native of Southeast Washington, confides that in playing Yvette she drew on her own experiences, recalling an abusive relationship that lasted eight years. "You know how sometimes you think you've gotten over something and, in actuality, what you've done is swept it under the carpet? Yvette is my hero, because she speaks up. In my situation, I wasn't able to speak my mind as she does."

When asked if this film, like *Boyz*, reflects the story of his life, Singleton looks slightly put off. "No, it's not autobiographical," he replies. "When I was twenty years old, I was at USC film school, you know?" And yet there are hard-to-ignore parallels. The film is, in part, about men having children with various women. When pressed, Singleton acknowledges that he has five children by four women.

"But that has nothing to do with my being a baby boy," he insists. "Those are two different things. [In the movie] we're talking about a twenty-year-old kid who's going through a dangerous rite of passage. He doesn't have the re-sources that I have, both economic and mental. . . . I'm a thirty-three year-old man," he adds. "With a job." Laughing, he adds: "I'm not walking around the mall with no shirt on, trying to talk to sixteen-year-olds."

Tosha Lewis, the mother of Singleton's oldest child, Justice, has garnered media attention in recent months with claims that the director was not pres-ent during the first three years of their daughter's life.

"That is a lie," responds Singleton, who adds that he is seeking full cus-tody of Justice. "You want to be real about it? This woman has been the bane of my existence because she's a scorned lover. She hasn't moved on, and it's been ten years. I'm man enough to admit that . . . dysfunctional relation-ships had to be explored," he adds. "You know, it is more the norm than the exception that these men and women are fighting."

Perhaps the most disturbing scene of *Baby Boy* is, in fact, a fight in which Yvette belittles and curses and hits Jody so persistently that the blow she finally receives in return feels inevitable. A jarring bedroom scene follows—sex as apology—accompanied by a montage of images in Yvette's mind: a fantasy wedding, an afternoon by the lake, an abortion, a funeral, prison.

What did Singleton mean to convey with such a scene?

"It's about her hopes," says the filmmaker. "And her worst fears if she con-tinues on in this relationship. A lot of women have told me that's the kind of thing they think about during sex."

In 1999, Singleton pleaded no contest to charges of assault and battery filed by Lewis. He was ordered by a Los Angeles Superior Court judge to un-dergo counseling and to make a short film against domestic violence. None-theless, he now calls the criminal charges "a lie, too." He adds, "I had to plead no contest just to get it off me."

The film Singleton was ordered to make is actually going to be about "vio-lent women," he says. "I'm a very passive guy, and I'm saying that there's this dangerous dysfunction that runs through all these relationships. No one would ever think that I was the one going through the abuse. So that's what my short film is going to be about."

Although Singleton says he did not want *Baby Boy* to have a "neat and tidy" ending, we last see Jody and Yvette as they were in the fantasy scenes: picnicking in the park, engaged and expecting another child.

"I felt that I at least needed to give this couple some hope," says Singleton. "At least I gave her a ring and they're probably going to get married. People can watch it and if they want to change their lives, they can change. Some people may look at it and are just happy to see themselves and their dysfunc-tion on the screen."

His fingers racing across an imaginary computer keyboard, he adds, "I wasn't thinking, 'I'm going to make a positive statement by doing this.' I just thought, 'I'm going to begin with an abortion and end with her pregnant again.' Why? Because it was inevitable."

With that, the director bursts into laughter. "They have sex constantly," he says. "It was inevitable."

Singled Out:
A Chat with Director John Singleton

DAN HEATON/2001

JOHN SINGLETON burst onto the scene in 1991 with the release of *Boyz N the Hood*, a powerful, touching tale of young life in South Central Los Angeles. Only twenty-four at the time, John became the youngest individual and first African American ever nominated for the Best Director Academy Award. He followed this success with a more low-key approach in *Poetic Justice*, then broadened his scope to a diverse college campus in *Higher Learning*. *Rosewood*'s historical tale of a real-life 1923 massacre represented his most impressive work to that point. In 2000, he undertook his first big budget project with an energetic remake of *Shaft*, starring Samuel L. Jackson.

John's most recent film is *Baby Boy*, the story of a young man struggling to face his responsibilities and become a man. This setting returns to South Central, the site of John's first two pictures, and represents his most accomplished work in terms of visual and emotional complexity. Released this past summer, *Baby Boy* stars Tyrese Gibson, A. J. Johnson, Ving Rhames, Snoop Dogg, Taraji P. Henson, and Omar Gooding. digitallyOBSESSED.com recently talked with John about his latest film, the DVD format, and his directing style.

DOC: *How did the story for* Baby Boy *originate, specifically in regards to the mother-son relationship?*
JOHN: It's just the converse of what went on in *Boyz N the Hood*. There's a lot more single-parent females trying to raise boys than there are men. So I felt "Why not do a story about that?"

From *DigitallyObsessed.com* (2001). Reprinted by permission.

DOC: *How did the opening womb image with the abortion arise?*
JOHN: It supports the theme of the whole film, with the young boy. I'm basically interested in the development, with trying to be a man. I felt that somehow I had to come up with some kind of defining opening image.

DOC: *You seem to do that pretty often, like with the stop sign in* Boyz N the Hood. *Do you think that's important to always have a really strong opening image?*
JOHN: Yeah, I think it's important to have strong images throughout the film. But with the opening image, if you can get the whole theme of the film, then you've got something. Like in the opening of *Jaws*, with the appearance of the shark. It's always affected me to see that.

DOC: *The characters in* Baby Boy *are very realistic, even more than in* Boyz N the Hood. *How have you matured as a writer over the years?*
JOHN: I think I've gotten more specific and more profound in the way in which I tell a story when I'm writing or directing. I'm more interested in showing the story than saying the story. I'm less interested in dialogue than I am in imagery.

DOC: *I noticed that in the way that the characters are placed within the frame. Can you discuss that, especially with the three: Melvin, Juanita, and Jody?*
JOHN: Yes, I use creative blocking to discuss thematically what's going on between the three of them. It's a love triangle.

DOC: *Can you discuss your writing process?*
JOHN: I just keep a journal and throw stuff in the journal and make notes for several years until I'm ready to write the script. Then I just throw the script out within a certain amount of time. I have so much material and so many notes.

DOC: Baby Boy *contains really strong female characters, which I think are actually the toughest in the film. Can you describe, especially in regards to Juanita, what your thoughts were as far as those characters?*
JOHN: Yes, I wanted to make these women that basically are holding up the whole community. They go through the burden of trying to take care of children and being moral supports for the men because the men have no power. They have no economic power; they have no power in the home. You see every guy moving into a woman's place and saying, "This is my house."

DOC: *You're constantly using new actors like Tyrese, Morris Chestnut, and Cuba Gooding Jr. Are you just looking for a fresh perspective?*
JOHN: I'm always looking for new faces. Always.

DOC: *You also use high profile music stars like Janet Jackson, Tupac, and Ice Cube. Is there a specific reason for this?*

JOHN: No, it just ends up that way. I like to use artists and performers, people who have some soul.

DOC: *The Tupac mural in Jody's bedroom is striking, almost like an angel watching over him.*

JOHN: Yes. His journey could possibly be Jody's journey.

DOC: *Tyrese Gibson and Taraji P. Henson have a great chemistry, especially in arguments where it doesn't feel like they're acting. What made you choose them for the roles?*

JOHN: They just did so well together in the audition process. It was inevitable.

DOC: *This was Tyrese's first film. You originally chose Tupac. What made Tyrese stand out with the qualities that Tupac had?*

JOHN: He was good looking, he had a lot of soul, and he had a lot of heart. I wanted a guy who girls would like, and he would do a lot of bad things, and they would still like him.

DOC: *How was it working with Snoop Dogg?*

JOHN: Oh, it was cool working with Snoop.

DOC: *He seems to be all over the place right now.*

JOHN: Yeah, he's a superstar.

DOC: *Let's talk about the music in your films. There's both older soul and hardcore rap songs. Being the music supervisor, how did you go about choosing them?*

JOHN: I just basically use music that I like, music that I wrote in the script and that was appropriate for the various scenes.

DOC: *How involved are you in the DVD releases of your films?*

JOHN: Very involved. I pick the artwork, I choose how the animation goes in it, and I choose what goes on the DVD. I'm very involved.

DOC: *Do you have approval over the image and the audio transfers?*

JOHN: Yes.

DOC: *How do you enjoy recording the audio commentaries?*

JOHN: I love it. I'm a fan of the whole format. I love taking part in it. I think it's great; it's for the people that really want to study the behind-the-scenes of the film.

DOC: *Do you have much of a DVD collection?*

JOHN: I have a huge DVD collection. I have thousands of DVDs.

DOC: *What are some of your favorites that you seem to watch all the time?*

JOHN: *Se7en.* I'm trying to think about which ones I really watch all the time because I have so many of them. The *Se7en* collection is really a good one, and the *Lawrence of Arabia* disc is very good.

DOC: Boyz N the Hood *was originally released without a commentary. Have you thought about going back and re-releasing it?*

JOHN: Yeah, we're doing a special edition of *Boyz N the Hood* coming out next year.

DOC: *In what way does DVD change your approach to filmmaking? Has it changed?*

JOHN: It hasn't, it's still the same. It's just that I know if I don't put everything in the movie, people will see it on the DVD.

DOC: *How much of* Baby Boy *reflects your own experiences growing up?*

JOHN: The characters reflect people I knew growing up in the neighborhood and people I know now.

DOC: *It seems that your films have a lot to do with parents and their roles.*

JOHN: I get into the non-traditional family mode with the characters in my films because I didn't grow up in a traditional family.

DOC: *The image of the garden appears to have a connection with where Juanita is going.*

JOHN: Yes. She's growing and she's healing. It's a whole new season for her in her life. Because she was a baby girl. She was a young mother.

DOC: *What originally made you decide to pursue a career in film?*

JOHN: The only thing I was very interested in growing up was movies.

DOC: *What movies really got you excited about film when you were a kid?*

JOHN: *Star Wars, E.T., Raiders of the Lost Ark*, basically those types of films when I was kid. And when I was in high school, I started going to revival theaters and seeing the work of Woody Allen, Martin Scorcese, and Stanley Kubrick.

DOC: *Can you talk about the origins of the buyer-seller discussion in* Baby Boy?

JOHN: That comes from just looking on the street and seeing how people are, and they can't get a job so they find something to sell.

DOC: *Who do you consider the major influences on your current directing style?*
JOHN: Kurosawa and Welles, very much Welles.

DOC: *Are there any current filmmakers that really catch your eye?*
JOHN: I like Soderbergh's work. I think he always does something interesting.

DOC: *You earned several Oscar nods for* Boyz N the Hood, *and they've pretty
much avoided you since. What are your opinions on the role of that show?*
JOHN: I don't really think about it that much, until it comes along.

DOC: *Spike Lee has said that he feels compelled to present a voice for the African-
American community similar to the Civil Rights movement. Do you feel compelled
in the same way?*
JOHN: No, I'm just speaking from the perspective of John Singleton. That's
all you can do.

DOC: *How was your experience making* Shaft?
JOHN: It was great. I had every toy that I needed to do the film.

DOC: *That's pretty different from your other work. Would you do it again?*
JOHN: Yes, of course. My next film will be like that. I might do a big adventure movie.

DOC: *Are you going to write that one too?*
JOHN: No, I'm going to hire someone else and just do the direction.

DOC: *What have you learned over the last ten years as a director?*
JOHN: I think I've learned to be more visual, to show the story instead of
telling the story. That's what makes a film.

An Interview with John Singleton

PHILLIP WILLIAMS/2001

WITH HIS NEW PICTURE, *Baby Boy*, writer-director John Singleton returns to his own backyard in South Central Los Angeles for an uncompromising look at the life of a handsome young African-American man, Jody (Tyrese), a case study in arrested development. Jody stands at the edge of adulthood, refusing to commit to the responsibilities of manhood; content to let others pick up the slack in his life. Bouncing between two women [with whom he has children], Jody still lives at home with mom. As screenwriter, Singleton hurls his protagonist one curveball after another, as friends, family, and the turbulent and often violent inner city world around him conspire to bring Jody across the threshold of manhood—if necessary, by force.

While ostensibly dealing with issues relevant to African-American families, *Baby Boy* addresses material that has clear universal resonance: commitment, family, and the fear of growing up. It's the coming of age story of a young man who refuses to come of age. Yet, one of the film's charms is the obvious affection that the director has for these characters, warts and all. It completes what Singleton calls his "Hood Trilogy," which includes *Poetic Justice* (1993) and *Boyz N the Hood* (1991). *Higher Learning* (1995), *Rosewood* (1997), and *Shaft* (2000) have kept him busy in between.

PHILLIP WILLIAMS (MM): *Can you talk about the origins of this movie; where the idea started for you?*

JOHN SINGLETON (JS): I came up with this film around the time I did my first film, *Boyz N the Hood*. I started thinking about different stories that I could do about South Central Los Angeles. It was called something else at

---

From *MovieMaker Magazine* (June 1, 2001). Reprinted courtesy of *MovieMaker Magazine* (www.moviemaker.com).

the time and the characters were different—I remember I was going to do it originally with Tupac [Shakur] as the lead. In fact, the last thing I said to Tupac before he passed was "I've got the movie we are going to do together." He was really excited and a couple of weeks later he was gone. So I put it away again. I didn't think I was going to be able to find the actor to play this part until Tyrese came along.

MM: *Would you consider* Baby Boy *a companion to* Boyz N the Hood?
JS: Yes, it's very much a companion to that film. Totally different characters, same environment.

MM: *How does your writing process generally work?*
JS: I write when I am inspired. If I come up with an idea, right then and there I'll write it on a piece of paper. I may write for hours at a time on a given day. I'll do a first draft in the course of three months. I just attack a story like that and pick at it until I get the first draft. Then I go back over it and figure out what matters in the story that I am telling and if I'm telling it in the clearest way; without a lot of dialogue. I try to tell the story visually.

MM: *Do you do an outline of your characters?*
JS: Yes, I do. I outline the characters and the set-up and I basically know where I want to end it.

MM: *What sort of research did you do for* Baby Boy?
JS: For *Baby Boy*, it was just talking to friends, talking to family, and life experience. I don't have to do much research for a film like this. It's casual research.

MM: Boyz N the Hood *felt like a very mature film for a first-time director. Which other moviemakers were influencing you?*
JS: At that time, probably Francis Coppola, Steven Spielberg, and Martin Scorsese.

MM: *Were there any films you were watching when you did* Boyz N the Hood?
JS: Luis Buñuel's *Los Olvidados* (1950) and Hector Babenco's *Pixote* (1981). I was looking at *Stand by Me* (1986) by Rob Reiner. I was looking at all these different movies—youth movies—from around the world and then applying that to South Central Los Angeles.

MM: *Was there anything specific you were picking up that was helpful?*
JS: The way the stories were told very simply; the director wasn't showing their hand. With *Boyz N the Hood*, my whole thing at the time, as a first-time filmmaker, was not to look like a first-time filmmaker. But it was literally the

first time I was behind the camera. I hadn't done anything with sync sound; I had only done Super8 films. So I studied *Citizen Kane*, everything I could about people who did films for the first time, and I learned that the successful ones didn't move the camera just for the sake of moving the camera. They moved the camera to serve the story. I tried to be very, very succinct in a way, and focused in the way I tell the story and not try to show how fancy I can be. I just move to move the story forward, to further the dramatic intent or the emotional intent of the story.

MM: *When you are writing, do you put less information and description in the scripts because you know that you are going to direct them?*
JS: I never put camera angles or any of that. I don't do that stuff. I was taught at school never to do that. I try to write the story as visually as possible, so when you are reading it, it lays itself bare.

MM: *Are there any screenwriters in particular that you like?*
JS: I took a lot from different writers: the early work of Larry Kasdan and Robert Benton—this is all when I was in school. I was a writing major, for films. Ernest Lehman and Woody Allen. I read a lot of different screenplays and wondered why the films were such great films. What makes these films work?

MM: *And what did you find out?*
JS: I picked up that the great thing about screenplays is that it's a film on paper and the less dialogue you have, nine times out of ten—unless it's a Woody Allen movie—the better the film. The more visual the film is, the better. I practice saying things without any words in my films.

MM: *Because of the experience you've gained in the film industry, how was the making of* Baby Boy *different than the making of your other films?*
JS: I was able to move faster and just cut to the chase. I have been doing this for eleven years, so I was more confident and, for some reason—shooting in my neighborhood—unencumbered. I had final cut and just did what I wanted to do.

MM: *Were there any surprise challenges on* Baby Boy?
JS: (laughing) Directing my one-and-a-half-year-old daughter.

MM: *How so?*
JS: Just getting her to do the things that I wanted her to do. It was very fun to have the whole crew around, holding her, telling her to laugh or smile or whatever. Sometimes she would do it, sometimes she wouldn't. There was

a time we decided, "Ok, we're not going to have her do it" because she was crying between each take—she would start crying in the middle of the takes. So we decided to get the double baby. So we had my daughter sit around and watch the double do it. My daughter got antsy, so we put her back in and she just did the take (laughs). She didn't want that double to do it.

MM: *Do you find yourself changing the script in rehearsals?*
JS: Very much so. I love to rewrite during rehearsals. I love to find out the organic base of a character and put it in the script.

MM: *Do you think the writing changes a bit when you know who the actors are going to be?*
JS: It does to a degree, but I had no idea who was going to be in *Baby Boy* when I was writing it.

MM: *Do you think that being the director of a film makes you a better writer?*
JS: Being a writer makes me a better director.

MM: *How so?*
JS: If it's not on the page, it's not in the film. You have to be sparse, not longwinded. You learn not to fall in love with a scene; you have to make it tight. I basically direct on the page.

MM: *Talk about the way you work with sound to support the story.*
JS: I really try to create what I call, instead of emulating reality, a hyper-reality. To take an ordinary moment and give it more of a hyper-realistic feel on the big screen in the way that it sounds, not only the way it looks.

MM: *So you might be using sounds that wouldn't naturally be there, but that work emotionally?*
JS: Let's say this guy is grabbing another guy and has him in a chokehold. Instead of just having him grunt, you put the sound of a little animal under there. You can't actually hear it, but you can feel it. Like a lion pouncing or something.

   Those are the things that we talk about all the time, in our spotting sessions: the sounds that are felt and not heard. They don't have to be heard to be effective, but they do have to be felt. The audience hears them but they don't know what they are. I learned that a long time ago in film school.

MM: *What do you think will surprise people the most about* Baby Boy?
JS: That it's really funny.

MM: *Did the comedy come about when you were writing the script?*

JS: It's something that was always there, but once we got the script done and started shooting it we found that the way the actors were playing these characters was just funnier than expected. When I say humor, I say humor in the sense that they are not trying to be funny, it's just the irony of it; it's an ironic humor. It's like the humor characters in a Woody Allen movie would have, except that this is an urban film. In a comedic movie you can tell that they are going for the laugh; with *Baby Boy* it comes more from irony.

Why We Make Movies:
Black Filmmakers Talk
about the Magic of Cinema

GEORGE ALEXANDER / 2003

FEW FILMS KNOCK ME out of my seat and haunt me for days. But John Singleton's first feature film, *Boyz N the Hood* (1991), was one of those films. The riveting, largely autobiographical, coming-of-age film about boys growing up in South Central Los Angeles brought me closer to young boys I knew from growing up but perhaps thought I didn't know so well but did nonetheless. Singleton's simple, honest portrayal of human life ignited a plethora of derivative urban films to follow, with few carrying the emotional intensity and integrity of *Boyz N the Hood*.

Boyz N the Hood garnered Singleton a place among the Hollywood elite, making him the first Black and the youngest person ever to be nominated for the Academy Award for directing in 1992. He also received an Oscar nomination for Best Screenplay.

A native of Inglewood, California, and a graduate of the University of Southern California School of Cinema, Singleton followed *Boyz* up with *Poetic Justice*, with Janet Jackson and Tupac Shakur; *Higher Learning* with Ice Cube; and *Rosewood*, with Ving Rhames. In 2000 came *Shaft*, with Samuel L. Jackson, which became Singleton's biggest box office success to date, grossing $70 million domestically. In 2001 came *Baby Boy*, starring Tyrese. The film is the final work of a trilogy of films dealing with urban Black young

From *Why We Make Movies: Black Filmmakers Talk about the Magic of Cinema* by George Alexander, copyright © 2003 by George Alexander. Used by permission of Broadway Books, a division of Random House, Inc.

men, which started with *Boyz* and was followed up with *Poetic Justice* (1993). He is currently at work on *Fast and the Furious 2* (2003) for Universal.

GA: *You grew up in Inglewood, California. Tell me about your childhood and the role movies played.*

JS: I was a latchkey kid, and I think I broke into movies because of that. My mother and father never married, but I was always close to both of them. My mother's apartment was adjacent to a drive-in theater called the Century Drive-in, which was an L.A. landmark, and I used to watch movies, including the slasher films, out of the back window of the apartment. And growing up, my father and mother would always take me to the movies. My mother actually took me to my first movie—*Rosemary's Baby*, but I was too young to remember. My father and I would always go to Hollywood to see the big films at Grauman's Chinese-Theater or the Egyptian. In the summer of 1977, when I was nine, he took me to see a film, but he didn't tell me what we were going to see, he just said that I'd like it. And the movie starts, the Twentieth Century Fox logo comes up, you hear the Fox theme song, then BOOM, it's the beginning of *Star Wars*, the opening of Episode IV. I remember the star cruiser coming down chasing a smaller ship and firing at it, and that was the defining moment for me. That's when I decided I wanted to be a filmmaker. I saw *Star Wars* about a dozen times over that next three years, and because I saw the movie again and again and again, I began to break down how a film was made. I learned that a film had to be written, shot and edited.

Another defining moment was watching Steven Spielberg on a late-night news program. I think he was discussing *Close Encounters of the Third Kind*, and I said, "Hmm, that's what a director is." At the time, I knew nothing about Black pioneers like Gordon Parks, Melvin Van Peebles, or Michael Schultz, whom I admire as a pioneer in studio filmmaking. I only knew about George Lucas and Spielberg. In elementary school I would take a notepad and draw slightly different images on each page and make these little animatics—little animated films on paper. My friend Aaron Spears and I would do this all the time from elementary school to junior high. But when I got to junior high I had problems because I wore glasses and I was picked on, but I wasn't about to be no punk. So I carried a box cutter to school, because this kid kept asking me for my money and my comic books. My dad worked at Thrifty's (the drugstore) as a manager, and they used box cutters at the store and I brought one from home. One day when this kid picked on me I slashed his jacket with the box cutter and I got suspended. When I came back to school they had a rule against bringing metal combs—cake cutters—to school, because they could be used as weapons, so this time I didn't bring a box cutter, it was just a comb to pick out my little afro. And this teacher saw me with the metal comb and he said, "Singleton, don't you realize you can't bring metal combs to school? Aren't you halfway intelligent enough to understand the rules?" So he took my comb and embarrassed me in front of the whole class and I threw it in his face and said, "Fuck you, motherfucker," and ran out of the school.

The next day I went from living with my mother to living with my father up the street on Century Boulevard. My friends in that neighborhood got up at 6:30 or 7:00 in the morning to take a school bus out to the San Fernando Valley where they went to school with all of these Jewish kids. My friend said, "They got all the white boys out there, you know, it's more fun and you don't have to worry about anything." So I got up early with my friend across the street and I walked to the bus stop with him, got on the bus, rolled out to the Valley and enrolled myself into that school. Janet Jackson also went to that school for a time, but I don't think she was there while I was there, but she came to visit. At my new school there were last names like Shapiro and Abramowitz, and that was my first time interacting socially with kids who weren't Black or Mexican. Actually, it was all very refreshing, because we all had the same interests—comic books and movies. A lot of the parents of the kids who went to this little public school, worked in the film business. The father of one of the kids in my class was a casting director who cast a lot of the movies in the seventies. So this kid would get to go to premieres for films like *Raiders of the Lost Ark* an *E.T.*

GA: *Lucky kid. Did he come back to school and tell you all about it?*
JS: Yeah, yeah. Because, see, in my neighborhood when we sat around talking about what we wanted to be when we grew up, everyone would say that they wanted to be a basketball player or a football player. When I'd say that I wanted to be a film director, they'd say, "Film director? What's that?" I'd tell them and they'd say, "Ain't no white people gonna let no Black people make no damn movies." I would get dashed, but at my school in the Valley, I could be a film geek, I could love movies, I could love comic books. We'd go to all types of movies. In my neighborhood Kung Fu movies were popular, and I had a very good friend named Carl Austin—Carl was significant, because in eighth grade when *Blade Runner* (1982) came out, he bought the Phillip K. Dick novelization of the film, which was called *Road Warrior*, and gave it to me to read. These cheap novelizations were basically just the screenplay transposed into novel form, and Carl would always read the novels quickly, then let me borrow them. He also gave me Syd Field's *The Screenwriter's Workbook*.

GA: *So you were exposed to Syd Field very early.*

JS: Yeah, *Screenplay* by Syd Field and *The Screenwriter's Workbook,* and all Carl and I would talk about was making movies. He'd get these books about the making of *Star Wars* and we would read about *Raiders of the Lost Ark* and how Spielberg used storyboards and everything. I had no film equipment but the kids in the Valley all had 8mm cameras and were shooting shit. I didn't have any of that shit; all I had were my animatic storyboards. So I went to that school for a year, then my father suggested that we move in with my grandmother out in La Puente, and I cried like a baby. I really wanted to go back to that school, because all of those cats who went to the school in the Valley were from different cultures, and one thing I learned from them was to be proud of where you're from. On weekends the Jewish kids studied Hebrew and the Japanese kids studied Japanese, and for African Americans it's important to be proud of our music, our heritage, and our culture. That's why I want my kids to be proud of being Black and to know that we built this country.

GA: *When did you start taking your filmmaking dreams seriously?*

JS: At Eisenhower High in California, I really began to get serious about my future, and whether or not I was going to go to college and I ended up writing film criticism for the school newspaper and I'd get preview passes to movies. I wrote reviews of *The Breakfast Club* (1985), *Ladyhawke* (1985), *Mask* (1985) and *Sixteen Candles* (1984). I also remember complaining to my mother during this time. I said, "I'm bored, I don't have nothing to do. I need some money." She said, "You're bored, why don't you take your ass over to South Pasadena and go to that old theater? They show old movies." So I started hanging out at this theater called the Rialto, and the first thing I saw there was Woody Allen's *Bananas* (1971), then *Annie Hall* (1977), and then I saw *A Clockwork Orange* (1971).

GA: *Kubrick, huh? That's heavy stuff.*

JS: Yeah, films were an escape from delinquency for me. Like François Truffaut, who said that films saved him from being a delinquent, films saved me from being a delinquent. The great epiphany for me was when I realized that all of the films that I went to see were basically big Hollywood movies. But in high school I got interested in art films and different forms, different types of cinema, when I realized that I could bring a lot of my own culture to my work and that's what would make me unique. During the summer between eleventh and twelfth grades, I took an 8mm cinematography class at Pasadena City College, and this was my first time using film equipment, and I learned about exposures and lenses and started shooting stuff.

GA: *And you eventually decided to go to film school at USC. How did your parents feel about your wanting to be a filmmaker?*

JS: My mother and father didn't really want me to go into film, they wanted me to go into business. My father said, "Go into real estate or go to business school." My mother's response was "Oh, shit!" Because in any family one generation works hard and the next generation wants to be artists. I don't know where you're from, but when you say that you want to be a writer most parents say, "Aw, man, how are you going to eat off of that? You're going to be coming and opening up my refrigerator and letting the cold out."

GA: *[Laughs] Of course, no one really encourages it.*

JS: Yeah, but before I went to film school, my mother had become friends with a woman in Pasadena named Tracy Willard, who had gone to Spelman College. Tracy was in charge of this NAACP film program, and I entered one of my 8mm films that I'd made at Pasadena City College to the program. My films were always controversial, even then. This film was about a Black dude who's so bent out on this blond girl that he kills himself over her. I don't think that went over too well with the NAACP. [Laughs]

GA: *[Laughs] I wonder why.*

JS: So I didn't get an award for it, but Tracy said that she liked my work and that I reminded her of a friend named Spike who went to Morehouse when she was at Spelman. She told me that he'd just made a movie, he'd be coming to L.A., and that I should meet him. And she gave me a flier for a *She's Gotta Have It* preview screening, and I asked my mom if I could borrow the car to go and hang out and meet this guy, but she wouldn't let me borrow the car. She figured it was an adult movie and she didn't want me going out there, hanging out with all of these suspicious Hollywood types. I later found out that the film had gone to Cannes, got an award and was coming out in August. It was the summer of 1986, and I went to see Kurosawa's *Ran* at a theater in Santa Monica, and a trailer came on that played the beat to the rap song *Set It Off*, and here was Spike Lee on the screen saying, "Tube socks, tube socks, tube socks. Wanna buy tube socks? I wanna tell you about my new movie, *She's Gotta Have It*. And I said, "That's the guy Tracy was talking about!" When the film came out, they showed it in a theater in Santa Monica and there were all these Black people going to see it on opening day, and I went out there, and who was in the front of the theater passing out buttons and talking to people? Spike. I said, "Hey, you know Tracy Willard? My name is John Singleton and I'm going to film school in two weeks, Tracy was trying to hook us up. I'm really looking forward to seeing your movie." I go in to see the movie, and I thought, "Wow! Black people on the screen acting like real Black people." I'm blown away, loving it, and so I came out of the theater afterwards—I'll never forget this. People always say that Spike is ornery and antisocial sometimes, whatever, but I'll always give him love for this. After the movie, all of these Hollywood types were surrounding him, and I walked out of the theater and was trying to get to him in the crowd, and he moved everyone aside and came to me and said, "What'd you think of the movie?" And I told him that I really liked it and was happy he'd made it, and I said, "I'm going to film school, watch out for me." [Laughs] It's a classic story.

GA: *Definitely a classic.*

JS: And so every year for the next four years, from *She's Gotta Have It* to *School Daze* to *Do the Right Thing*, I'd see Spike on his promotional tours, I'd go to his book signings and say hello and he'd ask me what was going on with me and how I was doing in school. And I was like, "Damn, I want to be like this guy, right?" But then something keyed into me because all the white boys at USC wanted to be like Spielberg and Lucas and they were telling me that they (the industry) were only going to let one Black person in the film business, and I used to be like, "Fuck all ya'll!"

GA: *You also later met actor Laurence Fishburne. Tell me about that?*

JS: Well, I got my first paying job in the business as a production assistant/security guard on a television show called *Pee Wee's Playhouse*, and I was cheese grinning because I was on a studio lot. My first day, this guy walked up to me and spoke, and we introduced ourselves and he said, "You can call me Fish." And we ended up grabbing coffee and donuts. And I said, "Wow, you're Larry Fishburne." Man! Larry, coffee, donuts? And so he came out to the stage periodically and we'd talk, and I'd tell him that I was going to be a filmmaker one day and that I might write something for him. And he said, "How old are you?" I told him that I was nineteen, and he said, "Go on, brother." And he gave me his number and everything and I went to school and I kept going to school and I kept looking at movies, and I really realized that the cheapest way to make a movie was to write a movie. If you don't have a pot to piss in, you can get paper and pen and you can write a movie. I also read a lot of screenplays, and I realized that your screenplay can't be boring to the reader. You have to write the screenplay so it's enjoyable to read. If you write your own movie, then you're not at the mercy of getting or finding a script. You can write your own script. That's the most powerful thing to have in this business—the ability to generate new ideas—I tell my kids that all the time. So I wrote a screenplay called *Twilight Time*, about these five women who get together for their mother's funeral and in cleaning up her house, discover that she wasn't such a good person at all. She was a real ornery chick. For it, I won the Jack Nicholson and the Robert Riskin Awards at USC. After that, I started making the rounds to agencies, but no one wanted to sign me and I was getting frustrated because I wanted to quit school for a while and go to Brooklyn to work on *Do the Right Thing*, but Spike's company 40 Acres didn't hire me. Thank God they didn't, right?

GA: *Yeah. Why did you want to quit school?*
JS: Because at the time, which was 1989, I was feeling a little resentful because I really wanted to make it happen. It was the best time. It was the golden age of hip-hop music—you had everyone from KRS-One, Eric B and Rakim, and Public Enemy was coming out. In L.A. the hottest group on the streets was NWA (Niggaz with Attitudes), and Ice-T was out here, the whole gangsta style was coming in. And as adverse as I was to growing up in gang-ridden streets and having to deal with all that bullshit, and the stress from real life, I saw what was happening and I said, "I'm gonna write about my experiences." And I got the title for my script *Boyz N the Hood* from the song off of Eazy-E's album, "Eazy Duz It," which was written by Ice Cube.

And that summer I went to a preview screening of *Do the Right Thing* and I came out of the theater and said, "I'm gonna make my fucking movie, watch this." That was June, and I started making my notes for the screenplay, and that fall I wrote *Boyz N the Hood*. I sat in the computer room at USC and I just started writing the script. I was basically doing what they said in film school that we should do—write what you know. I wanted to put L.A. on the fucking map. Spike was doing it in Brooklyn and I was going to do it in L.A. That was my whole mantra, and I would sit and listen to NWA and Eazy and write. When I pitched the script in class, I got up and said, "My script is called *Boyz N the Hood*. It's about South Central L.A. where you hear automatic gun fire and helicopters in the distance, it's about three boys growing up. It's my magnum opus. This is the movie I was born to make."

That year, I won the Jack Nicholson Award for a second time and started to get some notice. At the time I was interning at Columbia Pictures reading these stupid scripts, and I told Karen Teicher, who was in charge of the internship program, that I was a writer and she asked to see some of my work. So I gave her a copy of *Twilight Time*, and she liked it and I told her that she had to read *Boyz*. She read it, loved it, and asked me what I wanted to do with it, and I told her that I was going to direct it. She gave it to her boss, who said that he didn't think they could let me direct it. But Karen had some friends who were agents, and she gave them the script and set up some meetings, including meetings at CAA [Creative Artists Agency] and William Morris. I went to the CAA meeting, and a guy named Brad Smith was there and some other agents, and they said that they wanted to sign me. And I had adopted this kind of cool reserve about anything I was excited about and said, "Okay." But then the excitement hit me and I said, "I'm in film school and I got an agent! The top agency in Hollywood. CAA?! Mike Ovitz?!" So you can't tell me shit now. I'm a senior at USC, I'm represented by CAA, I'm Black, and they all hate me anyway because I'm the one on campus who plays loud music in the middle of campus, and thought: "Fuck all ya'll. I have something to talk about." That was my attitude, and I guess what got me through USC—that pre-dominantly white university—was the fact that I had something to prove. I had to prove that our stories were worth something and that was a combination of what was going on in hip-hop at the time and the fact that we were into it, because not a lot of white kids were listening to hip-hop then, or watching Spike and Robert Townsend's films. Eddie Murphy was at the height of his fame and stuff, but it was still small in comparison to what was happening in the mainstream. There was no real Black Hollywood.

GA: *What happened after you signed with CAA? Did you start taking meetings in Hollywood?*
JS: Yeah, my first meeting in the film business was a lunch meeting with Jasmine Guy, and I sat with her at a coffee shop, and she was talking about how she wanted to do the Dorothy Dandridge story, and I asked her to let me write something for her. I'm sitting there thinking to myself "I'm sitting here with fucking Jasmine Guy," and I go in the middle of campus and [snaps his fingers] tell some cats that I'd just had a meeting with Jasmine Guy and these niggers didn't believe me. Later, I ended up meeting with Russell Simmons. Now, there are different versions of this story, but this is the right version. I had a meeting with Russell, who was looking at doing a production deal with Columbia Pictures because he was thinking about getting in the film business. Stan Lathan [the producer/director] had read *Boyz N the Hood* and loved it, and he told me that I had to pitch it to Russell. So I went to the Mondrian Hotel up on Sunset where Russell was staying, and he's from New York and was standoffish, and had the attitude "prove yourself to me" or whatever. And I told him that the script was about L.A., and he wanted me to pitch it to him, and I said, "I don't need to pitch it to you, man. This is L.A., you're from New York, you wouldn't get this." I was basically just being as standoffish as he was. And so I said, "I tell you what, you know how in *Jaws* before the shark comes you hear the music 'DONNUM, DONNUM'? Well, before

there's a drive-by you hear the booming sounds of this car going by and you know something's going to happen." Then Russell keyed in and said, "I'm doing the L.L. Cool J album, *The Boomin' System*. I get that, I get that." And he wanted to read the script, and at the time there was an airline called the MGM Grand that flew from L.A. to New York, and Russell took that back to New York and read *Boyz N the Hood*, and flipped the fuck out. He said, "This is the best fucking script I've ever read in my life!" He calls Columbia, "You stupid white motherfuckers. This is the first script I want to produce; this is the best script I've ever read." And the folks at Columbia said, "*Boyz N the Hood*? Didn't John Singleton the intern write that script? Where is it? Where is it?" I had to call my agent at CAA, and my agent didn't want to give it to them because he wanted to hold on to it for himself, but we had already given it to all of these different production companies and none of them wanted to do it. They weren't feeling it.

But eventually a woman named Karen, who headed up the internship program, got the script to Stephanie Allaine, who was a creative executive at Columbia and the only Black working at the studio who could speak to the powers that be. And Stephanie thought that the script was phenomenal and tried to get Columbia to make it, but they didn't want to make it. She took the script to G-Peck, which was Guber Peters. Jon Peters was running Sony, and he and Peter Guber had their own production company at the same time they were running the studio, and they said that they wanted to do it for $5 million. If they didn't want to make it, Stacy Snider at Universal Pictures said that she wanted to make it.

So now after G-Peck decided that they would make it, Columbia decided that it would do it and wanted to meet with me. So I get my biggest meeting ever, with Frank Price and Michael Nathanson at Columbia. I came in wearing jeans and a Public Enemy T-shirt and acting like I was a bigwig but was really the smallest person on the street and had just caught the bus there, right? And they said, "So we liked your script and you want to direct it?" I said, "Yeah, I'm gonna direct it." And he asked me what I thought if they'd pay me $150,000 for the script and had someone else direct it. And I said, "Well, then, we'd have to end this meeting, because I'm directing this movie," and they asked me what made me think I could direct it. I said, "Because this is the movie I was born to make. It won't cost a lot of money. Instead of renting helicopters in the scenes where the helicopter flies over South Central, I'll use sound and light. I'll let light go past the window and put in the sound. I know who I want in the movie, and I'm gonna make this movie." I ended the meeting, and Frank Price used to say that I had more chutzpah than any other young person he'd met since Steven Spielberg.

GA: *[Laughs] He was probably right. You were pretty gutsy.*

JS: So my agent called me and told me that Columbia wanted to make *Boyz N the Hood*, they wanted me to direct it, and then I got scared. I also got my first office ever, in the Irving Thalberg Building at Columbia. Irving Thalberg was a movie mogul at a young age, so that was phenomenal for me to get my first office in that building, since I was only twenty-two at the time. And they say that it's great to operate from fear sometimes because you learn so much very quickly. I was very cavalier about being a filmmaker before, but I was really scared as hell because I had to fucking prove myself, so I just started watching movies upon movies and movies to figure out how I wanted to direct the film.

GA: *What movies did you watch?*

JS: I watched *Drugstore Cowboy*, *The Color Purple*, some Kurosawa films, and a lot of Coppola's work, because the first call I made was to Fish [Laurence Fishburne]. I sent Fish the script and he said, "Oh, this is beautiful, this is so beautiful. I was crying at the end." He told me that he wanted to do it and asked me if I could just add some more scenes with the father.

GA: *[Laughs] His part, eh?*

JS: Right, an actor's response.

GA: *How did you go about working with actors, since this was your first film?*

JS: I would ask Fishburne how Coppola rehearsed his actors, and Fishburne would tell me everything that Coppola did on the four or five films that he worked on with Francis, starting with *Apocalypse Now*. I would do acting exercises with the actors that had everything to do with the characters but had nothing to do with the movie. I dealt with the characters' past, present, and future and did some improvisation.

GA: *How did you run your set that critical first week?*

JS: The first day of production I'm shooting in my old neighborhood, in the Bottoms in Inglewood. In the movie you'll see my old neighborhood. I got to the set at five in the morning, the call time was 6:30 or 7:00 A.M. and there was fog everywhere and it's one of the worst neighborhoods in L.A. and I'm there early in the morning, I'm standing there shivering—not shivering because it's cold, I'm shivering because I'm nervous. Then I saw the trucks come and all the people arrive, and I said, "Okay, let's do it, I need the kids over here, I need you guys to start walking, rehearse. I'd look at the shot and they'd rehearse the shot. The first shot in the movie was the most basic of shots—it was a tracking shot with four little kids, and the main character,

Tre, is basically standing on the curb waiting for his friends to get there. His friends walk into the shot and they start walking. It's the first shot I ever shot in a movie ever. I went through the whole day shooting, and people were coming out of their apartments, people I hadn't seen since elementary school. They said, "John? What are you doing here?" And I told them I was directing a movie. And they said, "You're directing a movie?"

So we'd do scenes and stuff and there'd be about two hundred people standing to the side, and I'd yell, "Cut," and everybody in the neighborhood would yell, "Yay! Hooray!" And I'm on a roll, I'm shooting a movie, but I'm learning how to direct a movie while directing a movie. I shot most of the movie in continuity, which you never get a chance to do. But Steve Nicolaides, being the good producer that he was, knew that I had to basically shoot part of the film in continuity [the scenes shot in the order of the script, which is unusual], because I was new at it. So the film becomes a better film as it goes along, because I was becoming a better filmmaker day-to-day. I'd be up at two o'clock in the morning, making shot lists and figuring everything out in advance, the nuances and everything, and just poring over the whole thing. I had an outward appearance of confidence, but inside I was nervous for the first week and a half, but once I started watching the dailies, I was cool.

GA: Boyz N the Hood *was also accepted to the Cannes Film Festival in France, right?*

JS: Yeah, we got accepted to the Cannes Film Festival, and Spike had *Jungle Fever* there as well, and it was interesting, because my career was really getting started and Spike was going through some messy stuff with another Black director. It was just that whole nigger backbiting shit. Spike and I went to dinner the first night I was in Cannes and we later had lunch on the beach. We'd only known each other peripherally before, because I was in school and he was doing his thing, but then we sat there and we made a pact to never backbite each other in the media. We had a kind of mutual admiration because we both went to film school, and I'm not an elitist person or anything, I'm from the hood, but when you study your craft? When you study this shit? You really realize the strength of having knowledge about the past, and not only film form and film content and what filmmakers have done well, but you also study what they didn't do well and use it to do your own thing. It makes you a better filmmaker. To this day, Spike and I are so cool. I have a natural admiration for what he's accomplished, and it was really cool for us to sit down and talk candidly back then. At that time he was like a big brother to me, and I would say, "I want to grow up and be like you."

GA: *Let's talk about your hip-hop influence on movies?*

JS: I'm the first-generation hip-hop filmmaker. I was eleven years old when *Rapper's Delight* came out, so I've grown up with hip-hop, If you look at all of my movies, they're hip-hop films, because they have a different sensibility than the films from the filmmakers who came before me, like Melvin Van Peebles, Gordon Parks, Michael Schultz, Spike, and Eddie Murphy. These people really made inroads into this business. And I mentioned Eddie Murphy because of his phenomenal success as an actor. All of these people who came before me opened the door for me to be able to do what I do in the way that I do it. Nobody's doing it the way I do it even now, because there's a certain mind-set when you choose to do things on your own terms and to not act like you're happy just to have your foot in the door. I've never been like that. So I'm basically a brat, because the first thing I directed, *Boyz N the Hood*, was so phenomenally successful that it all led from there, and I've had varying degrees of success since I started doing my thing. When I sit in a meeting with a bunch of executives who just happen to not be Black, I'm thinking, "I'm gonna do what the fuck I want to, because I've been doing it this way and I've been successful." Why am I going to take your suggestion? I'll be polite, if it's good and constructive criticism, I'll do it, but I'm gonna do what the fuck I want to do. [Laughs]

GA: *After* Boyz N the Hood *there were a lot of other "hood" films, but none of the derivative films seemed to have the emotional fortitude of* Boyz. *Why?*

JS: I like that, emotional fortitude. I'm gonna write that down. From an emotional standpoint, when I wrote *Boyz N the Hood*, I was writing about myself. All of these other people were doing it in reaction to wanting success or because they had an excuse to put out a soundtrack. When *Jaws* was successful three or four *Jaws* movies were made, and it's the same thing. Whenever anything is successful in Hollywood, it's appropriated.

GA: *How were you able to transfer strong emotions to the page?*

JS: I don't know, man. I just remember writing the script for *Boyz N the Hood* crying at the computer and smiling. I was writing about my life, about how I was ornery towards my mother when I was twelve years old and she sent me to live with my father, and how that changed me. My father gave me responsibilities and basically said that I was going to take out the trash, wash dishes, and wash my ass. I was going to be a man. And he said, "I'm teaching you these things because all your little friends across the street don't have a daddy to teach them and you're going to see how they end up." So I basically just poured my life out. Right now I'm writing a script called *Flow*—about a young guy who makes a lot of money very quickly and his reaction to it. There're some personal things that I had to deal with when I had a change of lifestyle, and I can put that in the script. So I'm always trying to write from the heart, and that's what I think people key into.

GA: *How did it feel to be nominated for the Oscar the first time you directed a movie and to be the first African American director and the youngest person ever?*

JS: It was good, but at the time I couldn't really enjoy it, because I was very nervous about so much adulation so soon and I felt that I had to get another movie made quickly. The great thing about that was when I was nominated for the Oscar I was already in preproduction on *Poetic Justice.*

GA: *Did the early success put pressure on you to perform at that level again?*

JS: Until *Shaft,* I don't think I made a film where I didn't feel like I had to say something—I didn't know *Boyz* was going to be such a powerful thing—I felt that I had to do something powerful every time.

GA: *What inspired you to do* Rosewood?

JS: I met the survivors of the town of Rosewood, Florida, and they told me their stories and when someone in their seventies or eighties tells you that they saw their whole family killed, it's just so humbling. I was actually prepping another movie at the time—*Makes Me Wanna Holler,* based on Nathan McCall's book, which I had the rights to. I still want to make that film. I just felt that at the time I had to make *Rosewood.* A lady from Rosewood told me, "Baby, either you're gonna do this movie or Steven Spielberg's gonna do it."

GA: *But the film didn't perform well at the box office.*

JS: Warner Brothers basically shelved the movie. They were ashamed they made the film, and wouldn't even let me take it to the Baptist convention and show it to all the ministers so they could talk about it in their churches.

GA: *Why didn't they get behind it?*

JS: Because no one wants to hear about the Black struggle. You hear about the struggles of all different kinds of people, but it's like trying to get Germans to do a movie about the Holocaust in Germany. They don't have any empathy for that, because in the back of their minds some of them are very ashamed of what happened.

GA: *So why would they invest money to make the movie but not promote it?*

JS: I don't know. It was fucked up. I could have done a lot to promote it, and after a while I figured it's not my $30 or $40 million.

GA: *How'd you actually convince them to actually make it, though?*
JS: It really wasn't a struggle to get the film made, because Jon Peters, who later produced *Ali*, was a big powerhouse producer, so he got it made.

GA: *It seems that Blacks avoid films with difficult subject matter like* Rosewood. *Why is that?*
JS: The fallacy of African Americans in this country, and I say this with all my heart and soul, is that unlike Jews, Chinese, or Japanese or anybody, we don't lecture on the things that we've struggled through to make us stronger. We've gone through so much in this country to get to where we are today that every Black person should want to fucking read. Everyone should want to be a fucking genius, because it was illegal for us to learn how to read. We should never celebrate ignorance, because it was once illegal for us to have any type of knowledge at all. It's a case of our accepting that we're still being oppressed. Everybody's fucking oppressed, but rise above it. But *Rosewood* was a good experience for me, because I didn't make it to make money, but because I thought it was the right thing to do. Plus, what better way to get the monkey off my back about being the "urban" filmmaker than to do something radically different?

GA: *It's a disturbing film, but I highly recommend it. Why* Shaft?
JS: After *Rosewood* I felt like I needed a hit. In this business you're only one movie away from being out in the street. *Shaft* was one of my most successful films financially, and it was a big Hollywood movie and my first movie with a movie star—Samuel L. Jackson.

GA: *What are your hopes for Black cinema?*
JS: I'm trying to move Black cinema back into having something to say. Right now they're making these stupid-ass comedies. I don't want to blast anybody, but people know what they do is marginal and they know what they could do if they aspired to something more. You can make us laugh without having a minstrel show.

GA: *What are your favorite films?*
JS: Kurosawa's *The Seven Samurai, Jaws, Citizen Kane, E.T.: The Extra-terrestrial, Raiders of the Lost Ark,* and the first *Star Wars* and *The Empire Strikes Back.* And then *A Clockwork Orange, Annie Hall, The Godfather.* And I love westerns like *Red River.* They're the most American of movie conventions, and every movie I've done references westerns.

GA: *During the Jazz Age a lot of the Black musicians collaborated on projects, and many hip-hop artists collaborate today. Why don't we see the same in film?*

JS: Because everyone is out for themselves. When it does happen, it's beautiful: Denzel, Wesley, Sam, all of the huge stars who are working right now have done their best work with Black filmmakers. The relationship that Denzel and Spike have is phenomenal. Every movie that they've ever done together has been the best that either of them has done. Spike and Denzel did *Mo' Better Blues, Malcolm X,* and *He Got Game.* Look at those three performances from Denzel. But everyone is out for his own, and what I hate about this business is how it serves to keep successful Black people apart and how it serves to keep Black stars from working with hot Black directors.

GA: *And how's that?*

JS: It's just that some Black filmmakers have their agents and their managers telling them that they shouldn't do this movie or whatever. But Denzel Washington is a smart actor. On *Training Day,* Denzel said that he wanted Antoine Fuqua to direct. Antoine Fuqua hadn't had a hit, but he said he wanted Fuqua, and that helped Denzel and it helped Antoine's career. And I predicted that he would get his first Best Actor Academy Award, and he did. It's a beautiful thing, and that is the way it should work, because everybody looks out for each other in this business, and Black people need to do the same thing, and this is what I've been about since day one. I don't get on my soapbox and preach, I just do it, but none of these fucking stars, none of the actors that I've ever helped make a star have ever called me up and said that he's got this project, why don't we work together? We're both going to get paid [Laughs], and we're probably going to get paid more by collaborating. But none of those people have ever called me up. That's why every movie I make I invent new monsters.

GA: *If we could see more collaboration between Black directors, producers, and actors, Black cinema might really soar.*

JS: But look at it, man, the big thing in this business is when successful people collaborate, and that doesn't happen that much, but when it does happen, it's beautiful. Look at what Sam Jackson and I did with *Shaft.* We want to do another movie, and when that happens, it'll be powerful.

GA: *There's something about the psychology of Black men that is understood between each other; the subtext is understood.*

JS: Yeah. Because when they're acting on their own and it's a white director, no matter what the director's great intention, they're on their own. They're directing themselves.

GA: *How does fatherhood affect your creativity?*

JS: I have five kids, and fatherhood's made me a better filmmaker, it's given me more patience, and it's made me more compassionate. I thought that fatherhood was going to make me more conservative, more risk adverse and everything, but it's made me even more radical, because I want to try different things that excite me.

GA: *What advice do you have for aspiring directors?*

JS: Write your own scripts. That's the cheapest way to learn how to make a movie.

2 Fast 2 Furious:
An Interview with John Singleton

WILSON MORALES/2003

AFTER DIRECTING *Baby Boy*, the third film of the South Central films he's done (*Boyz N the Hood, Poetic Justice*), John Singleton is taking a break from hard-hitting subjects to do something fun and exciting. In his first PG-13 film, John Singleton is directing *2 Fast 2 Furious*, the sequel to the blockbuster hit *The Fast and the Furious*. In an interview with blackfilm. com, he talks about his input to the film and having musicians/rappers in his films.

WM: *Was the film fun to do?*
JS: It was definitely fun to do. The cool thing about this movie was that it was like hanging out with some good friends for eight months in a sexy city like Miami. We were working seven days a week but it didn't feel like a job.

WM: *Were there any concerns about doing the sequel?*
JS: No. At first I had concerns, but at the same time I thought that if I have to make a new movie I might as well make it as new as I can. Change it all up with a whole new cast and new cars and new location. Basically it's a whole different kind of film in the way that it is shot and the way that it looks, and in the way that in feels. There's more humor.

WM: *Can you talk about the casting of Tyrese?*
JS: Tyrese came on because the head of the studio, Stacey Snider, got a 35mm print of *Baby Boy* the opening day. She said we had to do something with this kid. She had the head of production call me when Vin (Diesel) fell out of the sequel to *The Fast and the Furious* and they said they wanted my

---

opinion on my putting Tyrese in the film. I told them to watch 'cause he's gonna be a huge star. I believed in him from the beginning. They asked if I would direct the film if he agreed to be in it. I said yes and that's how it happened.

WM: *Was it difficult to shut down South Beach while you shot several scenes there?*
JS: We didn't shut down South Beach at all. A lot of this movie is not even in South Beach. It's in different parts of Miami that you really don't see as much.

WM: *How much of the filming was CGI?*
JS: A little bit. There's some in the first race and there's a couple in the second race that's CGI, but a lot of it is practical shots with this thing called "mick-ray," basically a truck with a car shell mounted on it. The guys would drive for real because it's always good to see the actors do it. When Paul is doing a 180 car spin, he had to rehearse that several times. Some of this you can't create with CGI. It needed to look realistic.

WM: *Did you do research for this before you started shooting?*
JS: I did a lot of research. I learned a whole lot while I was making the picture. It was a great learning experience for me. I've always wanted to do a film where I can basically plan out a whole lot of stuff and be creative. Most of things I've done have been hard-hitting dramatic pieces, so I wanted to do something that was really more like an action adventure film.

WM: *Some of the action car scenes were similar to those scenes we see in video games. Were any games an influence to shooting those scenes?*
JS: Yeah, funny how you were able to pick that up. When I was formulating the way I wanted to shoot the film, I watched a lot of Japanese anime, and I watched *The Road Warrior* over and over again, which I feel is the best car movie ever made. I played a couple of video games where it allowed me to free my mind and shoot something different from the traditional way. I also played with "hot wheels" on my desk and I thought about how a camera can shoot this from different angles. I would come up with these cool ideas and then draw them out and put them in a sequence and then figure out how we would do this. It was cool for me because my whole goal for this movie was that from the beginning of my career I was only concerned about being a real serious filmmaker. I wanted to be taken seriously so that when I make a movie, it means something. I got this monkey of being too serious a filmmaker and saw all these cats coming out of the music world getting these cool jobs and I thought about not always doing serious pictures while these

guys are getting the fun work. So I was like "I'm going to do some popcorn work and make a film that's going to make a lot of money." I did *Shaft* which was a huge hit and felt like flipping it up 'cause the filmmakers I really admire from the old days like Howard Hawks and older filmmakers would go from a western to a comedy and to an adventure movie and I just felt like it was time for me to do that. I could always do another socially relevant film that's really hard-hitting. At least I have that. It would be different if I was just either or. Now, hopefully people will see me as being able to shoot anything. I went to USC film school, the best school in the country so I know cinema. I'm a student of cinema.

WM: *Can you talk the casting of Ludacris? You have a way of making musicians shine in your films such as Ice Cube, Tupac, Janet Jackson, and Tyrese.*
JS: It depends. Anyone that comes from any medium whether they come off the bus to Hollywood for the first time or they're established musicians, if they come to act, they have to have respect for the craft. There's been so much about too many hip-hop artists taking the work from actors. The artists that have worked for me, if you have noticed, have gone on to have careers in this business and doing other films. It's not like when they work for me, they're a flash in the pan. I have a rigorous process from which they learn the respect for the craft. They have an acting coach and go through some improvisation and scene study and stuff. It's like a boot camp for three or four weeks before they get to do the movie.

WM: *Is it surprising to you that Tyrese says that he doesn't like to watch films?*
JS: Yeah, he doesn't watch a whole lot of movies. While we were making *Baby Boy* I would watch about three or four films and he would fall asleep in the middle. He didn't even know the stars of *Raging Bull*. Keep in mind that he's only twenty-four years old.

WM: *How much did you work with him on the set?*
JS: I worked with him scene by scene. I lived vicariously through him. He's like my baby brother. It was cool that we did another movie before this because our goal was to show how funny he could be as opposed to how serious he was in *Baby Boy*. There was a little bit of humor in that film. But here we wanted to show how he's funny and magnetic.

WM: ˙ *Cole Hauser is also someone you have worked with before. Has he grown since you last saw him?*
JS: Cole first worked with me when he was eighteen years old on *Higher Learning* when he should have been in high school. He was a wild and crazy

166 JOHN SINGLETON: INTERVIEWS

kid. He played the lead skinhead in the movie and now he's twenty-seven and a young man and has come into his own as an actor. I really want to do another movie with him. He's got a cool vibe about him.

WM: *Tyrese mentioned that you wanted him to "leave the nest?" Is this true?*
JS: It's true. We're close friends, but he has to work with someone else besides me, and then he'll appreciate me better.

WM: *What kind of car do you drive?*
JS: I drive a Lexus truck. It's like a '98, but I just got a Mercedes. It's an SL500. It's hot as hell.

WM: *Paul is the one holdover from the first film. What's that like for you as a director? Is that character already done for him?*
JS: Not at all. What we did for Paul's character was I told Paul that "You can't be the nice white boy" like he was in the first film. He was going to be edgy, he's a criminal now, and the cops are after him. Once you see how he is in this movie, it's totally different from the first movie. We wanted to make the dialogue a bit realistic, and he and Tyrese would go over the script constantly to make it so. This film is still very much a fantasy action movie, but it was important for the audience to believe that these guys had a history together. Paul and Tyrese had such a good time on and off the set, that you feel it in the movie more than you felt of Paul and Vin in the first film. Paul and Vin weren't close and all that stuff in the back of the movie shows on film.

WM: *Can you compare the energy spirit between Tyrese and Tupac?*
JS: When I worked with 'Pac, he was twenty years old. He was a totally different person than he was years later. 'Pac was convoluted because of all of the stuff he went through before he got into show business. He and his mom went through a lot of issues before he got in the business. Tyrese has a whole lot of focus. He's not self-destructive and I give him a lot of respect for that because he knows what needs to be done in his career with singing or acting or whatever. He's the first kind of cat that I could kick it with. He takes my advice, and we've had some success together on it. He's now producing movies, and he's written a movie that Universal wants to make. They'll probably make it. It's really cool to see him grow in the entertainment medium.

WM: *How important was the look of each car?*
JS: Very important. When I first got this gig, we went to the auto show in the Staples Center and I checked out the cars. The cars are like dream cars and every sponsor wanted to be involved with this film. You should see the

amount of stickers on the cars. I was upset I didn't get any free stuff out of it.

WM: *Would you do the third film if asked?*
JS: Probably.

WM: *What are you working on next?*
JS: I'm writing something right now. I don't know if it will be my next project or not.

John Singleton

JAMES W. POWELL / 2003

WRITER/DIRECTOR JOHN SINGLETON was only twenty-three years old and fresh out of film school when he made his first feature film, the highly acclaimed *Boyz N the Hood*. Twelve years and many delays later, his debut is finally being revisited on DVD, this time with a number of bonus features improving on the initial lackluster DVD. I recently had a chance to sit down with Mr. Singleton to discuss the new DVD edition of *Boyz N the Hood*, his thoughts on the film, and how he feels the digital format is affecting Hollywood. Of course, for the comic book fans out there, I also got the inside scoop on the feature film debut of Marvel Comics' *Cage*.

JAMES W. POWELL: *Boyz N the Hood is finally getting the DVD treatment it deserves, but the special edition was announced two years ago.*
JOHN SINGLETON: Yeah, I know. It took forever to get out. I delayed it another year because not everything was on there that I wanted. Everything is on there now, except for the screen tests.

JWP: *Why aren't the screen tests included?*
JS: I don't know what happened with the screen tests. Something must've been lost in the translation. I had Ice Cube's and everybody's screen test. I don't know why, but we'll see. Maybe on another pass. (laughs)

JWP: *I was looking forward to the Ice Cube screen test. Is that the one that wasn't so good?*
JS: No, this was the second test, the one where he was good. Actually, [the second Ice Cube screen test] was on the Criterion release, years ago, when Criterion did laserdiscs. But then a lot of the elements that we did were lost

---

From *DVDTalk.com*. Reprinted by permission.

between the translation of Criterion and [the new DVD]. In home video back then, they didn't know what they had, you know? So they let Criterion put out the laserdisc and the laserdisc sold gangbusters. It had all the extra stuff on it, but the new DVD is great because we got a chance to do that documentary. Did you see the documentary?

JWP: *I did, and I loved it. It's the way all documentaries should be. None of this fluffy stuff.*
JS: Yeah. You know, we were dealing with the cast member that got killed, and one guy became a murderer. Did you hear that one?

JWP: *I didn't hear about that.*
JS: Oh, it's not on there? The guy who shot Ricky, he was a middle-class kid that became a killer after he made the movie. They probably edited it, who knows? But one friend of mine got killed. I know that's in the documentary. Dedrick [Gobert], you know, he had the pacifier—he was murdered. He was actually a street racer, like in *The Fast and the Furious*. And he was racing out in Riverside. Some Vietnamese guy shot him.

JWP: *That was an interesting portion of the documentary, and it was the first I had heard about the murder. It was a good tribute, I think.*
JS: Yeah.

JWP: *I watched the film last night for the first time in about eight years. It seems to me that, unlike some of the other movies that came out in the late '80s, early '90s, it's aged really well. What do you think made it so powerful that it could age like that?*
JS: I have no idea. I just think that the film has a kind of emotional resonance with the audience because it's so personal. It was made from a personal standpoint. It's like, it wasn't so much of a manufactured thing. It was something that came straight from the heart.

JWP: *I was surprised by how much of what was on screen was based on events from your own life.*
JS: Oh yeah, you listened to the commentary?

JWP: *Yeah, I did. Great commentary by the way.*
JS: Oh thanks, man. Oh yeah, this guy breaking into the house, that happened. And things that Furious says come right out of my father's mouth.

JWP: *When you sat down to write the film, did you intend for it to be autobiographical?*

JS: No, I just sat down and wrote the film over the course of a few weeks sitting in the computer room at USC.

JWP: *So you actually wrote* Boyz N the Hood *while you were still in school?*

JS: Yeah, I wrote it while I was in film school.

JWP: *Okay. So, you're twenty-three, you have a cast of nineteen-year-olds, you have $6 million, and you've never shot anything besides Super 8. That's got to be pretty exciting and scary at the same time.*

JS: (laughing) Yeah, it was scary. It was scary the first time because I was nervous, too, but I was like, you know, it's all about acting like I wasn't nervous at all. I was like, "Yeah, I got this." I remember the first time me and Ice Cube went to dailies. It was like, "Oh shit." But then we looked at the film, we were like, "Oh, okay. This is looking good."

JWP: *In either the documentary or the commentary, you mention how confident you were, but then somewhere else, you say you were scared as hell. That's quite a ride for a twenty-three-year-old.*

JS: (laughing) Yeah, yeah. My agent told me if you don't do it right, man, they can fire you. And after awhile, after I'm doing it, I was like, "Well shit, who are they going to get to come down to the 'hood to do this? They're not going to get anybody to come down and do this."

JWP: *It sounded pretty dangerous down there for awhile.*

JS: It's always like that. When I did *Boyz* or *Baby Boy* or whatever, after awhile, you know, once people found we're there, they're coming out of the woodwork. When you're not so visible, people don't care. When you're visible, you know, people come out like, you know, "Give me a $100 or I'm standin' here." (laughs)

JWP: *That's why all the trucks were in the background to protect the crew?*

JS: Oh, that story. (laughs) Yeah, that's right. They beat up that guy on the set, and then they were threatening to do a drive-by. And they put the trucks behind the camera crew. Yeah, true story, man.

JWP: *You must've had some balls, because at one point you just said, "Ah, don't worry about it. We'll deal with those guys later."*

JS: Yeah, well, we were like, "We're going to do this. You can't tell us where to shoot or not. This is our thing."

JWP: *In the infamous uzi scene, you didn't tell anyone you were going to shoot the gun. What kind of reaction did you get from the crew after it all settled down?*

JS: Everybody just laughed. People were scared, but they laughed. It was so funny because everybody thought somebody was going to drive by that night. So when we shot the gun, everyone just ran for real. I got the shot I wanted, man. (pause) I forgot what I said on the commentary and everything. It's interesting. One of these nights I'll have to watch it myself and put the commentary on.

JWP: *Actually, it sounds like that commentary was recorded eight years after the film. That wasn't from the laserdisc, was it?*

JS: No, that's what I did for this DVD. The laserdisc was Criterion, which is a whole other thing. I did that a year after I made the film. So I'm younger on that one. This one is me after I've done several films.

JWP: *The commentary is quite revealing. When you sat down, did you plan it out? Did you have any notes beforehand, or did you just wing it?*

JS: I just sat down and talked.

JWP: *Well, you're well spoken, and it's an entertaining listen. I can't say the same about most commentaries.*

JS: Well, that's what I try to do. I try to make sure my commentaries are entertaining.

JWP: *A lot of commentaries are pretty dry and—*

JS: Boring.

JWP: *(laughs) I have a question about the DVD. The image quality is great, but how come there's no 5.1 audio track? I mean, it sounds fine, but I was hoping for it to kick. You know, the music and such. And for the guns to really boom.*

JS: I didn't have any idea that was going to happen. Shit man, and I'm a stickler for that. Okay, I'll call 'em on it.

JWP: *So, seven films later, looking back on* Boyz N the Hood, *is there anything you'd do differently? Anything where you say, "Oh, I could've done that better. I could've shot that a little better today."*

JS: Naw. There's nothing in there that I would do differently. Because we did it in like forty days, and I think it looks good for the time that we did it and for how quickly we did it. We shot that movie quick, down, dirty, and easy, which was fun.

JWP: *The deleted scene with Furious confronting Doughboy. Can you tell me a little bit about why you deleted that?*

JS: It was a powerful scene but it didn't add to the whole thing. (quotes scene) "Who the fuck is they?" It's like, he said, "That's what they want you to do." Who the fuck is they? I remember writing that. I remember that one, man.

JWP: *Yeah, I don't know, it seemed like it could've fit. When did you decide to cut it?*
JS: During editing. I didn't have to cut it, but it kept the ending more powerful to keep them apart.

JWP: *The scene is powerful just as a deleted scene. I was amazed at how forty seconds could be like, "Whoa."*
JS: I know, it's like, "Whoa" when he tries to grab him, and he says, "Let me talk to him." The cool thing about that movie was, here it is, Ice Cube is just now learning how to act, you know what I'm saying? He's just exploring it as a new venture. All those kids, it was their first movie. They just really wanted to prove to themselves, and to me, that they were doing a good job. Morris [Chestnut] would come up to me afterward, and he'd be like, "How am I doing?" It's like "You're doing fine, man." It's like, "Would you get the fuck out of my face, you're doing good." And it was just fun, man, that's what I loved about the process of making that picture. It let me know what I needed to do with making my other films, which is create a kind of cool vibe while you're making the movie, you know what I mean?

JWP: *So how do you create that vibe in your direction?*
JS: I just keep my energy level up to the degree that everyone just has to follow what my energy level is.

JWP: *As far as your most recent films, while you're filming, do you think about the eventual DVD treatment? Do you make a special effort to shoot, for example, behind-the-scenes material?*
JS: I just try to make the best film possible and once the movie's done we deal with the DVD. But we do shoot some footage. Three weeks after the *Boyz N the Hood* DVD comes out, the *2 Fast 2 Furious* one comes out. And we have a lot of stuff on that, you know. A gag reel, and I think a little featurette on the making of it, and another commentary.

JWP: *DVD players are in pretty much everyone's home now. How do you think the rise in home entertainment has affected film in general?*
JS: I think it's helped filmmaking, because now you can't say there's any one film that can't be made because there's always an audience. There's a

huge, vast audience. I mean, the box office for home video has surpassed the box office for theatrical now. So, it's like phenomenal, man.

JWP: *How do you feel about the fact that movies are at the theater for a couple of months, then they're on DVD almost immediately? Do you have any concerns about that?*

JS: No, I think a film has a life from just being seen. I mean, the more people who see a film, the more life it has. But I don't like when people watch DVDs and look at two scenes but they don't look at the whole movie. Or they sit and talk to each other. You should always watch a movie all the way through. I can't watch a movie and watch just two minutes and turn it off, then go talk to my girlfriend. I'm like, "Don't say shit to me. I'm trying to concentrate."

JWP: *(laughing) Or the worst is when your girlfriend falls asleep halfway through.*

JS: Yeah, yeah. (laughs) You know, "Go upstairs and let me watch it by myself if you're going to fall asleep."

JWP: *Can you give us any information about what you're working on now? For example, what about* Cage?

JS: I don't know yet. We'll see. Neal Moritz, who produced *Fast*, is producing that so it looks like something we may do. I want to direct it. I want somebody to write it, but I may do some writing on it. We're going over that right now.

JWP: *Is it true that you're going to get a star on the Walk of Fame? What are your thoughts about that?*

JS: I'm honored. For some people it's just like a publicity thing when they do that. But for me it's huge because I grew up catching the bus up Vermont Avenue to get to Hollywood. I could go to the movies, and look down the street and look at all the stars from the '30s and '40s. And that's how I formulated my whole thing of wanting to become a filmmaker.

JWP: *When is the star going to be revealed?*

JS: Tuesday [August 26] at 11 o'clock in the morning. In front of the Chinese Theater. That's where my star's going to be.

JWP: *I read somewhere that you're quite a DVD fan.*

JS: I'm a huge DVD fan. I buy DVDs every Tuesday. I just got *All That Jazz*. I just bought the new one, that Wanda Sykes concert thing that was on Comedy Central [*Wanda Sykes: Tongue Untied*]. And *Casablanca*.

JWP: *Any chance we'll see a different edition of the* Rosewood *DVD?*
JS: It depends on Warner. They don't know what they have with that movie. That movie is a really special movie. They don't think it'll sell. But maybe with my higher profile, they'll tout it more.

JWP: *You were the first African American to be nominated for an Academy Award for Best Director. And you were also the youngest person. For the next couple of films you were doing, did you aspire to that goal again, or did you not care so much?*
JS: I think what it did for me was that I really took filmmaking very seriously. That culminated in *Rosewood*, with me being real fucking serious. It was an honor and then a crutch also, because at a young age, I was like, I guess I'm a serious filmmaker. I never set out to be a serious filmmaker. I just set out to make movies. And so if you look at *Higher Learning*, which I was twenty-five years old making it, I'm like chock full of everything that would concern young people: lesbianism, and racism, and everything I could put in that movie. It was a great movie. A fun movie to do. But you could never get that movie made now. Never. The guy shoots everybody, know what I mean? Then *Rosewood* hit with that, and it was too powerful for some people. So then I was like, you know what? I'm just going to go and have some fun, and approach filmmaking from an emotional standpoint. Whatever I feel like doing, whether or not it's a fun movie or a serious movie. I'm just gonna go and do it. That's what I'm doing now.

His Name, and Money, at Stake, Director Takes Producer's Risk

DRESSED IN A PUMA T-SHIRT, jeans, and white sneakers, John Singleton walked into the lobby of a building on the Paramount Pictures lot here and suddenly stopped in his tracks. Before him were two giant billboards: one for a film he had bankrolled and produced, *Hustle & Flow*, which hits theaters on July 22, the other for his latest directorial effort, *Four Brothers*, due in August.

"Wow," a smiling Mr. Singleton said, reveling in the double whammy. "That's pretty cool." Mr. Singleton is back in a big way, but to hear him tell it, he never left.

"My last film made $240 million," he quickly pointed out in a recent interview. He was referring to *2 Fast 2 Furious*, the critically lambasted blockbuster he directed in 2003. "Hello, I've been here."

Yes, Mr. Singleton has been here, churning out, on average, one film every two to three years. But none has managed to generate the buzz of his 1991 breakthrough, *Boyz N the Hood*—that is, until now. Written and directed by a newcomer, Craig Brewer, *Hustle & Flow*, which Mr. Singleton dropped more than $3 million of his own money to make, was the hit of this year's Sundance Film Festival, winning an audience award, a $9 million price tag and Mr. Singleton a $7 million two-movie deal with Paramount and MTV Films.

Equal parts *Rocky* and *8 Mile*, *Hustle & Flow* tells the tale of DJay, a Memphis pimp who has a midlife crisis and decides to become a rapper. The plot was a hard sell at first. Mr. Brewer and the producer Stephanie Allain knocked on doors for two years trying to land a deal in Hollywood, but to no avail.

From the *New York Times* (July 21, 2005). Reprinted by permission of Lola Ogunnaike.

Ms. Allain turned to Mr. Singleton, hoping his pull would open doors. "They shot us down again," Mr. Singleton said. "I was surprised by that."

He was more than surprised, Ms. Allain said: "It was like a slap in the face. It upset him so much. He felt like his name value was on the line."

Studio executives "couldn't see past the stereotypes and see the humanity in these characters," Mr. Singleton said. It did not help that they had Terrence Howard, a relative unknown, in the lead and Mr. Brewer, a first-time director, at the helm. So Mr. Singleton, inspired by Mel Gibson and the hip-hop entrepreneur Damon Dash, decided to finance the film himself, thus violating Hollywood's Rule No. 1: Never ever spend your own money.

"Everybody thought I was crazy," Mr. Singleton said. "Everybody."

Though he has been vindicated, Mr. Singleton is not out of the woods just yet. The road from Sundance to box office glory is littered with the carcasses of small films that were supposed to hit it big. So, Mr. Singleton has been tirelessly promoting the movie. During filming last August, he flew journalists to Memphis to visit the set. Friends like Spike Lee and Will Smith have held private screenings for tastemakers. And Mr. Singleton has guarded prints of the movie with the ferociousness of rabid pit bull. "If it gets pirated it will be after the movie comes out," he said.

On the day of the interview, Mr. Singleton, a consummate multitasker, had a power breakfast with executives at E! and a lunch with an executive at DreamWorks. He then dashed over to a meeting about the soundtrack for *Four Brothers*, which stars Mark Wahlberg, Garrett Hedlund, the R&B singer Tyrese, and Andre 3000, one half of the hip-hop duo OutKast. Because the film is set in Detroit, Mr. Singleton wanted a lot of old school soul. The studio was asking for more contemporary urban hits.

"There was a time when executives wanted to only put rock in everything," he said. "Then it was techno and now it's hip-hop."

Mr. Singleton may have inadvertently had something to do with this turn of events. It was his poignant depiction of life in the gang-ravaged streets of Compton, California, *Boyz N the Hood*, that established Mr. Singleton as one of Hollywood's most promising talents. While the world of drive-bys and Crips and Bloods had been chronicled in rap lyrics by groups like N.W.A., it had never been captured on celluloid. At only twenty-four, Mr. Singleton became the youngest person ever nominated for a best director Academy Award. He followed two years later with *Poetic Justice*, starring Janet Jackson and Tupac Shakur. *Higher Learning*, his next project, dealt with life on a socially segregated college campus.

In each of these films, main characters meet violent deaths. Mr. Singleton was out to do more than tug at heartstrings; he was eager to provoke thought, to advance the conversation whether it be about race relations, gender bias, date rape, single parent homes, or, preferably, all of the above.

"I wanted to be taken seriously as a filmmaker and my first film was taken so seriously," Mr. Singleton said, "so I kept feeling like each film had to be more serious than the last one."

It doesn't get more serious than *Rosewood*, Mr. Singleton's 1997 film about an African-American town in Florida that was burned to the ground by a white mob in the 1920s. The film received tepid reviews and was a commercial flop. And even worse, Mr. Singleton said, it was trounced by *Booty Call*, which was released the same month.

"You've got to understand, before that I was a golden boy," the director said. "*Rosewood* was a whole different thing. The studio didn't support it. They were afraid of the picture. You're talking about black genocide."

Mr. Singleton took some time off to gather his thoughts, travel, marry and divorce, and have more children (five in total, with four mothers). Unlike other young directors, he was not grappling with how to break into the business, but what exactly he wanted to do in the business. The answer was simple: Have fun.

"Finally I said, you know what, I'm in this business because movies saved me from delinquency, movies saved my life," he said. "I just want to make movies. It doesn't matter if they're serious or not." Mr. Singleton went on to make films like *Shaft*, a remake of the 1971 action movie, and *Baby Boy*, a commentary on the infantilizing of the black man.

Mr. Singleton has grown fond of telling interviewers that he greenlighted *Hustle & Flow*, and while that makes for a compelling sound bite it is a bit of a stretch. His inability to get the film made within the system speaks to an even bigger issue in Hollywood, the director Spike Lee said.

"Very few studios have people of color deciding what films get made," Mr. Lee said. "There's not one African American at a studio in a position to greenlight a film. When that happens that will be landmark. That will have far more impact than two black people winning Academy Awards in one year."

Though Mr. Singleton agreed with Mr. Lee's assessment, he does say that blacks have made strides in front of and behind the camera in recent years. "When I came in the game it was more of a novelty to be a young, black male making movies," he said. "Now it's not a novelty, which is good."

Mr. Singleton said he wanted to continue to guide other young filmmakers through the moviemaking process. "There are a lot of talented kids making films on video," he said with the fervor of someone who struck oil once and is eager to drill again. "I'm looking for the next new stars."

Now that he's got the hang of this producing thing, Mr. Singleton, who is teaming with Mr. Brewer again for *Black Snake Moan*, about a girl who suffers from a sexual addiction, said he was ready to tackle movie moguldom.

"I just want to be able to make the type of movies that I want to make and I don't ever want anyone to tell me that if I really feel passionate about something I can't make that movie," Mr. Singleton said. "I've got to be able to say, well, I'm making it anyway, bye." He threw his head back in laughter. "Now that's power."

John Singleton:
Hollywood's Star Maker and Rule Breaker

JAWN MURRAY/2005

"THIS KID IS a f—king star," raves John Daniel Singleton as he plays
back footage on the set of his most recent film, *Four Brothers*, reviewing a
scene with actor Andre Benjamin, known musically as Andre 3000, the ec-
centric half of the hip-hop duo OutKast. "When people see him in this film
they're going to be f—king blown away," Singleton continues while exiting
a screening room where the film is shooting in Toronto. "He's the next big
thing! Trust me on this."

Trusting Singleton on talent waiting to be discovered is not difficult to
do. Whether actors such as Nia Long, Ice Cube, and Academy Award winner Cuba Gooding Jr. credit him or not, it can be argued that the celebrated
Hollywood director-producer helped launch their now-thriving film careers.
He prides himself on having both an eye for talent and a touch to make it
shine, so his praise for Benjamin is twice as nice, coming from the heart and
a straight, no chaser ego.

"He's got that thing. You'll see. He did four movies before mine, and he's
never come off like this before. When people see his performance in this film
they're going to be all over him," Singleton says. "Just watch!"

Singleton's first film, *Boyz N the Hood*, released in 1991, made a hefty $100
million, earned stellar reviews and made him the youngest person—he was
twenty-four at the time—and first African American to be nominated for an
Oscar for Best Director. He experienced quite an entree into the movie business, one most skeptics felt he would never top.

From *Savoy* (June/July 2005). Reprinted by permission of Jawn Murray.

Like his mentor, Spike Lee, Singleton knew early on that he was more concerned about conveying the African American voice through cinematography and less interested in adapting to the Hollywood system. Such principals would serve Singleton well later in his career when "Black" wasn't the flavor of the month in La La Land and studios were only interested in financing slapstick comedies like *Soul Plane*. Understanding the bigger picture and not bowing to the bigger paycheck was a practice that would pay off for Singleton in the years to come.

Following the success of *Boyz N the Hood*, in 1992 Michael Jackson tapped Singleton to direct his "Remember the Time" video. Over the next three years, the young director made two additional movies, *Poetic Justice* (1993) and *Higher Learning* (1995). Although *Poetic Justice* was nominated for an Academy Award for Best Original Song, "Again," neither movie was critically or commercially successful. The critics raved about Singleton's next movie, the 1997 drama *Rosewood*, which was based on the real-life 1923 massacre and destruction of an African American town in Florida by whites from a neighboring community. Although the film garnered rave reviews, it fared poorly at the box office.

Singleton's big-budget remake of *Shaft*, starring Samuel L. Jackson as the title character and nephew of the original Shaft, Richard Roundtree, received lukewarm reviews but generated strong ticket sales. Next came the semiautobiographical *Baby Boy*, which was released almost ten years after *Boyz N the Hood* and was also shot in South Central Los Angeles, where he grew up. That film was succeeded by *2 Fast 2 Furious*, the sequel to the 2001 box office smash *The Fast and the Furious;* Singleton's follow-up was a blockbuster as well. In August 2003, he received a star on the Hollywood Walk of Fame in front of Graumann's Chinese Theater.

Despite the critical strokes and box office successes, Singleton has rarely worked with actors who are the top draws—the Denzel Washingtons and John Travoltas of the business.

"I haven't had the luxury, like a lot of directors have, of working with established talent. Like a friend of mine said, instead of working with the monsters, I had to make the monsters. I've had to find new talent, nurture it, and capitalize on it. It's been both a blessing and a curse. Samuel L. Jackson and Mark Wahlberg (who costars in *Four Brothers*) are the only people who were big before I worked with them," he boasts. "The rest of the people have been people I made."

Although Singleton is credited for also giving breaks to once-fresh Hollywood faces like Taraji P. Henson in *Baby Boy* and Morris Chestnut in *Boyz N the Hood*, he's best known for having launched the careers of hip-hop heavyweights. "I see myself as the first filmmaker of the hip-hop generation. I've probably made my career working off of hip-hop artists," he says.

Ice Cube in *Boyz N the Hood*, Busta Rhymes in *Higher Learning*, Q-Tip in *Poetic Justice*, Ludacris in *2 Fast 2 Furious*, and singer Tyrese in *Baby Boy* were all introduced to Hollywood via Singleton projects. "Every single person I've worked with that's a hip-hop artist that has crossed over into acting with me has had a career in film. None of them has been a flash in the pan. Everybody has worked again and again and again and has a career. It's because of what I do with them," Singleton says.

And what is that? "I just tell them to keep all of the record industry pretentious music bulls—t out of the way. I don't care about your album or whatever, you work as an actor," he says.

There's more to Singleton's coaching than just his frank approach, says singer-turned-actor Tyrese. "He creates a comfortable environment. I have to be me even when working on a film. Some people don't understand me and my energy. It's real big and sometimes overwhelming. He creates the type of environment where I feel like I can be me."

Henson, who starred opposite Tyrese in *Baby Boy*, believes Singleton's analysis of characters has helped make him both successful and easy to work with. "He's brilliant because he understands casting," she explains. "You can have a great script and go out and hire a bunch of OK actors, but John understands that chemistry on film is important, so casting is important. All of the characters are believable, and he totally gets casting."

Baby Boy was Henson's breakout role in Hollywood, and Singleton later tapped her to costar in the upcoming *Hustle & Flow*—on which he served as producer and not director or screenwriter—where her performance was so riveting that he also had a part written in the script of his next movie, *Four Brothers*, just for her. "He told me that as long as he's making films, I've got a job," Henson says. "It's amazing to have someone who believes in you like that."

Singleton wants to empower actors and filmmakers in Black Hollywood, mainly by developing a camp of talent that, he says, "work when [he] works," another lesson learned from Lee.

When studio executives in Hollywood opted to pass on *Hustle & Flow*, a film about a thirty-something pimp having an epiphany about fulfilling his dream of becoming a rapper, it changed Singleton's entire approach to filmmaking. He realized that he could not solely rely on Hollywood to tell stories relevant to an African American audience or depend on it to embrace projects that he was passionate about.

What was it about newcomer Craig Brewer's script that so intrigued Singleton? "[The script is about] a guy who had a vision and a dream, and who realized that his dream changed other peoples' lives. That's why I gravitated to it in the first place," says Singleton. "The second part of what drew me to it was the fact that this guy was a pimp, and everyone in Hollywood was afraid to do a movie with the character being a pimp. And I said if everyone is afraid to do it, then I have to do it. That means that nobody will copy it. Well, they probably will now, if it's successful. But there hasn't been a really cool movie in that world in more than thirty years."

Despite his determination to get *Hustle & Flow* made, Singleton, along with screenwriter/director Brewer and fellow producer Stephanie Allain (who brought the project to Singleton and also started him in the business), faced the biggest obstacle in Hollywood: No one would finance it.

"We went around pitching this film to everybody in town, and they turned it down. I said, 'I am going to put up the money myself.' Everyone was like, 'You're f—king crazy!'" he says. "I was like, 'F—k all of you guys.'"

Production began on *Hustle & Flow* last summer in Memphis. Word quickly spread through Los Angeles that Singleton and Brewer had a hit on their hands. "As we were doing the movie, people were like, 'I heard it was good, I heard it was good,'" laughs Singleton.

The grass-roots chatter about the film only intensified once shooting wrapped in September. "I started stroking the waters. We showed it to a couple of people, and then you know how this business is . . . the people who turned us down were calling months before we screened it at Sundance, and I was like, 'No, none of you can see it!'"

Even with his high hopes for the film, Singleton and the best of psychics couldn't have foreseen what was coming next: *Hustle & Flow* made history earlier this year at the Sundance Film Festival in Utah when Paramount Pictures paid a record price, $10 million, to acquire the movie. "That's the whole thing for me and why I feel vindicated. I'm like Michael Jordan or Muhammad Ali in the way I do this s—t," Singleton says. The film also received a resounding ovation and won the coveted Audience Award at the festival.

The entire Paramount deal came to nearly $15 million, which included development financing of two more features for Singleton's production company, New Deal Productions. This is the outcome for a man who couldn't get financing for a film nearly two years prior. "I don't like being doubted! Especially about knowing what's hip and knowing what people want to see. It's like calling me the 'n' word—it ain't cool with me. I have an innate thing of knowing what people want to see. I've proven that over and over again," Singleton exclaims.

Hustle & Flow, which stars Terrence Dashon Howard, Taryn Manning, Anthony Anderson, Elise Neal, and Taraji Henson, has critics predicting a return to the Oscars for Singleton. "Arguably, one could say this was the best film John has been involved with since *Rosewood*. It's a dynamic movie that could certainly take him back to the Oscars in addition to every other award show of importance in Hollywood," says Gil Robertson IV, president of the African American Film Critics Association.

Singleton brushes aside any mention of Oscar buzz. "I don't know about all that," he says. "We'll see. I can't even think about that. It would be the icing, but I don't know."

One thing Singleton does know is that the experience has changed his perspective on filmmaking. "I've learned now that I have to do this s—t on my own despite what any studio says and make them beg for the s—t later," he boasts.

There's also talk that *Hustle & Flow* could catapult star Howard, who has appeared in more than thirty movies in supporting roles, into the league with Hollywood leading men Denzel Washington, Don Cheadle, Will Smith, Jeffrey Wright, and Djimon Hounsou. Creating a vehicle to take Howard to the "next level" is something that Singleton wanted to do years ago. "I saw a preview of *The Best Man* before it even came out. I said to Terrence, 'You've got to be in my movie *Shaft*.' I brought him up from Philly to New York. In the interim of us rehearsing *Shaft. The Best Man* came out and everyone was on him, so he went and did a Disney movie about Muhammad Ali," says Singleton. "It was a bad Disney movie. They offered him all of this money. I hammered him and said, 'You can't leave me.' Then his career meandered down for a few years and I told him, 'See, you should have been f—king with me.'"

Director John Singleton Labors in Shadow of His Debut Hit

JOYCE J. PERSICO/2005

N E W   Y O R K—Fourteen years ago, John Singleton was the Great Black Hope, a new, young director whose first film, *Boyz N the Hood*, turned him into an overnight success and, at age twenty-four, into the youngest person ever nominated for a Best Director Oscar. But fourteen years is a long time, and Singleton has never equaled the critical success of his debut movie. Yet, at the suggestion that he's in need of a bit of career revival, the thirty-seven-year-old Los Angeles native quickly points out that his last film, the 2003 sequel *2 Fast 2 Furious*, made $240 million worldwide. What that action film lacked in critical acclaim has been made up by the widely praised *Hustle & Flow*, which opened August 5. Singleton produced and financed the film with $3 million of his own money.

Singleton's latest film, a Detroit-based action-drama titled *Four Brothers*, opened last Friday and earned the No. 1 spot at the box office, bringing in $21.2 million. Starring Mark Wahlberg, Garrett Hedlund, Tyrese Gibson, and Andre Benjamin as a quartet of adopted brothers, it's a story of revenge fashioned in the style of a shoot-'m-up Western.

"There's no system in place to help new filmmakers get into the business," Singleton says. "My inspiration for making movies is to make them the way (independent) directors John Sayles and (the late) John Cassavetes did. I make interesting pictures that may seem out of the norm, but are really commercial movies," adds the director, dressed in jeans and a Sean

John T-shirt for a round of interviews in New York prior to the opening of *Brothers*.

Singleton also has become the unofficial conduit of pop stars, rockers, hip-hop artists, and rappers who want to make the transition to a career in film. Model-turned-R&B singer Tyrese and Outkast member Andre 3000 (Benjamin) co-star in *Four Brothers*. Tyrese and rapper Snoop Dog were featured in the director's *Baby Boy*. His *Higher Learning* co-starred rapper Ice Cube and Singleton's *Poetic Justice* starred Janet Jackson and the late rapper Tupac Shakur.

"I met John ten years ago when I was eighteen and he called me in about the music for *Higher Learning*," Benjamin says. "He kind of blew me off. But I've always said he's the best director for musicians trying to make the transition to film. I felt honored. I tried out for *2 Fast 2 Furious* and didn't get the part."

Singleton described himself to Benjamin as "an old school director" who said he didn't want to use "tricks and gadgets" to make a film work. "He said, 'I want emotion out of the piece,'" Benjamin says.

The director has another way of describing himself—and his cast. "I'm a man's man," he says. "They're (the stars of *Four Brothers*) good-looking guys who are not trying to look better than their female co-stars. "I know certain people as people," he says of his casting method, "and I can gauge what they're capable of. I've made a point of working with hip-hop artists."

Gibson says of Singleton, "I pretty much do whatever he calls me about."

Born to a mortgage broker and a pharmaceutical company representative who never married, Singleton was raised in separate households. After high school, he attended the University of Southern California's film-writing program, winning writing awards that led to his signing with an agent during his sophomore year. His *Boyz N the Hood* script, drawn from his years growing up in South Central Los Angeles, sold for $7 million. The film won him nominations for directing and original writing. The director doesn't think much has changed in South Central L.A. since his 1991 film was made there, only the color of the faces there.

"*Boyz N the Hood* wouldn't be made today unless I did it," he says. "Now it's all about Mexicans, Latinos, or Vietnamese."

The success of *Hustle & Flow*, with its star-making performance by Terrence Howard, began at this year's Sundance Film Festival, where the movie won the audience favorite award and was sold for $9 million. Singleton also picked up a $7 million, two-movie deal with Paramount and MTV Films as a result. This was achieved only after major studios turned down *Hustle & Flow*, even with Singleton's name attached. With *The Four Brothers*, Singleton has referenced movies he remembers from his childhood.

"I'm also a real student of American film," Singleton says. "In the early '70s, they took Western archetypes and put them in an urban milieu. That was kind of lost over this generation."

John Singleton Still Lives in the 'Hood He Films

TERRY ARMOUR / 2005

JOHN SINGLETON has a confession to make.
"In some ways, *Four Brothers* is actually socially irresponsible," the filmmaker
joked about his latest film, which in its opening weekend topped box office
numbers with an estimated $20 million. "I've made films advocating against
taking action upon action. But this is more like a western, or a *Dirty Harry*."

Yes, the thirty-seven-year-old Singleton has dealt with the cause-and-
effect issues of violence before, particularly in his directorial debut, at age
twenty-three, with 1991's *Boyz N the Hood*. If *Four Brothers*—which stars
Mark Wahlberg, Andre Benjamin, Tyrese Gibson, and Garrett Hedlund as four
adopted kids reunited to avenge their mother's murder—could be deemed
socially irresponsible fare, *Boyz* was lauded for providing an unflinching social commentary on gang life in South Central Los Angeles. It is a life that
Singleton knows all too well. Not only was he raised by his father in South
Central (Laurence Fishburne's character in Boyz was based on his dad), Singleton still lives there.

"There are a lot of directors who make big money and do big things and
then move out of the 'hood," said Gibson, who also worked with Singleton
on *2 Fast 2 Furious* and *Baby Boy*, another film set in South Central. "They try
to tell 'hood stories from a Beverly Hills perspective. That's not what John's
about."

When Singleton tells those so-called "'hood stories," many of them provide moviegoers with a look into a world they might not know, or understand.

And Singleton readily admits that world is sometimes shaped by violence. But what bugs Singleton, whose credits include Poetic Justice, Shaft, and the critically acclaimed Hustle & *Flow*, which he produced and bankrolled, is a perception that he might be glorifying that often violent world.

This is a touchy subject for the filmmaker, who says he's well aware of that fine line between social commentary and the glorification of mindless violence in movies.

"Americans, we grew up with cowboy movies and westerns, but we've become even more desensitized to the violence," he said as he settled into a chair at a North Side coffee shop recently. "And it's not necessarily just in the movies. It's the music, the video games, and everything else. Violence is glorified in a way that people are not sensitized to it."

Particularly when it comes to teens and pre-teens. According to a recent study conducted, in part, by Dartmouth College's Department of Psychological and Brain Sciences, 28 percent of 5,000 kids between the age of ten and fifteen had seen what researchers described as "especially violent" R-rated movies. Though these films are not supposed to be viewed by audiences under seventeen, the study found that many of the subjects were still able to view the movies via DVD, videotapes, or cable television. Jane Tallim, director of education for the Federal Media Awareness Network, a Canadian non-profit organization that collects data to educate families about issues surrounding violence and children, says exposure to these types of films continues to be a growing problem.

"It really comes down to access to entertainment that is intended for adults," said Tallim, who has three children of her own. "Whether a movie has a social moral message, or it's a gun-slinging movie, as adults, we can put into context what we are seeing. The issue is when children have access to these forms of entertainment. It's the notion of immersion. It's not just one violent movie or TV show; it's the music videos or the CDs they listen to. You see it in advertising. You have to look at our whole media culture. [Violence] becomes wallpaper."

Singleton, the father of five children between the ages five and twelve, is quick to point out his movies are not for kids. He also puts the onus on parents to keep track of how children are spending their leisure time.

"Hey, I don't let my kids watch my movies," he said. "I don't let my kids play violent video games. Children, for better or worse, are a reflection of who we are. There's a positive and a negative to it. It's just a matter of how much of a guiding force you want to be in your children's lives. Parents can't put that off on anything other than themselves."

As for his critics, Singleton says *Boys N the Hood* isn't trumpeting the gang-banging lifestyle and *Hustle & Flow*, starring Terrence Howard, isn't giving plaudits to a lifestyle that degrades women.

"Why would anybody want to live the life of that character in [*Hustle & Flow*]?" Singleton said. "That isn't some feel-good story. It's funny because back in the day, the guy on the street or the guy who was the gangster, he was an anomaly. Now you have generations of kids who aspire to that. It's out of control. Anybody who is really from the 'hood doesn't want to be in the 'hood. They want to get out and live a better life."

And then there is *Four Brothers*. Hedlund, who at twenty is the youngest member of the ensemble cast, says that for all its shoot-'em-up bluster, the film is not as socially irresponsible as one might think. "The unique part of this is that these guys are the bad guys at the same time as being the good guys," he said. "In this film, you know the intentions of these guys, but you also see the cause and effect of what they do."

Gibson agreed. "Shooting guns is a part of a lot of movies," he said. "But the difference with John's movies is that at the end of the movie, you find yourself saying, 'Would I have done the same thing?'"

That's all Singleton wants people to take away from his work.

"The thing about it is there's nobody really making films that comment on where they are, where they live," he said. "All the violence I've ever had in the movies is always to make a commentary about violence. When things happen that happen to be violent, they are played out for the reality of it, for the consequence of it."

In the Mouth of Jaws

HENRY SHEEHAN/2006

JOHN SINGLETON IS rocking back and forth in his seat in delight. "Look at all that blood!" he points out with a laugh, pointing at a screen where poor Robert Shaw is getting bitten in half by a giant great white shark. "Hear it? Grrrrr! Rooaaarrr!"

The filmmaker, who in 1991 became the youngest person ever to earn a best director Oscar nomination, is truly reliving a moment from his childhood. As a kid, he saw *Jaws* under what might have been optimum conditions for its time (1974): At a drive-in theater, specifically the Vineland Drive-In, a pastel outpost in the grungy City of Industry (now the only operating open-air cinema in Los Angeles County). But Singleton's exclamations aren't just a flash from his youth. He's also analyzing the use of sound by another young filmmaker, Steven Spielberg, who was only twenty-six at the time he made *Jaws*. As Singleton points out, sharks don't growl, but Spielberg had cleverly mixed down the threatening, animalistic rumbles into the soundtrack's orchestrated cacophony of music, splashing, and human shouting. The result might have been zoologically wrong, but cinematically oh-so right.

"It was the first Spielberg movie I ever saw and I remember just being so intrigued by how great the movie was," Singleton says, viewing the film again in a DGA screening room. "Later on, when I was nine years old and *Close Encounters* came out, I recognized the name of the guy who did it. I saw him on [ABC newsmagazine] *20-20* directing *Close Encounters* and I was like, 'Wow, I want to be a director.' What I loved about *Jaws* was that he really told the story with the camera. You know, it's not like filmmakers now where every movie they make is from another movie. No one had done a movie like

---

From *DGA Quarterly* (Spring 2006). Reprinted by permission of the Directors Guild of America.

this up till then. It's just the sustained tension of it, the excitement of it, and the pure voyeuristic pleasure of it."

The tale of a marauding shark snacking on the inhabitants of an East Coast vacation colony may seem an odd choice for Singleton to point to as a crucial influence on his own work. His debut, *Boyz N the Hood*, set an example for films to come, works embracing open engagement with African American themes and settings, a preoccupation with relationships between fathers (or father-figures) and sons, and frequent threats—even occasional outbursts—of tragic violence. That may be to undersell, though, the pervasive influence *Jaws* had on the cinematic culture at-large. Spielberg's megahit was instantly recognized for the directorial playground it was, an exaltation of imaginative technique over a humdrum monster story with a smattering of character bits. But not playfulness devoid of intellectual intention. It's that youthful combination of thoughtfulness and virtuosity that is, for Singleton, the hallmark of the film.

"There's simultaneous action, there's foreground action, and background action that happens in this picture and I do that a lot," he says. "Then you can play with that back and forth. I learned that from watching this movie over and over again: Moving the camera for the sake of moving the story forward. I'm thirty-eight now, my first movie was sixteen years ago, and I've realized that a lot of young filmmakers move the camera just for the sake of moving the camera. Or they're afraid to move the camera. The filmmakers I always admire, they move the camera to tell the story. Everything is in service of telling the story. It's like set-up and then pay-off. You can do that within the shot and within a sequence."

Singleton finds an example right in the film's opening minutes. The film's famed midnight skinny-dipper has already suffered her ghoulish fate, and Amity Island Police Chief Brody (Roy Scheider), has been summoned the next morning to check on her still mysterious disappearance. A sequence begins with Scheider and the victim's boyfriend walking along the top of a sand dune in a mid-long shot.

"This master shot starts with a tracking shot," Singleton points out as the camera discreetly tracks along with the two characters, taking in the solitary, lonely dune. "There's choreography with the camera as they come up towards it [a 180 degree pan] and then it continues to track [this time with an open expanse of beach and ocean]. You're getting so much visual information with minimal amount of coverage and then, boom, the cut [to another shot.]"

Having noted a pattern of two-shots with mostly wide-open backdrops, Singleton analyzes how Spielberg soon cuts to a reverse of Brody and the young man now approaching the camera from a distance.

"Then another upset cop drops right into the frame's foreground and, boom, the music changes. You don't see what he sees, and the other two stop, they're still far away, and then Brody comes into the foreground—see, the foreground and background. Then, all of a sudden, it cuts to a close-up of the hand and the crabs all over the hand. Then a cut to Brody; the camera's still not all the way up on his face, but you get his grief, you get his emotion. He looks over to the ocean. If the camera was in a close-up you wouldn't get the fact that he looked over the ocean like, 'What is in there?'"

A close look at *Boyz N the Hood* instantly reveals how the director employed what he learned from *Jaws*. The movie's opening, in particular, consists of a series of long tracking shots that introduce the characters and their social milieu. The film's hero, a kid named Tre, shown at ages ten and seventeen (when he's played by Cuba Gooding Jr.), often finds himself cosseted by the safety of the foreground, but confronted by emerging figures in the background. These figures can turn out to be friendly, hostile, or even fatal, but this visual tension, especially during the first half, is the movie's dominant motif.

The relationships between *Jaws* and *Boyz* can be surprisingly sharp once you're attuned to Singleton's source of influence. He becomes particularly excited in his play-by-play when Quint, the salty dog played by Robert Shaw, is introduced during a meeting of Amity's alarmed politicos and merchants. The whole scene takes place in a commandeered schoolroom.

Spielberg shoots the sequence with a long, focus-shifting dolly shot through the tiny throng before, in perfect sync, ending up with a loose, but precise, close medium shot on Quint. Quint then famously gets everyone's attention by scratching his fingers on a blackboard. Even without the typically flamboyant stylistic flourish, Spielberg was clearly building tension through the use of shifting fields of action.

"Look at this, see?" Singleton says, gesturing at the beginning of a shot that encompasses nearly the entire scene. "The speaker's in the close background but it's a good composition." Working up a head of steam, Singleton's specific and general observations now collide and careen. "The thing about it is, a lot of filmmakers don't readily, even when they're planning the camera, they're not thinking pictorially in a thematic way, in the way that they're setting up. Look at that! Hear the sound? And you haven't even seen Quint. I love this. 'You all know me, you all know how I earn a living.' Robert Shaw's across the room. Then look, someone tells him to sit up. See how he looks around?"

Oddly—or perhaps logically—*Boyz* also has an early classroom scene set up in much the way Spielberg did his. There are virtually no close-ups. "It's easier to shoot this way because you're being economical with the time,"

Singleton says, describing his method of working as much as possible with long, usually mobile shots. "The thing is, you have to work out the choreography. Then you can shoot a whole master shot. If the first part of the master is good, and the second part not good, a cutaway allows you to use the first part of the shot with the second part of the master from another take.

"What I love about Steven's work is he still does set-up, pay-off—the basic filmic elements that tell a story, and not the pyrotechnics or whatever," Singleton says with eyes firmly fixed on the screen. "Still does it now. That's filmmaking. That's telling a story with pictures. One thing I've learned from watching *Jaws* is that the audience is actively involved with watching the movie. Watching the movie is a participatory act. It's not a passive act. Depending if you shoot in a certain way, the audience is either laid back or they're sitting up in their seats in rapt attention. And that's what I've tried to do with my work: Try to find ways in which scenes or sequences capture the audience in such a way that emotionally, suspense-wise, they're at rapt attention."

Even a cursory comparison of Spielberg's and Singleton's films reveals another point of comparison: Both deal with, either directly or indirectly, the role and influence of the father. But Singleton demurs when it's suggested this is another lesson he learned from Spielberg. "No, not really," he says. "That comes from my own personal life."

Nonetheless, one of Singleton's favorite moments in *Jaws* is really nothing more than a couple of shots which preface Brody's inability to function as a protective "dad" for Amity Island's children. The scene precedes a brief ferry ride that Brody makes with Amity's mayor (Murray Hamilton) and a few other town bigwigs. The sequence starts with a simple medium shot of Brody on the shore and a cutaway POV shot of some kids out on the water.

"Now that we've had the shark attack, we got the children swimming. There's no inherent tension, but there's tension that the audience puts on it," Singleton says. "You set something up and the pay-off is you see Brody's anxiety. You see his anxiety as he's looking at those kids in the water. And the audience is looking at those kids in the water."

The ferry ride itself occurs as a sort of coda, implicitly recalling Brody's morbid fear of water in a bit Singleton also tags as a technical and narrative feat, the characters grouping and regrouping in front of a stationary camera.

When Singleton describes the film's thematic thrust, it's as a timeless odyssey to manhood. The key moment comes, he says, when Brody looks out to sea after one final shark attack at the beach, one that nearly cost his own son his life.

"He looks at the ocean and he's afraid, he can't swim, but he has to face it. He has to face his fears. It's classic heroic art."

The Big Picture

PATRICK GOLDSTEIN/2006

HOLLYWOOD, TO PARAPHRASE the old James Brown song, it's a white, white, very white world. Sometimes when I sit in on a production meeting or visit a movie set or have lunch at the Grill, I'm struck by the fact that in an industry with an ever-growing roster of African American and Latino actors and filmmakers, the odds of my seeing a black or Latino executive are about as good as seeing a studio chief pumping gas at a truck stop in Wyoming.

Having made movies about multiethnic subjects his entire career, both as a hit director (*Boyz N the Hood*, *Four Brothers*, and *2 Fast 2 Furious*) as well as a producer (*Hustle & Flow*), John Singleton knows exactly what it's like to pitch an idea that revolves around people of color to a roomful of white executives. "Basically the American studio structure is the same as it's been since Louis B. Mayer and Jack Warner ran the business," he says. "This is not one of these businesses run by affirmative action. In Hollywood, affirmative action is all about—how much money can you make?"

After his success bankrolling *Hustle & Flow* with his own money, Singleton is rolling the dice again, having earned a rare opportunity to bypass the stodgy studio greenlighting process and make the kind of movies that reflect an increasingly diverse country. Singleton and Universal Pictures are announcing this week that Universal will market and distribute five films financed and produced by Singleton. Each made for less than $15 million, the films will be distributed either by Universal or its Focus and Rogue divisions. The importance of the deal is that the studio has agreed to release the finished pictures; all the creative decisions are made by Singleton.

The first film in Universal's agreement with Singleton's New Deal Productions is *Illegal Tender*, a family drama about a young man and his mother who try to escape the drug-fueled violence of their old neighborhood in the Bronx. Directed by Franc. Reyes, it is now filming in New York and Puerto Rico. Singleton is providing the funding for the $8-million picture, while lining up money for future projects.

It's clear that the new slate of films will reflect Singleton's interests as a filmmaker, which have evolved from such personal projects as *Rosewood* to more genre-oriented films such as *Four Brothers* and *Shaft*. "If you make a movie for less than $15 million with the right genre elements and a young, multiethnic cast, you can make a nice profit," he says. "These aren't movies where people are sitting around talking all the time. Franc.'s film is a lot like *Scarface*, but with a Latino mother and son. It's got a lot of heart, but Franc jokes that whenever he sees me, I'm going, 'Can't we have more guns in this shot?'"

Singleton says he approached Paramount Pictures, which released *Hustle & Flow*, but the studio wasn't interested in a deal. Universal was a perfect fit, not only because the studio has already made a number of multiethnic pictures, but because Singleton has a close relationship with new Universal Chairman Marc Shmuger.

"I've known Marc for sixteen years and I consider him a friend," Singleton says. In fact, *Boyz N the Hood* was the first picture Shmuger worked on when he came to Sony in 1991 as an advertising executive. When Shmuger later moved to Universal, he worked with Singleton on *2 Fast 2 Furious*.

"From the very beginning of his career, John has crossed over to all kinds of audiences," Shmuger says. "He's always stood out as someone who's not only in touch with the youth culture, but who has a great eye for casting and finding new talent. It's no secret that our industry is badly in need of discovering fresh actors and filmmakers, and we expect that John will be a bridge to help us connect with them."

Shmuger is especially excited about reaching the Latino audience, which he says is the fastest-growing demographic in the country. (Latinos were a big force behind *Nacho Libre's* $27.5-million opening this past weekend.) "They way over-index for moviegoing, so they're going to be an increasingly big force in pop culture. They come to the broad-based movies we make, but we haven't been successfully focused on creating the movies that speak to them, which is what John's trying to do."

Singleton, who studied film at USC, sees a historical link between today's Latino moviegoers and the immigrants who made up the bulk of the moviegoing audience in the industry's early nickelodeon era. "The first great boom in American cinema was fueled by the immigrants from Europe who didn't speak English, but went to the movies in droves in the early 1900s," he explains. "It's totally analogous to the millions of cool young bilingual Latinos who go see *Saw* and *The Fast and the Furious* and the youth comedies. They drive a big chunk of the box office."

The problem, as Singleton sees it, is that Hollywood isn't always comfortable with new faces from unfamiliar cultures. Reyes' last film, *Empire*, was a low-budget hit in 2002. But he hasn't directed a film since. When I asked Singleton why, he answered: "He's almost six feet tall, he's Puerto Rican, and he's opinionated. Being Puerto Rican has made it tougher for him, no doubt."

Wouldn't Hollywood do a better job of creating movies that speak to this multiethnic audience if the studio executive suites weren't so lily white? It's an especially embarrassing question for the film industry, which is full of supporters of all sorts of progressive causes, but when it comes to hiring people of color, betrays a huge gap between its ideals and its actions.

"Forget about what's right, if you're dealing with a pop culture that's so driven by Latinos and African Americans, you'd think it would just be good practice to have people of color in those jobs," says Spike Lee, who's been a longtime advocate of improved Hollywood minority hiring practices. "But when they are making the big decisions, about greenlighting movies and TV shows, we're not participating.

"I've been meeting with executives who can make movies for twenty years and I've never sat across the table from someone who looked like me. When I do see a young black face, I think—did they pull 'em in from the mailroom? It's like they have someone in a glass case on the shelf that says, 'Break the glass in case Spike Lee comes into the room!'"

The head count is pretty dismal. A survey of African American or Latino production executives at a vice president level or higher found one executive at 20th Century Fox, New Line, and Paramount, none at Universal, Warner Bros., and Sony Pictures. After three days of trying, I couldn't get an answer out of Disney's corporate publicity staff, so I'm guessing they're at zero too. Whenever I would ask studio chiefs for an explanation, there was usually a long, awkward silence.

"We haven't done a good enough job to get better representation of African Americans and other minorities inside the company," Shmuger says. "Obviously this partnership with John is a big step forward in terms of bringing in more diverse points of view. But it's a fair criticism. We've got a long way to go."

20th Century Fox Co-Chairman Jim Gianopulos says, "It's not for lack of interest or desire, because we're constantly searching for creative people. But it's a really difficult question and we haven't found an answer yet."

Some executives believe progress is being made, even if it is painfully slow. "I think if you look at our company or at the talent agencies, you're starting to see more faces of color," says New Line production chief Toby Emmerich. "This certainly isn't something that's under the radar with our human resources department."

What the studio executives won't say, at least on the record, is that it isn't easy to attract minority talent to the studio system. This is in part because studios are an incredibly insular world, but also because minorities don't necessarily see the job of studio employee as such an enviable goal in an era where the real action is in new technology, hip-hop, and other more entrepreneurial, ownership-oriented arenas.

Much of the creative energy today is on the outside of corporate systems, not the inside. "John isn't going to put on a suit and go to the office," says Shmuger, adding with a laugh, "He knows he has a better job than me."

In the music business, for example, a variety of black artists and producers have successfully made the leap to running record labels, including Sean "Diddy" Combs, Dr. Dre, L. A. Reid, Jermaine Dupri, and Jay-Z. Singleton sees Jay-Z as an intriguing role model.

"I want to do for the movie business what Jay-Z did in the music business," he says. "He's the guy everyone goes to for guidance, which is a role I want to embrace, being a godfather to a new generation of filmmakers."

Hip-hop has remained relevant, Singleton says, because it is always embracing new talent. "The studios are always two years behind," he says. "They say they want to be in the new talent business, but if you're sitting at Morton's, you're not out helping a young filmmaker learn how to fix their script or get a shot right."

At thirty-eight, Singleton may not be as young or brash as he once was, but he still knows talent when he sees it. And talent attracts money, which is one thing the executives in the white world of today's studios understand. "I want to nurture the next generation, which is where our future will come from," Singleton says. "I'm hoping I can give them what I always wanted, which is some real-life advice."

INDEX

CPSIA information can be obtained
at www.ICGtesting.com
Printed in the USA
BVHW032301270920
589721BV00024B/86